THE PEDDLING PERIL INDEX (PPI) 2017

THE FIRST RANKING OF NATIONAL STRATEGIC EXPORT CONTROL SYSTEMS

DAVID ALBRIGHT, SARAH BURKHARD, ALLISON LACH, AND ANDREA STRICKER

INSTITUTE FOR SCIENCE AND INTERNATIONAL SECURITY

2018

Institute for Science and International Security

The Institute for Science and International Security is a non-profit, non-partisan institution dedicated to informing the public about science and policy issues affecting international security. Its primary focus is on stopping the spread of nuclear weapons and related technology to additional nations and to terrorists, bringing about greater transparency of nuclear activities worldwide, strengthening the international non-proliferation regime, and achieving deep cuts in nuclear arsenals.

Institute for Science and International Security (ISIS) Press

440 1ST Street NW
Suite 800
Washington, DC 20001
USA

www.isis-online.org
@TheGoodISIS

Library of Congress Control Number: 2018904649

Cover design: Stewart A. Williams Design
Back cover photograph credits: Korea Central News Agency and DigitalGlobe

CreateSpace Independent Publishing Platform
North Charleston, SC

ISBN-13: 978-1987781397
ISBN-10: 1987781392

CREDITS AND ACKNOWLEDGEMENTS

The Peddling Peril Index (PPI) project is a result of hundreds, if not thousands, of hours of data collection, research, and analysis by Institute for Science and International Security staff. The PPI project grew out of more than two decades of work by the Institute on understanding and characterizing illicit nuclear and other strategic commodity trafficking. A 2010 book, *Peddling Peril*, by Institute founder and president David Albright, furthered this work and is the project's namesake.

We want to especially thank Samta Savla who contributed many months of assistance to the project as a visiting research fellow. She in particular contributed to the development of information about national legislation, the specific criteria for all five super criteria, the streamlining of super criteria, development of the tiering system, and composed initial writeups on methodology. We sincerely thank her for her significant contribution to the project.

Ivy Yang, Mary Cate Duff, and Summer Gary contributed to the project as talented and appreciated interns.

The Institute also wishes to thank several expert consultants on the project including: Renaud Chatelus, Timothy Gildea, Kenneth MacDonald, and other experts who wish to remain anonymous.

We extend very special thanks to Michael Rosenthal for his substantive contributions to the methodology used in the PPI and his review of the report, and to Mark Dubowitz who first envisioned this project during a meeting in November 2015.

The book benefited greatly from the layout and design of Rob Siders of 52 Novels.

*Dedicated to all those who strive to stop the spread of
nuclear weapons and the wherewithal to make them.*

TABLE OF CONTENTS

INTRODUCTION

A critical strategy to stop Iran's and North Korea's dangerous nuclear endeavors is thwarting their ability to acquire goods needed to build nuclear weapons and other weapons of mass destruction (WMD) and the means to deliver them. Case studies, many of which the Institute has published on its web site, have shown that countries seeking nuclear weapons capabilities have depended on acquisition from abroad of a wide range of critical know-how, raw materials, equipment, and components.

Since the creation of the Nuclear Non-Proliferation Treaty (NPT) in 1968,[1] one case after another, from Pakistan to India, Iraq to Iran, and Argentina to Brazil have shown that almost all countries that have sought nuclear weapons face an essential challenge in that they cannot produce all that they need domestically or afford to create the indigenous industrial wherewithal to make thousands of required goods. For example, the dangerous nuclear programs of Iran and North Korea would have ground to a halt without access to goods from abroad.

Strategic export controls have developed into a critical countermeasure against commodity trafficking in nuclear, missile, WMD, and military-related goods. Although no one tool can completely stop determined countries like Iran and North Korea from acquiring illicitly the goods they seek, strategic export controls have proven important in slowing and complicating those efforts. They have also stimulated and provided tools to responsible nations for better and earlier detection of secret efforts to create, for example, the nuclear weapons capabilities our Institute focuses most on, particularly those in regions of tension such as the Middle East, South Asia, and Northeast Asia. By detecting these programs earlier and causing delays, export control systems have provided more time for diplomacy and other counter-proliferation tools to seek solutions to the fundamental problem of nuclear proliferation.

Today, strategic export control laws are well implemented in supplier countries. For example, members of the Nuclear Suppliers Group (NSG) have established a wide range of norms and principles over several decades for its members as well as extensive lists of equipment, materials, and technology relevant to nuclear proliferation. However, cases of nuclear commodity trafficking show that some NSG countries implement and enforce their laws far better than other members. About three quarters of all countries and territories are not members of the NSG. These non-NSG states often have far less comprehensive strategic export control laws, or none at all.

In response to the enactment and improvement of export controls, states whose aim is to acquire weapons of mass destruction have developed increasingly sophisticated national and transnational networks to acquire goods illicitly for unsafeguarded or sanctioned nuclear programs, as well as missile, other WMD, and military efforts. Thus, supplier states need to continually improve their strategic export controls to counter these steps. Moreover, case studies make clear that it is not enough for just a few countries to have adequate controls over the export of key goods. In fact, Iran, North Korea, and others often base their efforts in countries with less effective controls as they seek to acquire goods from countries with advanced technological sectors, like the United States and Germany. They often declare a false end-user and transship and finance the purchase of goods through other countries that also have less effective or nonexistent controls. These "pariah" countries in essence look for the weak links in the fabric or net of international strategic trade controls. The Institute's experience is that they find many opportunities to bypass controls.

These issues arose at a 2015 Institute for Science and International Security workshop involving a unique range of law enforcement officials, Congressional staff, and non-governmental experts. These experts could not agree on how to better target efforts to prevent the spread of strategic commodities and gauge weak links in the fabric of global trade controls. There was agreement that there is little chance of thwarting strategic commodity trafficking efforts without knowing the sufficiency of export control systems around the world. Participants concluded that there was a deep need for a better way to evaluate national export control systems worldwide, and thereby establish a basis from which policymakers could mitigate gaps and develop counter-proliferation initiatives. The Peddling Peril Index (PPI) was envisioned at this workshop as a way to help do this. At the workshop, Mark Dubowitz recommended this name as a follow-on to Albright's 2010 book, *Peddling Peril*, on illicit nuclear trade and the A.Q. Khan network out of Pakistan.[2]

This report is the result of a one-and-a-half-year project that ranks 200 countries, territories, and entities according to their adoption and implementation of export controls and assesses how well those systems are performing at preventing the trafficking in nuclear and other strategic commodities.[3] As expected, the PPI found that less than half of the world's nations have export control systems that are sufficient for preventing trafficking in these commodities. Nearly a decade and a half has passed since the passage of United Nations Security Council resolution (UNSCR) 1540, which mandated in 2004 that all nations must put in place appropriate, effective export control systems to prevent the spread of the wherewithal to make weapons of mass destruction. Yet, the resolution today remains under-implemented and levels of state compliance are irregularly reported. Moreover, the resolution contains no measure that mandates the evaluation of the effectiveness of national export controls.

This is where the PPI steps in. The PPI assesses numerous indicators pertinent to non-proliferation. Its data and analysis allow for comprehensive, straightforward assessments that help to better characterize the sufficiency of strategic export control systems and other globally-recognized best practices for implementing and maximizing the performance of export control systems. Section I includes information on the index's development, methodology, data, and scoring. Section II provides what the project views as the key rankings of countries in the index, grouping countries into three distinct tiers, each of which represents countries that are alike in their supply potential, economic development, and other measures. In brief, Tier One includes those nations that can supply, at least partially but significantly, the wherewithal to make nuclear weapons, other WMD, or the means to deliver them. Tier Two includes transshipment countries, and Tier Three includes the rest of the countries. Section III contains the findings and recommendations derived from the project and its rankings. Section IV assesses and compares countries in special groupings or applications of interest to the project and likely to many readers. Finally, the Annex provides a full ranking and score for all 200 countries, territories, and entities.

We offer this first version of the Peddling Peril Index with optimism that we will have the opportunity to produce future versions that improve upon it. It is our hope that the PPI will be valuable to states, organizations, researchers, and the general public. We aspire for it to motivate strengthened export control efforts worldwide and reduce the chances that additional states or non-state actors will obtain the wherewithal to fabricate nuclear and other destructive weapons. The printed version is available only in black and white. A color version is available at www. isis-online.org/ppi.

NOTES

1. Countries seeking nuclear weapons prior to the signature of the Nuclear Non-Proliferation Treaty depended on imports for their nuclear weapons efforts but at that time there were few laws controlling exports.

2. David Albright, *Peddling Peril: How the Secret Nuclear Trade Arms America's Enemies* (New York: Free Press, 2010).

3. A shortened United Nations-derived name for each country is used throughout the report. We also use an abbreviated name for non-UN recognized territories or provinces.

SECTION I
PEDDLING PERIL INDEX METHODOLOGY

CHAPTER 1
INTRODUCTION TO THE METHODOLOGY

At the core of the Peddling Peril Index is an evaluation of a set of criteria designed to measure the extent and performance of strategic export controls in 200 nations, territories, and entities. The goal of the PPI is to determine not just the existence of strategic export controls but also the extent of their implementation and enforcement. This endeavor is weighted toward nuclear and nuclear-related export controls but factors in other forms of export controls, such as those covering strategic commodities relevant to the development of missiles, non-nuclear weapons of mass destruction (WMD), and conventional military programs.

A central purpose of the PPI is to provide guidance for efforts to improve states' strategic trade control systems and aid in capacity building efforts. The PPI also provides an indication of a state's vulnerability to illicit procurement schemes and measures the extent of a country's compliance with international obligations, such as United Nations Security Council resolution 1540.

In the first phase of this 18-month project, about 150 sub-criteria in 13 major categories (later titled "super criteria") were identified. A goal was to identify criteria that provide simple answers and are quantifiable, since the PPI assigns points to determine rankings. Another goal was to minimize expert judgment, although this was not possible to do completely, as will be discussed in subsequent chapters.

A priority was not to model criteria used in the U.S. export control system, but to look more broadly and with an open mind at trade controls in a wide variety of countries. Many countries do not have export controls that are as extensive as the United States' but still have effective systems targeted to their level of international trade engagement or nascent systems that could support the development effective strategic export controls in the future, when they are more needed.

An early challenge was optimizing the set of criteria. For example, in the area of trade control legislation, a decision, based on expert advice, was made to identify a finite list of indicators of countries having in place sufficient strategic export control legislation. These included having in place national legislation, national authorities relating to export controls, export control lists, catch-all clauses, and signs of implementation of legislation, to name a few.

After the selection of the basic list of sub-criteria, and the initiation of the data collection phase of the project, we found that adequate data were lacking for many sub-criteria, at least at the level needed to be able to use them in the PPI's comprehensive scoring system. In some cases, data were not available for enough countries to warrant using certain sub-criteria. Moreover, as data were sought and found for sub-criteria, some of the definitions needed to be revised or broadened. In the end, the project settled on a total of 88 sub-criteria, in five major areas, or overarching super criteria.

The **five major super criteria** categories are, and include information about, a country's:

1. International Commitment to preventing strategic commodity trafficking;
2. Legislation in place that regulates and oversees trade in strategic commodities, and criminalizes and aims to prevent strategic commodity trafficking;
3. Ability to Monitor and Detect Strategic Trade;
4. Ability to Prevent Proliferation Financing; and
5. Adequacy of Enforcement against strategic commodity trafficking.

The sub-criteria under each super criteria category are listed and explained in subsequent chapters in Section I. Each sub-criterion is appropriately weighted by the project to derive a ranking for each country under the super criteria. We do not include a ranking of countries under each super criterion. The Legislation super criterion is the only super criterion that includes a breakdown into five groups of countries by the comprehensiveness of their export control legislation.

Countries are assigned a full final score and a resulting ranking by combining all individual super criteria scores. The full ranking and scores included in Annex I compare all 200 countries, entities, and territories. To obtain the full ranking, the super criteria are themselves weighted differently as to their significance. The Ability to Prevent Proliferation Financing and Adequacy of Enforcement super criteria were weighted the most; Legislation and Ability to Monitor and Detect Strategic Trade were given half the impact of those; and International Commitment was given a quarter of the impact of Ability to Prevent Proliferation Financing and Enforcement. In total, countries could receive a maximum of 1,300 points.

An original goal in the final phase of the project methodology development process was to qualitatively assign each country to one of four areas of adequacy. However, as the project developed, another approach was created, one of evaluating groupings of similar countries and performance metrics that aim to guide the improvement of export control systems of countries that are alike in many ways.

Instead of only assessing countries by a full ranking and comparing them against one another – for example, regardless of whether they are small island nations without much participation in international trade or major world economies, or comparing non-nuclear weapon states without access to domestic nuclear technology to nuclear weapon states that have a higher capacity to transfer this technology – the project decided to separate countries into Three Tiers, discussed in the Introduction and detailed in Section II. This manner of evaluating countries acknowledges that smaller countries and countries that trade less, and those that have fewer resources to devote to export controls, are not realistically expected to match the export control performance of major world economies. The tiering system allows for a fairer ranking and shows better how comparable countries rank next to their peers in their potential to prevent the trafficking of nuclear-related and strategic commodities.

A key source of data for the sub-criteria was the UN Security Council resolution 1540 matrices. However, the PPI project sought to confirm, and as necessary, supplement these data. For example, the attributes of legislation declared in the 1540 matrices were confirmed individually by looking at primary source documents, unless otherwise specified in the sub-criteria definition. If there was no entry in the matrix or it was not possible to confirm the source, government websites and other legislation databases were consulted until the PPI team could identify and evaluate each country's export control legislation or approach. In the end, export legislation (or lack thereof) for almost all of the 200 countries and territories were identified and evaluated. Because many laws were not in English, PPI project staff and consultants performed a great deal of translation from a variety of languages, including Chinese, French, Arabic, Spanish, German, and Hindi, among others.

The project depended on open source data, in particular information available online. This approach has limitations. Many of the sub-criteria that were not used would have depended on data held by governments that is not typically published. Some data are classified. A few examples of proposed but rejected sub-criteria where the project encountered problems in finding information are: a government's knowledge of supply chains in its country; the existence of technical reachback capabilities such as drawing on information and expertise from more knowledgeable countries; the transfer of internal investigations into export control enforcement efforts; and internal capabilities such as those of domestic intelligence agencies to detect illicit trade networks.

Sending project staff to visit all 200 countries or even a significant number of them was judged as too costly. The project also decided not to send out survey questionnaires to all the countries, at least for this round. Part of the reason was that the 1540 matrices and Financial Action Task Force (FATF) evaluation reports, which were used, already contain a considerable amount of national self-reporting that is directly relevant to the PPI sub-criteria. In addition, the project did not believe that enough countries would have an incentive to respond any more differently or completely than they do to the 1540 Committee, particularly concerning more sensitive export control enforcement information. Moreover, the project lacked the resources to verify survey information.

To compensate for some of these limitations, the project utilized the Institute's extensive in-house resources and expertise of staff on nuclear and strategic commodity controls and trafficking. In particular, the project benefited from hundreds of Institute case studies on commodity trafficking that shed light on specific countries' capabilities to control exports and detect, prevent, or prosecute those making illicit exports.

Project staff also conducted a number of interviews with experts from a range of countries. Those interviews focused on gaining information from people with specific, direct knowledge of countries' export control systems and their implementation. Many had provided capacity building or expert consultation in a number of countries or worked on programs that extend capacity building assistance. Information on over 60 countries was collected from these experts. The interviews helped add to the evaluation of the effectiveness and enforcement efforts of countries' export control systems.

No index is without limitations. Given that the PPI is the first attempt ever at comprehensively evaluating the effectiveness of national strategic export controls, at least publicly or as far as we could determine, we are fully cognizant of the limitations of the index. We treat this first edition of the PPI as a beta version and as a useful starting point to initiate a broader discussion, including on developing additional information that can improve the index and on incentivizing countries to improve their export control systems.

CHAPTER 2
SUPER CRITERION INTERNATIONAL COMMITMENT

Super Criterion International Commitment focuses on a state's international commitment to non-proliferation of nuclear weapons and other weapons programs, as well as strategic commodity-related materials and equipment. It measures memberships and adherence to a range of non-proliferation conventions, treaties, regimes, and groups. Commitment is not a measure of effectiveness or implementation of the principles or provisions of these instruments on a national level, but it is an important first step. It shows a willingness of a state to follow international standards, potentially improve their own performance, dedicate resources to doing so, share information with other countries and regimes, and allow susceptibility to international pressure.

A state's international commitment to non-proliferation related treaties and conventions is seen in the quality and quantity of the regimes it is party to. Super Criterion International Commitment includes an evaluation of a country's adherence to 22 sub-criteria, in this case key international regimes or agreements, as indicators of performance. Each of the sub-criteria is weighted as low, medium, or high impact by the project to determine a sufficiency rank under the super criterion. Of the 22 sub-criteria, four are considered low impact, nine are medium impact, and nine are high impact. They are worth 5, 10, and 15 points, respectively. A country could receive a raw total of 245 points. This raw score is used later to arrive at a total, weighted score and rank. It is also used to derive a ranking under the Three Tiers of countries discussed in detail in Section II.

International Commitment is the super criterion where countries have the greatest opportunity to score points, since it factors in the most sub-criteria. However, International Commitment does not assess performance, only membership and participation in international regimes or being a party to legal instruments, such as the Treaty on the Non-Proliferation of Nuclear Weapons or Nuclear Weapon Free Zones (NWFZs). Partial credit (usually half of the possible sub-criterion points) was given if a country has only signed but not yet ratified an agreement. It should be noted that, in general, an individual country might not be able to achieve 100 percent of the available points. For example, membership in export control arrangements such as the Nuclear Suppliers Group is by invitation, which might not be forthcoming for some. A country might also be in a location for which there is no relevant nuclear weapon-free zone, such as most of Europe and the Middle East, for example. In addition, the PPI has been constructed for a number of entities whose status makes them ineligible to adhere formally to international legal instruments, for example, Hong Kong and Taiwan.

SUB-CRITERIA[1]:

• Member of Nuclear Suppliers Group[2]

While not legally binding, NSG members are expected to follow certain guidelines regarding the export of sensitive nuclear and nuclear-related facilities, commodities, and material. Specific membership requirements apply, including the adoption of a comprehensive export control list into national legislation. Members generally have the capability of supplying goods classified as nuclear or nuclear dual-use.[3] It should be noted that some countries, such as Israel, adhere to the NSG guidelines, but are not official members. The PPI did not assign points in this case. NSG membership is a high impact sub-criterion.

• Member of the International Maritime Organization (IMO)[4]

Membership in the IMO has no direct legal implications; however, the IMO assists with the drafting and implementation of legally binding conventions to promote lawful, secure, and safe trade via sea routes. Of these, most relevant for the PPI is the Convention for the Suppression of Unlawful Acts Against the Safety of Maritime Navigation, which, among other things, makes it a criminal offence to transport via sea nuclear material and equipment without adequate control or permission by a state party or other applicable governing body. It is a high impact sub-criterion.

- **Party to IAEA Additional Protocol (AP) and participation in voluntary reporting scheme for the import and export of a list of items on the 2015 AP control list, INFCIRC/540 Annex II[5]**

State participants make a voluntary agreement to report to the IAEA annually on all nuclear-related exports they have made, following a control list in the AP Appendix. This voluntary reporting involves reporting by states "of nuclear material not otherwise required to be reported to the IAEA under safeguards agreements, and of exports and imports of specified equipment and non-nuclear material." While only few countries choose to report, it meets the IAEA's desirable level of information sharing and assists it with its safeguarding mission. AP voluntary reporting on sensitive nuclear-related exports is a high impact sub-criterion.

- **Party to the Convention for the Suppression of Acts of Nuclear Terrorism[6]**

This legally binding convention requires countries to actively counter and prevent the possibility of nuclear terrorism. States parties are required to make a wide range of activities related to nuclear and other radioactive material and nuclear facilities criminal offenses, which results in stronger deterrence of illicit conduct by individuals. It is a high impact sub-criterion.

- **Member of the Missile Technology Control Regime (MTCR)[7]**

Although not legally binding, members of the MTCR commit to adhere to stringent export control measures for a specific set of missile-related technologies. Joining the MTCR shows awareness and openness to regulations relating to the spread of ballistic and cruise missiles and their technologies. Membership eligibility also depends on a country's Nuclear Non-Proliferation Treaty, Chemical Weapons Convention (CWC), and Biological Weapons Convention (BWC) statuses. Some countries adhere to the regime but are not official members. In that case, no points were awarded by the PPI. It is a high impact sub-criterion.

- **Participant in the Wassenaar Arrangement on Export Controls for Conventional Arms and Dual-Use Goods**[8]

The Wassenaar Arrangement is a voluntary, non-legally binding multilateral agreement where state nuclear and conventional arms suppliers agree to adhere to recommendations and guidelines on their exports. Specifically, parties agree not to export lists of dual-use goods and technologies and munitions to parties that would not enhance the goal of international security. They also agree to use the guidelines in the drafting of their national export control legislation. Membership eligibility also depends on a country's NPT, CWC, and BWC statuses. Some countries adhere to the arrangement but are not official members. In that case, no points were awarded by the PPI. It is a high impact sub-criterion.

- **Participant in the Proliferation Security Initiative (PSI)**[9]

Not legally binding, the PSI is a voluntary initiative to network with other states to prevent WMD related illicit trade by land, sea, or air. States commit to "impede and stop shipments of WMD, delivery systems, and related materials" based on a set of "Interdiction Principles." This is arguably one of the most directly relevant international agreements for the PPI. As such, it is a high impact sub-criterion.

- **Member of the World Customs Organization (WCO)**[10]

Being a member of the WCO has no direct legal implications, however, the WCO introduces recommendations, declarations, and initiatives, and sponsors legally-binding conventions administered by its Customs Cooperation Council. State willingness to maintain high customs safeguards and standards plays a crucial role in the prevention of commodity trafficking. WCO membership is a high impact sub-criterion.

- **Member of the Financial Action Task Force (FATF) and FATF Regional Body member**[11]

While measuring a state's commitment to preventing the financing of proliferation is its own super criterion under the PPI, membership to the FATF and its regional bodies shows commitment that ideally filters down into a state's development of legislation regarding this matter. Before a country can become a FATF member, its financial practices must undergo a rigorous review process. It is a high impact sub-criterion.

- **Party to the Treaty on the Non-Proliferation of Nuclear Weapons**[12]

The NPT is a foundational step for a country in committing to never manufacture, otherwise acquire, or transfer nuclear weapons. Only five states are not parties to the NPT. It is a medium impact sub-criterion.

- **Member of the International Atomic Energy Agency (IAEA)**[13]

This is a medium impact sub-criterion.

- **Has an IAEA Comprehensive Safeguards Agreement (CSA) in force**[14]

A comprehensive safeguards agreement allows the IAEA to safeguard all nuclear facilities and material in peaceful uses within a country to ensure their exclusively non-military use. The CSA allows the IAEA to implement safeguards on all such nuclear material to ensure they are not diverted to the manufacture of nuclear weapons or nuclear explosive devices for purposes unknown. All non-nuclear weapons states that are parties to the NPT are required to conclude a CSA. This is a medium impact sub-criterion.

- **Has an IAEA Additional Protocol to CSA in force**[15]

Although states conclude Additional Protocols on a voluntary basis, the AP is a binding agreement. It provides the IAEA with enhanced verification tools designed to detect undeclared nuclear material and activities. According to the IAEA, it is granted legal "expanded rights of access to information and locations in the States. For States with a CSA, the Additional Protocol aims to fill the gaps in the information reported under a CSA." It is a medium impact sub-criterion.

- **Has in place a Small Quantities Protocol (SQP) to CSA**[16]

The SQP can be concluded along with a CSA. According to the IAEA, starting in 1974, a standardized small quantities protocol was made available to states with minimal or no nuclear material and no nuclear material in a "facility." It suspends the application of many provisions of the comprehensive safeguards agreement. In 2005, the IAEA Board of Governors decided that any future small quantities protocols should use a revised small quantities protocol that reduces the number of provisions of the comprehensive safeguards agreement that are held in abeyance and key provisions related to reporting nuclear material and the conduct of inspections are operative.

Often the SQP is in effect for states that use limited quantities of nuclear material at research or academic facilities or at medical venues. It is a medium impact sub-criterion.

• IAEA reached a positive Safeguards Conclusion for the country in 2015[17]

A safeguards conclusion is a public IAEA evaluation made each year for all safeguarded states. If a country has a CSA but no AP in place, the IAEA can reach a "conclusion" that *all declared nuclear material* remained in peaceful uses. The IAEA can also try to reach the more time consuming "broader conclusion," for those countries, meaning the IAEA confirms that in general, there is no evidence of diversion of nuclear material and all nuclear material remains in peaceful uses in the state as a whole. No conclusions can be reached for countries that have not signed a CSA or have signed but not ratified it. The PPI used the safeguards conclusion data for 2015. It is a medium impact sub-criterion.

• Party to a Nuclear Weapon Free Zone treaty[18]

A NWFZ Treaty is a regional, legally binding agreement where individual countries commit to keeping the whole region nuclear weapons-free. While countries in certain zones (North America, the Middle East, and Europe) have not yet established NWFZs, there are five successful, established NWFZs: the Treaty of Tlatelolco for Latin America and the Caribbean, Treaty of Rarotonga for the South Pacific, Treaty of Bangkok for Southeast Asia, Treaty of Pelindaba for Africa, and the Central Asian NWFZ for Central Asia. These zones include countries that once pursued or inherited but then renounced nuclear weapons programs and indicate a strong commitment to non-proliferation. It is a medium impact sub-criterion.

• Has in place a Customs Mutual Assistance Agreement (CMAA) with the United States[19]

A country can enter this legally binding, bilateral agreement with the United States to improve collaboration between the two parties' customs systems. This is especially important and beneficial for countries with otherwise weak border control measures and capabilities. It is a medium impact sub-criterion.

- **Party to the Convention on the Physical Protection of Nuclear Material (CPPNM)[20]**

Through this legally binding IAEA convention, states commit to adhere to international standards governing the protection of nuclear facilities and materials during use, storage, and transport. It is a medium impact sub-criterion.

- **Reports to the IAEA Incident and Trafficking Database (ITDB)[21]**

Countries that report incidents involving trafficking of nuclear-related materials or other incidents within their territories increase international collaboration and help the IAEA and all other countries identify strengths and weaknesses regarding abilities to monitor and secure nuclear equipment and material. It is a low impact sub-criterion.

- **Party to the Chemical Weapons Convention[22]**

and

- **Party to the Biological Weapons Convention[23]**

Legally binding adherence to these treaties commits countries to not pursue chemical and biological weapons and to collaborate internationally to eliminate chemical and biological WMD. Adherence to these treaties results in greater information sharing, as well as access to training and equipment in many areas that are applicable to countering nuclear trafficking, such as improved export and border-control measures. Each is considered a low impact sub-criterion.

- **Party to the Hague Code of Conduct against Ballistic Missile Proliferation (HCOC)[24]**

Not legally binding, this voluntary effort strengthens state efforts against ballistic missile proliferation, specifically the proliferation of missiles capable of delivering a nuclear warhead. Signature to the Code of Conduct shows commitment to preventing the spread of ballistic missile technology. It is a low impact sub-criterion.

IMPACT OF SUB-CRITERIA:

As discussed above, the PPI assigns a low to high impact for weighting each of the sub-criteria. **Table 2.1** compiles how each indicator is weighted in the evaluation and how much of an impact it therefore has on a country's score and rank within the super criteria.

SCORING:

Of the 22 sub-criteria, four are considered low impact, nine are medium impact, and nine are high impact. They are worth 5, 10, and 15 points, respectively. A country could receive a raw total of 245 points. This raw score is used later to arrive at a total, weighted score and rank. It is also used to derive a ranking under the Three Tiers.

HIGH IMPACT	MEDIUM IMPACT	LOW IMPACT
NSG	NPT	Reporting to IAEA ITDB
IMO	IAEA member	CWC
AP voluntary reporting scheme	IAEA CSA	BWC
Convention for the Suppression of Acts of Nuclear Terrorism	AP	HCOC
MTCR	SQP	
Wassenaar Arrangement	IAEA Safeguards Conclusion for 2015	
PSI	NWFZ	
WCO	CMAA	
FATF	CPPNM	

Table 2.1. The impact of each International Commitment sub-criterion.

NOTES

1. We considered an additional sub-criterion, namely being a party to the Convention on Combating Bribery of Foreign Public Officials in International Business Transactions. However, it has fewer than 50 signatories (all 35 Organization for Economic Co-operation and Development (OECD) members and eight non-member countries), so it was not included in scoring. It may be used in a future version of the PPI. This convention is administered by the OECD and "establishes legally binding standards to criminalize bribery of foreign public officials in international business transactions." It also established a Working Group to monitor implementation and publishes country implementation reports and recommendations. The PPI assessed that signature to the convention would likely ensure more regulated trade of strategic commodities and equipment by reducing corruption and bribery of officials involved in regulating export processes. Information on the convention is available on the OECD's website: "OECD Convention on Combating Bribery of Foreign Public Officials in International Business Transactions" http://www.oecd.org/corruption/oecdantibriberyconvention.htm.

2. Nuclear Suppliers Group, http://www.nuclearsuppliersgroup.org/en/

3. According to the NSG, factors taken into account for participation include the following:

- The ability to supply items (including items in transit) covered by the Annexes to Parts 1 and 2 of the NSG Guidelines;
- Adherence to the Guidelines and action in accordance with them;
- Enforcement of a legally based domestic export control system which gives effect to the commitment to act in accordance with the Guidelines;
- Adherence to one or more of the NPT, the Treaties of Pelindaba, Rarotonga, Tlatelolco, Bangkok, Semipalatinsk or an equivalent international nuclear non-proliferation agreement, and full compliance with the obligations of such agreement(s);
- Support of international efforts towards non-proliferation of weapons of mass destruction and of their delivery vehicles.

4. International Maritime Organization, http://www.imo.org/en/About/Conventions/ListOfConventions/Pages/SUA-Treaties.aspx

5. Information on the IAEA AP Voluntary Reporting Scheme can be found in *IAEA Safeguards Glossary,* International Verification Series No. 3, 2001 ed., p. 97, http://www-pub.iaea.org/books/IAEABooks/6570/IAEA-Safeguards-Glossary

6. *International Convention for the Suppression of Acts of Nuclear Terrorism,* http://legal.un.org/avl/ha/icsant/icsant.html

7. Missile Technology Control Regime, http://mtcr.info/

8. Wassenaar Arrangement, http://www.wassenaar.org/

9. Proliferation Security Initiative, http://www.psi-online.info/

10. World Customs Organization, http://www.wcoomd.org/

11. Financial Action Task Force, http://www.fatf-gafi.org/

12. *Treaty on the Non-Proliferation of Nuclear Weapons,* Adopted June 12, 1968, https://www.iaea.org/publications/documents/treaties/npt

13. International Atomic Energy Agency, https://www.iaea.org/about/governance/list-of-member-states

14. International Atomic Energy Agency Comprehensive Safeguards Agreement, https://www.iaea.org/safeguards/safeguards-legal-framework/safeguards-agreements

15. International Atomic Energy Agency Additional Protocol, https://www.iaea.org/topics/additional-protocol

16. IAEA, "More on Safeguards Agreements–Small Quantities Protocol," https://www.iaea.org/topics/safeguards-legal-framework/more-on-safeguards-agreements

17. International Atomic Energy Agency Safeguards Conclusion for 2015, https://www.iaea.org/sites/default/files/16/08/statement_sir_2015.pdf

18. Nuclear Weapon Free Zones, https://www.un.org/disarmament/wmd/nuclear/nwfz/

19. United States Customs Mutual Assistance Agreement, https://www.cbp.gov/border-security/international-initiatives/international-agreements/cmaa

20. International Atomic Energy Agency, *Convention on the Physical Protection of Nuclear Material,* https://www.iaea.org/publications/documents/conventions/convention-physical-protection-nuclear-material. The CPPNM entered into force in 1987. It addressed international transport of nuclear material. It was amended in 2005 to extend its reach to nuclear material in domestic use and to nuclear facilities. The amendment entered into force in 2016. The amendment calls for the amended treaty to be named the Convention on Nuclear Material and Facilities. However, the IAEA Secretariat, in line with established depositary practice, will continue to refer to the "CPPNM" and to the "Amendment to the CPPNM" until *all* States Parties to the CPPNM have consented to be bound by the amendment in order to not give the impression that, alongside the original convention, there is now a new convention and that states could now join either one or the other. (https://www.iaea.org/newscenter/news/update-eight-questions-and-answers-on-the-amendment-to-the-convention-on-the-physical-protection-of-nuclear-material).

21. International Atomic Energy Agency Incident and Trafficking Database,http://www-ns.iaea.org/security/itdb.asp

22. *United Nations Chemical Weapons Convention,* https://www.opcw.org/chemical-weapons-convention/

23. *United Nations Biological Weapons Convention,* https://www.un.org/disarmament/wmd/bio/

24. *United Nations Hague Code of Conduct,* http://www.hcoc.at/

CHAPTER 3
SUPER CRITERION LEGISLATION

Super Criterion Legislation focuses on a state's legislation, regulations, and related national authorities that are tools or capabilities to control strategic trade in sensitive commodities, with a focus on nuclear and nuclear-related goods. It assesses 13 sub-criteria, or indicators of performance. The ability of a country to act to prevent strategic commodity trafficking lies at the heart of the PPI. Without the legal basis and tools to act against illicit procurement, such efforts cannot be detected, investigated, and shut down, and key actors cannot be prosecuted. Legislation does not need to be the same for each country, but legislation that is adequate to achieve its mission should include, to name a few, provisions addressing import and export controls including licensing of controlled goods, the transfer and transport of sensitive commodities, and necessitating financing regulations to prevent illicit purchases. It should also provide for the national use of proper documentation to control imports and exports and information sharing systems that help with regulation, such as automated customs systems.

The Legislation super criterion assesses whether a country has legislation, authorities, and regulations in place to control strategic or sensitive trade according to 13 sub-criteria. Experts were consulted in the development of the list of legislative sub-criteria. The goal was to develop a list of key indicators of strategic trade control laws, which could show the extent of control legislation and differentiate between countries' controls.

All countries, and not only major economies involved in international trade or NSG member countries, have an opportunity to score highly under this super criterion if they strongly police imports and exports in general, rather than only strategic commodities. Less than one third of the sub-criteria are considered high impact; the majority are medium impact. Of the 13 sub-criteria, four are considered low impact, five are medium impact, and four are high impact sub-criteria. They are worth 5, 10, and 15 points, respectively. A country could receive a raw total of 130 points under this super criterion. This raw score is used later to arrive at a total, weighted score and rank for each country. It is also used to derive a ranking for the country under the Three Tiers. In addition, the project scores the comprehensiveness of all 200 countries,' territories,' and entities' export control legislation and divides them into five sub-categories.

Significant effort was put into finding all relevant legislation or confirming its existence by a reliable third party (such as the IAEA or European Parliament). Effort was made to ensure that non-English legislation and scanned documents, which are non-searchable, were detected and included. In addition to government websites, helpful resources were the UN Office for Disarmament Affairs database, 1540 matrices, International Labour Organization database, Arms Trade Treaty Baseline Assessment Project, and GunPolicy.org.[1]

SUB-CRITERIA[2]:

• **National export control legislation includes a catch-all clause[3]**

A catch-all clause is a component of legislation that is designed to "catch" the export of goods that may not be listed on export control lists but that may be used in sensitive weapons, sanctioned, or unsafeguarded programs. As such, they require authorization for export. The 1540 matrix provides information on which countries include a catch-all clause as a part of their national export control legislation. For countries that did not report a catch-all clause to the 1540 Committee, an effort was made to individually verify whether similar legislation exists in the country. This is a high impact sub-criterion.

- **Comprehensiveness of export control legislation such as encapsulating NSG Parts 1 and 2 lists**

The most rigorous national export control legislation encapsulates a comprehensive list of controlled items that include the NSG Parts 1 and 2 lists, and goes even further by adding additional items. An attempt was made to find a list of export-controlled items for each country. However, in some cases, national legislation refers to a set of controlled items without a country making a detailed list easily and publicly available. In that case, the PPI team looked at the comprehensiveness of the law referring to the list. This is a high impact sub-criterion.

- **Transit control legislation is in place[4]**

This indicator sought to collect trade regulations for each country addressing the treatment of goods that are in transit. Many countries have reported the existence of such regulations to the 1540 Committee. For the PPI, the data are taken from the 1540 matrices, and not individually collected. For existing legislation not reported to the 1540 Committee, no points were assigned. By this decision, the PPI supports the 1540 Committee's request for information and encourages countries to report fully and accurately. This is a high impact sub-criterion.

- **Transshipment control legislation is in place[5]**

This indicator sought to collect trade regulations for each country addressing the treatment of goods that are being transshipped through the country. Many countries have reported the existence of such regulations to the 1540 Committee. The PPI used data in the 1540 matrices, and not data individually collected. For existing legislation not reported to the 1540 Committee, no points were assigned. By this decision, the PPI supports the 1540 Committee's request for information and encourages countries to report fully and accurately. This is a high impact sub-criterion.

- **Presence of licensing process for export licenses**

Presence of a licensing process for export licenses refers to whether a country has a formal process to adjudicate decisions on making or rejecting applications for export permits or licenses for companies to export any type of controlled good. This is a medium impact sub-criterion.

• Use of automated customs system

Having an automated or electronic customs system versus one that uses paper documents indicates a more efficient and advanced customs system. It usually implies that a country inspects packages or cargo based on information about shipments that allows it to optimize inspections under a risk-based approach. A majority of countries use automated customs systems, particularly since the United Nations Conference on Trade and Development started to promote and assist with the implementation of its ASYCUDA software (Automated System for Customs Data). The PPI collected information for each country individually. It did not discern that certain types of electronic systems are better or worse. This is a medium impact sub-criterion.

• An authority regarding civil and criminal investigations is designated by law[6]

This indicator refers to the existence of a government body that deals with violations of export control laws and regulations, and whether it has civil and criminal investigation authorities. Members of Interpol list their respective authorities in a publicly available database. For most countries the investigative authority is the federal police. This is a medium impact sub-criterion.

• Import control legislation includes a list of controlled goods

This indicator refers to legislation in place that lists all controlled and banned imports, especially with regard to nuclear direct- and dual-use goods, radioactive materials, or goods that are capable of being used in WMD. This data includes an itemized list of controlled imports for countries. Sufficient import controls are especially relevant for countries in Tiers 2 and 3, which pose a transit or diversion concern rather than a supplier concern for strategic commodity trafficking. This is a medium impact sub-criterion.

• End-use statements are required for export licenses

An end-use statement is a legal declaration made by an importing party and discloses the final destination and intended use of a good. This is especially important to have in place for countries that can supply nuclear direct- and dual-use goods or those countries in Tier 1. End-use statements can be used to later check whether the good is being used by the party and for the use that was intended. This is a medium-impact sub-criterion.

• Import license or declaration is required to import goods

This indicator refers to whether or not an import license or declaration is required to import goods. The PPI assigned the same points for those countries that require an import permit or license and those that only require an import declaration at customs. This is especially important for countries that are heavily involved in the re-export of goods, or Tier Two countries, because it allows authorities the chance to detect illicit goods crossing their territories. Of note, rigorous import controls seemed more common than rigorous export controls.

• Certificates of Origin are required for imports or re-exports[7]

The International Chamber of Commerce defines a Certificate of Origin as "an important international trade document that certifies that goods in a particular export shipment are wholly obtained, produced, manufactured or processed in a particular country."[8] The World Bank's "Ease of Doing Business" database provides information for almost all countries on whether a Certificate of Origin is required for the import or re-export of certain goods. As the requirement is not specified for nuclear direct- or dual-use goods, but all goods in general, this indicator was weighed as having low impact.

• Bills of Lading (BOL) are required for carriers during transport[9]

A BOL assigns legal responsibility for goods during transport. According to a definition published by *The Economic Times*, a BOL "...acts as a receipt and a contract. A completed BOL legally shows that the carrier has received the freight as described and is obligated to deliver that freight in good condition to the consignee."[10] It is relevant for preventing strategic commodity trafficking as it adds accountability and monitoring of goods during transport. The World Bank's "Ease of Doing Business" database provides information for almost all countries on whether a Bill of Lading is required for the shipment of goods. As the requirement is not specifically for nuclear direct- or dual-use goods, but all goods in general, this indicator was weighed as having low impact.

• **Intellectual Property Rights are protected**[11]

The protection of sensitive information is highly valuable in sectors that both use and export nuclear-related and other sensitive commodities. Ideally, the PPI team would try to compare how countries protect in particular nuclear-related knowledge and information, including, for example, electronic information, designs, or calculations, from unintended use. This was too difficult to determine for each country, so the regulation and protection of know-how was assessed in general using the 2016 Intellectual Property Rights scores calculated by the Property Rights Alliance. As these scores are used for their potential implications only, this indicator was determined to be low impact.

IMPACT OF SUB-CRITERIA:

The PPI assigned a low to high impact for weighting each of the sub-criteria. **Table 3.1** shows how each indicator was weighted in the evaluation and how much of an impact it therefore had on a country's score and rank within the super criteria.

HIGH IMPACT	MEDIUM IMPACT	LOW IMPACT
Catch-all clause in legislation	Licensing process for export licenses	Import license or declaration required
Comprehensive export control legislation	Use of automated customs system	Certificates of Origin required
Transit control legislation	Civil and criminal investigations authority	Bills of Lading required
Transshipment control legislation	Import control legislation incl. list of controlled goods	Intellectual property rights protected
	End-use statements required for exports	

Table 3.1. High, Medium, and Low Impact of Legislation sub-criteria.

SCORING AND SUFFICIENCY RANK:

Of the 13 sub-criteria, four are considered low impact, five are medium impact, and four are high impact sub-criteria. They are worth 5, 10, and 15 points, respectively. A country could receive a raw total of 130 points under this super criterion. This raw score is used later to arrive at a total, weighted score and rank for each country. It is also used to derive a ranking for the country under the Three Tiers.

The comprehensiveness of the 200 countries', territories' and entities' export control legislation is divided into the following five sub-categories. Existence of comprehensive legislation is not to be confused with its effective implementation, which will be discussed in subsequent super criteria chapters.

- **Green (legislation is comprehensive):** Export control legislation or agreements includes controls or clauses relating to nuclear direct-use and nuclear dual-use goods, (nuclear and nuclear-dual use commodity controls such as implementation of NSG Parts 1 & 2 or their equivalent), in addition to conventional weapons. The most commonly used lists are the European Union (EU) Control List and Wassenaar Arrangement list. This category counted 75 countries.

- **Light Green (legislation is somewhat comprehensive):** Export control legislation or agreements includes controls or clauses relating to nuclear direct-use goods (nuclear commodity controls such as implementation of NSG Part 1 list or an equivalent), in addition to conventional weapons. This category counted 9 countries.

- **Yellow (legislation is deficient):** Countries have comprehensive, overarching nuclear safety and security laws which place transfer controls on nuclear material and equipment. If the PPI team was unable to locate relevant legislation, the 2016 Nuclear Threat Initiative (NTI) Nuclear Security Index was consulted, specifically its data on whether a country has or does not have a national legal framework for the Convention on the Physical Protection of Nuclear Material. These countries are not viewed as having effective export control laws governing nuclear and nuclear-related commodities, but their existing legislation is viewed as better in a relevant export control sense than the legislation or lack of legislation in the Red and Orange categories. This category counted 22 countries.

- **Orange (legislation has serious deficiencies):** Export control legislation covers only conventional weapons as laid out under the Arms Trade Treaty. This is not considered comprehensive export control legislation for the PPI. This category counted 41 countries.

- **Red (legislation is non-existent or severely deficient):** Export control legislation includes small arms and light weapons (SALW), and/

or radioactive materials under environmental laws. This is not considered comprehensive export control legislation for the PPI. This category counted 53 countries.

The project collected data on legislation from the summer of 2016 to the spring of 2017. An important development that occurred after this cutoff date, and is not reflected in the PPI, was the introduction of the Caribbean Control and Focus List. This initiative implemented a dual-use control list customized for the Caribbean countries. This project welcomes the progress and targeted approach that was taken by all of the participants. It should move the Caribbean countries to a green legislation color category in a future PPI version.

Table 3.2. Export control legislation sufficiency rank by color category

Green (legislation is comprehensive)

Albania, Andorra, Argentina, Armenia, Australia, Austria, Azerbaijan, Belarus, Belgium, Bosnia and Herzegovina, Brazil, Bulgaria, Canada, China, Croatia, Cyprus, Czech Republic, Denmark, Estonia, Finland, France, Georgia, Germany, Greece, Holy See, Hong Kong, Hungary, Iceland, India, Iraq, Ireland, Israel, Italy, Japan, Jordan, Kazakhstan, Kyrgyzstan, Latvia, Liechtenstein, Lithuania, Luxembourg, Macedonia, Malaysia, Malta, Mexico, Moldova (Rep of the), Monaco, Montenegro, Namibia, Netherlands, New Zealand, Norway, Pakistan, Philippines, Poland, Portugal, Republic of Korea, Romania, Russian Federation, San Marino, Serbia, Singapore, Slovakia, Slovenia, South Africa, Spain, Sweden, Switzerland, Taiwan, Thailand, Turkey, Ukraine, United Arab Emirates, United Kingdom of Great Britain and Northern Ireland, United States of America

Light Green (legislation is somewhat comprehensive)

Brunei Darussalam, Cambodia, Kosovo, Lebanon, Libya, Myanmar, Tajikistan, Uzbekistan, Viet Nam

Yellow (legislation is deficient)

Algeria, Bangladesh, Botswana, Cape Verde, Chile, Cuba, Ghana, Guatemala, Indonesia, Jamaica, Morocco, Nicaragua, Nigeria, Niue, Peru, Qatar, Rwanda, Sierra Leone, Sri Lanka, Tanzania (United Republic of), Uganda, Uruguay

Orange (legislation has serious deficiencies)

Barbados, Benin, Bhutan, Bolivia, Burkina Faso, Costa Rica, Côte d'Ivoire, Dominican Republic, Ecuador, El Salvador, Ethiopia, Fiji, Gabon, Gambia, Grenada, Kuwait, Lao People's Democratic Republic, Lesotho, Malawi, Mauritania, Mongolia, Nauru, Niger, Palau, Panama, Paraguay, Saint Kitts and Nevis, Samoa, Saudi Arabia, Senegal, Seychelles, Solomon Islands, Suriname, Syrian Arab Republic, Timor-Leste, Trinidad and Tobago, Turkmenistan, Tuvalu, Vanuatu, Venezuela (Bolivarian Republic of), Zambia

Red (legislation is non-existent or severely deficient)

Afghanistan, Angola, Antigua and Barbuda, Bahamas, Bahrain, Belize, Burundi, Cameroon, Central African Republic, Chad, Colombia, Comoros, Congo (Dem Rep of the), Congo (Rep of the), Cook Islands, Djibouti, Dominica, Democratic People's Republic of Korea, (DPRK), Egypt, Equatorial Guinea, Eritrea, Guinea, Guinea-Bissau, Guyana, Haiti, Honduras, Iran (Islamic Republic of), Kenya, Kiribati, Liberia, Madagascar, Maldives, Mali, Marshall Islands, Mauritius, Micronesia (Federated States of), Mozambique, Nepal, Oman, Palestine (State of), Papua New Guinea, Saint Lucia, Saint Vincent and the Grenadines, Sao Tome and Principe, Somalia, South Sudan, Sudan, Swaziland, Togo, Tonga, Tunisia, Yemen, Zimbabwe

NOTES

1. Unfortunately, some countries report environmental laws or similar as WMD-relevant export control laws to the 1540 Committee. See Section III, Chapter 12 for the PPI team's recommendations including those to the 1540 Committee.

2. Project staff considered four additional sub-criteria but they were unable to find enough information for a sufficient number of countries, so they were not included in scoring:

   1. An authority to enforce land border security is designated by national law: An attempt was made to identify the authority in each country that is responsible for controlling goods coming and going across land borders. Most countries did not differentiate between land, sea, or air authorities so this sub-criterion was dropped. Customs officials were the most commonly seen land border enforcement authority.

   2. End use verification for dual-use goods: The verification of end-user declarations can have significant impact on detecting the unintended diversion of exported goods. An end-use verification is a physical check made by a government or company at the site of the good's stated end destination. It seeks to determine that the stated buyer is an actual physical entity and that it is using the good for the stated end-use. While many exporters require an end-use statement prior to finalizing a sale and making an export, few countries (or their companies) use end-use verification as a monitoring tool against the illicit diversion of sensitive goods. Germany and the United States stand out as two of few countries that use this tool. Tier 1 countries should especially use end-use verification to check the location and use of nuclear-related goods. Few other countries have the financial and technical resources that would be needed to carry out such checks. A risk-based approach should be used to determine priority goods and destinations for post-shipment end-use verification.

   3. A specific nuclear-related licensing agency exists within the country: This authority refers to a government body in charge of granting export licenses for the export of nuclear-related goods. An attempt was made to assign points for countries that have a specific nuclear-related export body or office, but the majority of countries use a general export control or customs agency, so this sub-criterion was dropped.

   4. Implementation of additional, unilateral sanctions: The PPI team attempted to assign points for countries that employ and implement additional sanctions against known proliferant states or illicit networks that supplement UN sanctions. Not enough countries deployed additional unilateral sanctions to make this sub-criterion usable.

3. 1540 Committee Approved Matrices, Dated December 23, 2015, http://www.un.org/en/sc/1540/national-implementation/1540-matrices/committee-approved-matrices.shtml; internet searches.

4. 1540 Committee Approved Matrices, Dated December 23, 2015, http://www.un.org/en/sc/1540/national-implementation/1540-matrices/committee-approved-matrices.shtml. For example, 1540 Committee Matrix for Afghanistan, in row 20 of Table OP 3 (c) and (d), http://www.un.org/en/sc/1540/documents/Afghanistan%20revised%20matrix.pdf. An "X" in the "National Legal Framework" cell relating to NW (nuclear weapons) was taken as confirmation that sufficient enforcement mechanisms exist. A question mark was given partial credit. An empty cell received no points.

5. For example, see the 1540 Committee Matrix of Afghanistan, row 21, http://www.un.org/en/sc/1540/documents/Afghanistan%20revised%20matrix.pdf. In row 21 of a specific country's matrix, an "X" in the "National Legal Framework" cell relating to NW (nuclear weapons) was taken as confirmation that sufficient enforcement mechanisms exist. A question mark was given partial credit. An empty cell received no points.

6. The authorities for 190 countries were found in the respective country profiles published by the International Criminal Police Organization. Access to the country profiles is available here: Interpol, "World–A global presence," Member Countries, https://www.interpol.int/Member-countries/World

7. Whether a Certificate of Origin is required can be found in the World Bank's "Ease of Doing Business" database, by searching on a country-by-country case basis. Access to the database is available here: http://data.worldbank.org/indicator/IC.EXP.DOCS?end=2014&name_desc=false&start=2013

8. International Chamber of Commerce, "Certificates of Origin," https://iccwbo.org/resources-for-business/certificates-of-origin/ (Accessed June 2017).

9. Whether a BOL is required can be found in the World Bank's "Ease of Doing Business" database by searching on a country-by-country case basis. Access to the database is available here: http://data.worldbank.org/indicator/IC.EXP.DOCS?end=2014&name_desc=false&start=2013

10. "Definition of 'Bill of Lading,'" *The Economic Times,* https://economictimes.indiatimes.com/definition/bill-of-lading (Accessed November 2017).

11. Property Rights Alliance, *The Intellectual Property Rights Index 2016,* http://ec2.digitalliberty.net/. Individual country scores are published in the index.

CHAPTER 4
SUPER CRITERION ABILITY TO MONITOR AND DETECT STRATEGIC TRADE

Super Criterion Ability to Monitor and Detect Strategic Trade assesses the mechanisms that allow a state to monitor and control strategic or sensitive trade, and the hospitableness of the state environment to achieving the mission. It focuses mostly on tangible outcomes under 15 sub-criteria, rather than simply on the theoretical abilities of a country, by factoring in various performance metrics or views about performance such as statistics, surveys, expert observations, and rankings conducted by other non-governmental organizations or international organizations. For example, quantitative assessments about countries' relative governmental transparency, internal stability, and customs diligence are included. These factors can significantly add to or take away from a country's ability to monitor and detect strategic trade.

This super criterion is one of the most challenging for countries to score highly on as it measures tangible outcomes rather than pledges or intentions made in treaties or laws. It measures under the 15 sub-criteria actions, efficiencies, transparencies, and stability. Most countries can only improve their performance under this super criterion through systematic and long-term improvements. Many of the sub-criteria are medium impact, however, so they are not eligible for the most points. Of the 15 sub-criteria, two are considered low impact, ten are medium impact, and three are high impact. They are worth 5, 10, and 15 points, respectively. A country could receive a total of 155 points under this super criterion. This raw score is used later to arrive at a total, weighted score and rank for each country. It is also used to derive a ranking for the country under the Three Tiers.

SUB-CRITERIA[1]:

• **Has ability to track and trace consignments[2]**

The 2016 Logistics Performance Index produced by the World Bank provides a score for countries on their ability to track and trace consignments. Countries with higher scores under "tracking and tracing" demonstrate a greater capacity to perform this function, which indicates a country's capacity to monitor and control the movement of strategic goods inside and out of the country. As such, this indicator is given a high impact.

• **Percentage of import shipments physically inspected[3]**

The 2016 Logistics Performance Index by the World Bank also estimates the percentage of import shipments that are inspected in each country. While inspecting each container or every shipment is not practical, random inspections and inspections of known strategic commodity shipments are necessary to effectively monitor the transit of potentially sensitive shipments and detect illicit activity. This is a high impact sub-criterion.

• **Percentage of import shipments physically inspected multiple times[4]**

The 2016 Logistics Performance Index estimates the percentage of shipments that are physically inspected multiple times by each country. The World Bank finds multiple inspections to be a poor means of policing imports because it renders the entire customs system inefficient; for the PPI team, multiple inspections increase the chances that a sensitive commodity will be detected in transit. This sub-criterion allows countries that are weak in their Ability to Monitor and Detect Strategic Trade a chance to attain points. It is assessed as high impact.

• Use of automated customs system

Also used in Super Criterion Legislation, having an automated or electronic customs system versus one that uses paper documents typically indicates a more efficient and advanced customs system. This sub-criterion is used twice because of its fundamental importance to tracking the nature and movement of commodities. It usually implies that a country inspects packages or cargo based on information about shipments that allows it to optimize inspections under a risk-based approach. A majority of countries use automated customs systems, particularly since the United Nations Conference on Trade and Development started to promote and assist with the implementation of its ASYCUDA software. The PPI collected information for each country individually. The PPI did not discern that certain types of electronic systems are better or worse. It is a medium impact sub-criterion.

• Ease of starting a business[5]

Countries that make starting a business straightforward generally have a transparent and well-regulated process in place, such as obtaining legitimate licenses and documents. The PPI team assessed that such countries may be less likely to have companies engaged in illicit activities. The World Bank ranks 190 countries on the ability to start a business. This is a medium impact sub-criterion.

• World Economic Forum Ranking[6]

This ranking is taken from the Global Enabling Trade Report for 2014, produced by the World Economic Forum. The report ranks 138 countries on their ability to provide "faster and more efficient customs procedures through effective cooperation between customs and other appropriate authorities on trade facilitation and customs compliance issues. It also contains provisions for technical assistance and capacity building." These provisions are outlined in the World Trade Organization's Trade Facilitation Agreement. States with a higher rank are more likely to have implemented such provisions and have a broader capacity to monitor and detect illicit trade. This is a medium impact sub-criterion.

• Efficiency of customs clearance process[7]

As part of the World Economic Forum's Global Enabling Trade Report for 2014, countries were given a score for the efficiency of their customs clearance process on a scale from 1 to 5, with 5 being the most efficient. Countries with efficient clearance processes have the mechanisms in place to clear imports and exports and, thus, would be more likely to have trained and knowledgeable customs officials able to identify illicit imports and exports. This is a medium impact sub-criterion.

• Internal stability/Absence of violence/terrorism – World Bank estimate[8]

Countries that are described by the World Bank as more stable and have less violence and terrorism are correlated by the PPI as more able to effectively implement mechanisms to monitor exports and imports and detect illicit activity. These processes and related organizations are less likely to be negatively influenced by corruption, high turnover, and other disrupting factors. The World Bank 2014 Worldwide Governance Indicator on political stability and absence of violence/terrorism is used to calculate points for this sub-criterion. It is assigned a medium impact.

• Government Outreach[9]

To prevent nuclear-related and strategic commodities from being mistakenly or purposefully exported to sanctioned or nefarious end users, government agencies must conduct outreach to train and inform officials at companies about the country's laws and procedures for licensing, as well as detecting and preventing illicit procurement attempts. Government agencies should also have a point of contact to deal with 1540 implementation. Countries with greater outreach efforts are more likely to effectively monitor and detect illicit trading activity. The 1540 Committee's 2015 matrix includes resources that would be needed to carry out such checks and information about countries on these sub-criteria. Each is assigned a medium impact by the PPI, but could they could be considered high impact in future versions:

- State works with and informs industry about strategic trade
- State works with and informs the public about strategic trade
- State has point of contact for 1540 implementation

• Lack of denied parties by United States and the European Union[10]

Countries with entities sanctioned by the United States Treasury Department's Office of Foreign Assets Control (OFAC), Bureau of Industry and Security (BIS), or the European Union's sanctions lists likely failed to detect illicit activity until after it occurred. Thus, for the PPI, these countries are viewed as less capable of monitoring and detecting illicit activities. When assigning points for this sub-criterion, the number of entities was not taken into consideration, and points were only awarded if a country did not have a single entity on these sanctions lists. This sub-criterion allows for a rough measure of what a country knows about its internal business. It is measured as medium impact.

**• Party to the Convention on Transit of Land-locked States/Party
  to the UN Convention on the Law of the Sea**[11]

These two conventions are taken as a single sub-criterion. They have similar provisions regarding transshipment regulations. They are relevant for the PPI as they add clarity to countries' legal responsibilities and rights regarding the transport of goods through one or more countries. According to the Convention on the Law of the Sea, Article 125 *Right of access to and from the sea and freedom of transit*:

1. *Land-locked States shall have the right of access to and from the sea for the purpose of exercising the rights provided for in this Convention including those relating to the freedom of the high seas and the common heritage of mankind. To this end, land-locked States shall enjoy freedom of transit through the territory of transit States by all means of transport.*
2. *The terms and modalities for exercising freedom of transit shall be agreed between the land-locked States and transit States concerned through bilateral, subregional or regional agreements.*
3. *Transit States, in the exercise of their full sovereignty over their territory, shall have the right to take all measures necessary to ensure that the rights and facilities provided for in this Part for land-locked States shall in no way infringe their legitimate interests.*

Additionally, the Convention on the Law of the Sea introduces language in Article 25 that gives transit countries the legal authority for interdicting cargo. Specifically, the coastal state (transit country) may "take the necessary steps in its territorial sea to prevent passage which is not innocent." This language could be used as a basis to learn more about shipments of strategically-controlled goods.

This sub-criterion is of medium impact.

• Logistics Performance Index Rank[12]

The PPI team took into account a country's overall ranking in the World Bank's 2016 Logistics Performance Index. In addition to measuring countries' Tracking and Tracing of shipments, the World Bank measures a country's logistics performance through evaluating such indicators as Customs, Infrastructure, International shipments, Logistics competence, and Timeliness. It is a low impact sub-criterion.

• Level of state control of the economy[13]

The Heritage Foundation's Index of Economic Freedom for 2015 measures the level of state control of the economy, or "economic freedom," based on 10 factors in four categories: Rule of Law (property rights, freedom from corruption); Government Size (fiscal freedom, government spending); Regulatory Efficiency (business freedom, labor freedom, monetary freedom); and Open Markets (trade freedom, investment freedom, financial freedom)." These pillars support an efficient and reliable export control system. Since they support, but do not guarantee efficiency and reliability, this indicator was judged by the PPI team as having a low impact on overall Ability to Monitor and Detect Strategic Trade.

IMPACT OF SUB-CRITERIA:

The PPI assigned a low to high impact for weighting each of the sub-criteria. **Table 4.1** shows how each indicator was weighted in the evaluation and how much of an impact it therefore had on a country's score and rank within the super criteria.

SCORING:

Of the 15 sub-criteria, two are considered low impact, ten are medium impact, and three are high impact. They are worth 5, 10, and 15 points, respectively. A country could receive a total of 155 points under this super criterion. This raw score is used later to arrive at a total, weighted score and rank for each country. It is also used to derive a ranking for the country under the Three Tiers.

HIGH IMPACT	MEDIUM IMPACT	LOW IMPACT
Ability to track and trace consignments	Use of automated customs system	Logistics Performance Index Rank
Percentage of import shipments physically inspected	Ease of starting a business	Level of state control of the economy
Percentage of shipments physically inspected multiple times	World Economic Forum Ranking	
	Efficiency of customs clearance process	
	Internal stability	
	Government Outreach: State works with and informs industry	
	Government Outreach: State works with and informs the public	
	Government Outreach: State has point of contact for 1540	
	Lack of denied parties by US and EU	
	Convention on Transit of Land-locked States/UN Convention on Law of the Sea	

Table 4.1. The impact of each sub-criterion under Super Criterion Ability to Monitor and Detect Strategic Trade.

NOTES

1. Project staff considered five additional sub-criteria but were unable to find enough information, so they were not included in scoring: 1) Post-shipment end-use verification capacity, 2) Level of customs awareness and involvement in strategic trade control, 3) Knowledge by governments of own domestic supply potential, 4) Demonstrated capability to detect at borders illicit or unauthorized radioactive imports or exports, for example, deployed, effective radiation portal monitors (RPMs), scanners, or other means of hazardous material identification, and 5) National databases containing cases of nuclear-related trafficking detected or prosecuted by authorities.

2. The World Bank, "Global Rankings 2016," *Logistics Performance Index,* 2016, https://lpi.worldbank.org/international/global

3. "Global Rankings 2016."

4. Ibid.

5. The World Bank, "Starting a Business," *Doing Business: Measuring Business Regulations,* June 2017, http://www.doingbusiness.org/data/exploretopics/ starting-a-business

6. World Economic Forum, "Global Enabling Trade Report 2014," http://www3. weforum.org/docs/WEF_GlobalEnablingTrade_Report_2014.pdf

7. Ibid. The scores can be found in the individual country profiles under the report's discussion of Pillar 3: Efficiency and transparency of border administration.

8. The World Bank, "Worldwide Governance Indicators," DataBank: Series: Political Stability and Absence of Violence/Terrorism Estimate, 2014, http://databank. worldbank.org/data/reports.aspx?source=worldwide-governance-indicators

9. 1540 Committee Approved Matrices, Dated December 23, 2015, http://www.un.org/ en/sc/1540/national-implementation/1540-matrices/committee-approved-matrices. shtml

10. United States Department of the Treasury, Office of Foreign Assets Control, "SDN List by Country," https://www.treasury.gov/ofac/downloads/ctrylst.txt; United States Department of Commerce, Bureau of Industry and Security, "Supplement No. 4 to Part 744–ENTITY LIST," *Export Administration Regulations,* https://www.bis.doc. gov/index.php/forms-documents/regulations-docs/federal-register-notices/federal-register-2014/957-744-supp-4-1/file (Accessed Winter 2016); European Commission, "European Union - Restrictive measures (sanctions) in force," updated April 26, 2017, https://eeas.europa.eu/sites/eeas/files/restrictive_measures-2017-04-26-clean.pdf

11. United Nations Treaty Collection, *Convention on Transit Trade of Land-locked States,* New York, July 8, 1965, updated June 11, 2017, https://treaties.un.org/pages/viewdetails.aspx?src=treaty&mtdsg_no=x-3&chapter=10&lang=en; United Nations Division for Ocean Affairs and the Law of the Sea, *United Nations Convention on the Law of the Sea,* December 10, 1982, http://www.un.org/Depts/los/convention_agreements/texts/unclos/unclos_e.pdf

12. The World Bank, "Global Rankings 2016," *Logistics Performance Index,* 2016, https://lpi.worldbank.org/international/global

13. Chapter 1 in Terry Miller and Anthony B. Kim, "Principles of Economic Freedom," *2015 Index of Economic Freedom,* (Washington, D.C.: Heritage Foundation, 2015), http://www.heritage.org/index/pdf/2015/book/chapter1.pdf

CHAPTER 5
SUPER CRITERION ABILITY TO PREVENT PROLIFERATION FINANCING

Super Criterion Ability to Prevent Proliferation Financing evaluates a country's ability to prevent Financing of Proliferation, a relatively new approach to stopping commodity trafficking. This super criterion uses evaluations conducted by the Financial Action Task Force, the major international organization seeking to establish standards and assess efforts at preventing money laundering and financial crime. Early in the sub-criteria development process, experts with knowledge of proliferation financing advised the project on the most relevant FATF-collected data. In addition to FATF data, the super criterion Ability to Prevent Proliferation Financing utilizes real world measures and information about countries' susceptibility to being exploited or involved in proliferation financing, including violations of international sanctions. Of note, it is the super criterion under which countries collectively performed the worst. Moreover, this super criterion offers the fewest sub-criteria for measuring countries' performance because of a lack of data involving this newer approach.

This super criterion first *assigns* points to countries based on sub-criteria derived mostly from FATF determinations. These sub-criteria assess countries' theoretical capabilities to prevent money laundering and proliferation financing based on their financial regulatory systems and counter-illicit financing programs. The eleven sub-criteria are characterized as "positive indicators." The PPI then *takes away* points according to five "negative indicator" sub-criteria, or real-world information and examples of poor controls, such as when countries are known to have been involved in illicit finance, they are sanctioned by major world economies for illicit financing activities, they have assisted others in proliferation financing, or they consistently do not act to prevent illicit financing efforts. The positive and negative indicators are assigned a low, medium, or high impact for scoring purposes. The project next assigns or takes away available "extra credit" points according to two other FATF-related sub-criteria. Finally, the judgment of experts in proliferation financing who were consulted for the PPI is used to take away or assign points based on their knowledge of proliferation financing in certain countries. Of the 11 positive sub-criteria, two are considered low impact, seven are medium impact, and two are high impact. They are worth 5, 10, and 15 points, respectively. Of the five negative sub-criteria, four are medium impact and one is high impact. After extra credit and expert knowledge points, a country could receive a total of 110 points under this super criterion. This raw score is used later to arrive at a total, weighted score and rank for each country. It is also used to derive a ranking for the country under the Three Tiers.

Overall, there is little international effort devoted to assessing proliferation financing, which is why the PPI relies heavily on FATF evaluations. However, much of the FATF's information applies to broader illicit financing activities rather than specifically to proliferation financing. FATF only added proliferation financing as a focus in 2012. Since then, FATF evaluations include looking at countries' theoretical ability to implement international financial sanctions and the effectiveness of the controls against those countries under international financial sanctions, including investigation and enforcement actions. These evaluation data were only available for a limited number of countries. Thus, the PPI team decided to factor in the other point addition and subtraction categories.

POSITIVE INDICATORS[1]:

• **Compliance with selected FATF recommendations**

FATF is the organization that provides the most data regarding a country's banking regulations and practices. The objectives of the FATF are to set standards and promote effective implementation of legal, regulatory, and operational measures for combating money laundering, terrorist financing, and other related threats to the integrity of the international financial system. It publishes a periodically updated set of recommendations that all member countries should follow to prevent financial crimes and publishes evaluations of individual counties' compliance with each recommendation. The evaluations are conducted by FATF or its regional FATF bodies and are titled "Mutual Evaluation Reports." For each recommendation, potential deficiencies are listed, and a final conclusion is drawn, which can be that the country is Not Compliant, Partially Compliant, Largely Compliant, or Compliant with the specific recommendation. With the emergence of additional threats to the international financial system, including terrorist financing, and subsequently proliferation financing, FATF recognized the need to update its recommendations in 2003, and again in 2012. The mutual evaluation reports based on 2003 guidelines versus 2012 guidelines often number their recommendations differently, and as a result the PPI lists a recommendation and its associated year, such as FATF Recommendation 2 (2012), meaning it is the one from the 2012 guidelines. As of April 2017, only 31 countries have undergone an evaluation based on the 2012 standards.[2] To establish common ground between countries that have undergone a FATF evaluation before and after 2012, the PPI team only took into consideration recommendations found in both the new and old guidelines. The following FATF recommendations (FATF R.'s) have been carefully evaluated and selected by consulting financing of proliferation experts as most relevant to preventing proliferation financing, based on their experience with what governments need the most to prevent this illicit activity[3]:

- **FATF Recommendation 2 (2012) 31 (2003) National Coordination**[4]: "Countries should have national [anti-money laundering/ counter-terrorist financing] policies [...]. Countries should ensure that relevant competent authorities, at the policymaking and operational levels, have effective mechanisms in place which enable them to cooperate, and, where appropriate, coordinate domestically with each other concerning the development and implementation of policies and activities to combat money laundering, terrorist financing and the financing of proliferation of weapons of mass destruction." This is a high impact indicator.

- **FATF Recommendation 40 (2012 and 2003) International Cooperation / Other Forms of Cooperation:** "Countries should ensure that their competent authorities can rapidly, constructively, and effectively provide the widest range of international cooperation in relation to money laundering, associated predicate offences and terrorist financing." This is a high impact sub-criterion.

- **FATF Recommendation 10 (2012) 5 (2003) Customer Due Diligence (CDD):** "Financial institutions should be prohibited from keeping anonymous accounts or accounts in obviously fictitious names. [...] The principle that financial institutions should conduct CDD should be set out in law. [...] Financial institutions should be required to verify the identity of the customer and beneficial owner before or during the course of establishing a business relationship or conducting transactions for occasional customers." This is a medium impact indicator.

- **FATF Recommendation 13 (2012) 7 (2003) Correspondent Banking:** Financial institutions should collect additional information before conducting cross-border correspondent banking, and they "should be prohibited from entering into, or continuing, a correspondent banking relationship with shell banks." It is a medium impact sub-criterion.

- **FATF Recommendation 26 (2012) 23 (2003) Regulation and Supervision:** Financial institutions should be licensed, registered, regulated, and subject to monitoring. "[...] Countries should not approve the establishment, or continued operation, of shell banks." This is a medium impact sub-criterion.

- **FATF Recommendation 30 (2012) 27 (2003) Law Enforcement Responsibilities:** "Countries should ensure that designated law enforcement authorities have responsibility for money laundering and terrorist financing investigations [...]." This is a low impact indicator.

The PPI assigned points (with a maximum score of 65 points) based on country compliance with this selected set of FATF recommendations that encapsulate critical elements or essential features of a system that prevents proliferation financing.

• Unavailability of trade financing

The World Economic Forum, as part of its 2014 Global Enabling Trade Index, measures how easily a business can finance trade at an affordable cost, based on conducted Executive Opinion Surveys. According to the World Economic Forum definition, the cost of financing trade includes trade credit insurance and trade credit, such as letters of credit, bank acceptances, advanced payments, and open account arrangements. Countries are ranked out of 138, with 1 being the easiest country in which to obtain trade financing and 138 being the most difficult. For the PPI, this as a low impact indicator to assess how attractive a country is as an illicit finance hub. In other words, the *un*availability of trade finance can be a small deterrent to proliferation financing.

The reasons for this include: 1) 80 percent of trade financing takes place through "open accounts," i.e. wire transfers, so the unavailability of trade finance can render only 20 percent of all transactions in a country susceptible to illicit financing activities[5]; 2) Trade financing applies mainly to countries at the origin and end point of transactions and not to countries in-between, limiting the opportunities for exploitation; and 3) State-sponsored proliferation networks are likely willing to dedicate more financial resources than profit-seeking businesses, which could make unavailability of trade financing a deterrent because of the additional time, documentation, and paper trail required. Many developing countries have such an unavailability of trade financing, but surprisingly, also some small, developed countries, such as Lithuania or Portugal, have an unavailability of trade financing. Greater availability of trade financing is seen in common trading hubs such as Hong Kong and Malaysia, but also in smaller, inconspicuous countries such as Malta, Oman, and Bahrain. It is a medium impact indicator.

• Low cumulative illicit financial outflows[6]

This indicator measures illicit financial outflows from developing countries in 2013. Data are collected and published by Global Financial Integrity. According to the organization:

Illicit outflow, measured in millions of U.S. dollars, is money illegally earned, transferred, and/or utilized. Some examples of illicit financial outflows listed might include:

- *A drug cartel using trade-based money laundering techniques to mix legal money from the sale of used cars with illegal money from drug sales;*
- *An importer using trade misinvoicing to evade customs duties, value added taxes (VAT), or income taxes;*
- *A corrupt public official using an anonymous shell company to transfer dirty money to a bank account in the United States;*
- *A human trafficker carrying a briefcase of cash across the border and depositing it in a foreign bank; or*
- *A terrorist wiring money from the Middle East to an operative in Europe.*

As none of these is directly related to proliferation financing, the measure is deemed a medium impact indicator. Data are only collected for developing countries, which is in a sense useful as it balances out points that countries may have undeservedly received for having unavailable trade financing. Although illicit outflow is measured in absolute values, the PPI team took into account the size of illicit financial outflows in relation to a country's gross domestic product (GDP). Countries are awarded more points for not having large cumulative illicit outflows.

• Country has FATF or FATF Regional Body Membership[7]

FATF has established eight regional bodies to promote global dissemination and coordination in order to promote better understanding and implementation of its international standards as highlighted in the FATF 40 (49 for post-2003) recommendations. Most countries are either FATF members or members of a FATF-style regional body. Some are members of both. The level of organization and dynamic varies within the different groups. Before being able to become a FATF member, countries undergo a rigorous review process. FATF membership is awarded more points than regional body membership. The regional bodies are:

- The Eurasian Group (EAG)
- Asia/Pacific Group (APG)

- Caribbean Financial Action Task Force (CFATF)
- Committee of Experts on the Evaluation of Anti-Money Laundering Measures and the Financing of Terrorism of the Council of Europe (MONEYVAL)
- Eastern and Southern Africa Anti-Money Laundering Group (ESAAMLG)
- Financial Action Task Force on Latin America (GAFILAT)
- Intergovernmental Action Group Against Money Laundering in West Africa (GIABA).
- Middle East and North Africa Financial Action Task Force (MENAFATF)
- The Task Force on Money Laundering in Central Africa (GABAC)

This is a medium impact indicator.

• FATF compliance score[8]

The FATF compliance score is available for 90 countries on the 2015 Financial Secrecy Index (FSI), published by the Tax Justice Network. In the FSI, FATF compliance is indicator 11, "Anti-Money Laundering." According to the FSI report, compliance with all available recommendations (49 recommendations post-2003, or 40 recommendations post-2012) was calculated as a percentage, where "a 100% rating indicates that all recommendations have been rated as 'compliant', whereas a 0% rating indicates that the jurisdiction is wholly 'non-compliant.'"[9] Working with FATF to comply with general recommendations by implementing regulations and best practices is the first step for a country to prove its full commitment to financial transparency and anti-money laundering efforts. Despite some degree of duplication with the FATF recommendations above, this is a good indicator of general ability to prevent financial crimes. This is a medium impact indicator.

• Lack of denied parties by United States and European Union[10]

Countries without entities sanctioned by the United States' OFAC, BIS, or the European Union's sanctions lists are likely better at detecting illicit activity and stopping it. Thus, for the PPI, these countries are viewed as capable of monitoring and detecting illicit activities and gain points. This sub-criterion allows for a rough measure of what a country knows about its internal business. Since it is only a rough measure, it is assigned low impact.

VARIABILITY IN FATF COMPLIANCE EVALUATIONS

In ranking the 31 countries that underwent the 2012 FATF evaluation, the PPI team noted that the way compliance judgments are made is not standardized throughout the regional FATF bodies. While some FATF bodies appear very strict and require that all deficiencies are removed before awarding a country with the two highest levels of compliance (largely compliant and compliant), other evaluating bodies seem to be more generous in assigning compliance levels. For example, the PPI team found that the European regional FATF body tends to be harsher in its assessments. The CFATF, or Caribbean regional body, and GAFILAT, or Latin American regional body, seem more generous in their assessments, which skews the outcome for a ranking.

The countries were grouped by FATF membership in regional FATF organizations or FATF itself. If a country was in a regional organization, the PPI team established that the evaluation was done by that regional body. The graph (Figure 5.1) shows a distribution of these countries with their assigned score but in their regional bodies. The graph suggests that some FATF regional bodies, such as CFATF and GAFILAT, appear to be artificially ranking countries higher compared to the other regional bodies. Cuba and Guatemala, for example, which are listed as money laundering countries by the State Department, rank as high as or higher than the United States and all but one European country if only FATF data are used.

Key to Membership by geographic region: *APG: Asia/Pacific; MONEYVAL: Europe; MENAFATF: Middle East and North Africa; ESAAMLG: Eastern and Southern Africa; CFATF: Caribbean; EAG: Eurasia; GIABA: West Africa; GAFILAT: Latin America; GABAC: Central Africa.*

Figure 5.1. The vertical axis represents a country's performance based on a ranking that only relies on FATF evaluation reports, where a high score represents high performance. The horizontal axis represents the different FATF regional bodies.

EXPLANATION FOR THE NEED FOR ADDITIONAL, NEGATIVE INDICATORS:

If only the positive FATF-derived sub-criteria above were used to derive a ranking in this super criterion, the final ranking would be less reliable. Although FATF is the only organization that systematically tracks countries' actions to improve legal financial controls aimed at reducing threats to the integrity of the international financial system, its reporting contains many gaps. As discussed above, not all countries have been evaluated based on the 2012 standards, in particular FATF Recommendation 7 and Outcome 11, which directly relate to preventing proliferation finance. These gaps complicate gaining insights into what many countries do to prevent financial crime. The extent to which these gaps impacted the PPI ranking is difficult to evaluate.

Another issue concerns the FATF's evaluation methodology. Although the FATF evaluations are strong, there appear to be some potential weaknesses or biases that argue for the use of more sub-criteria. Compliance judgments published in follow-up FATF reports, for example, are derived based on a less rigorous evaluation process than the full reports. In follow-up reports, self-reporting plays a much greater role.[11] In addition, there are differences in how regional FATF organizations evaluate countries, as discussed above. This issue could risk that countries in certain FATF regions are ranked higher than what would be expected, based on other indicators such as money laundering. Lastly, FATF does not include in its evaluations the impact of enforcing UN financial sanctions on Iran and the DPRK. Those sanctions include a number of financial measures such as activity-based sanctions, vigilance requirements, and many others. Although these are described in non-binding FATF Guidance dated June 2013, they are not formally evaluated during the mutual evaluation processes. This issue could imply that countries may be doing better than the mutual evaluation reports conclude.

Because the number of positive sub-criteria based on FATF information is already relatively low and FATF information is not complete, the method was developed to more effectively rank countries under this super criterion. This additional set of sub-criteria focus on negative outcomes, such as the existence of substantial black markets in countries or countries having a high number of sanctioned entities. A negative sub-criterion means that points are subtracted instead of added. Ten or 15 points are subtracted for a negative performance under these indicators since they are all medium or high impact.

NEGATIVE INDICATORS:

- **Presence of denied parties by United States and European Union**[12]

Countries with entities sanctioned by the United States' OFAC, BIS, or the European Union's sanctions lists likely failed to detect illicit activity until after it occurred. Thus, for the PPI, these countries are viewed as less capable of monitoring and detecting illicit activities. When assigning points for this sub-criterion, the number of entities was not taken into consideration, but more points were taken away for a country having entities on multiple sanctions lists. It is measured as a negative indicator with high impact, since it indicates actual instances where illicit activities have been detected.

- **Appearance on the 2017 State Department List of Countries posing Money Laundering and Financial Crime concerns**[13]

The State Department Bureau for International Narcotics and Law Enforcement Affairs identifies in its March 2017 report "Countries/Jurisdictions of Primary Concern" for "Money Laundering and Financial Crimes." Using country profiles, the report points out weaknesses in those countries' enforcement or justice systems which pose challenges to the implementation of financing regulations. Examples of observed implementation challenges include "limited resources, lack of technical expertise, and poor infrastructure" as well as "administrative hurdles" and "corruption." This sub-criterion is medium impact.

- **Worldwide Biggest Black Markets ranking**[14]

This indicator is a ranking of the world's 93 biggest black markets published by Havoscope, measured by their size in U.S. dollars. Although the size was measured in absolute values, the PPI team took into account the size of the black market in relation to a country's GDP. Black markets are linked to financial proliferation because they facilitate the financing of the illicit procurement of goods, which require secretive means. It is a medium impact sub-criterion.

- **Significant illicit financial outflows**[15]

This indicator again uses data collected and published by Global Financial Integrity, measuring illicit financial outflows from developing countries in 2013. The PPI team decided that significant illicit financial outflows should be penalized. Points are taken off for countries that had more than $100 million in illicit financial outflows in 2013. As above, it is a medium impact indicator.

- **Lack of influence of corruption**[16]

Corruption can interfere significantly in the implementation of financial controls and their implementation. Companies engaged in exporting may believe they can simply ignore any legal export or financial requirements if they believe there is little likelihood of being investigated or prosecuted. Corruption would likely inhibit strong financial controls and enforcement.

In this sub-criterion, the 2016 Corruption Perceptions Index (CPI) by Transparency International is used as a measure for corruption in 176 countries. This index was selected from a variety of corruption measures and indices, mainly because this index lists the most countries and is widely respected. The PPI team used the rank of a country in the CPI to assign points, rather than its score derived by Transparency International. The points in this sub-criterion were assigned in an inversely proportional way to their relative rank. If the country or entity did not appear on the CPI, it was not assigned points. This sub-criterion has a medium impact.

"EXTRA-CREDIT" OPPORTUNITY:

For the 31 countries that were evaluated according to post-2012 FATF standards, the PPI offered an "extra credit opportunity," which allowed for the addition (or in a few cases the subtraction) of points. Information on those countries is included in the PPI scoring because the 2012 standards are of higher relevance than the previous sets of recommendations. For the first time, a recommendation specifically addresses a country's ability to implement targeted financial sanctions related to proliferation as laid out under relevant UN Security Council resolutions. Normally, if data were available for only about 30 countries, the PPI would not include this sub-criterion in the total. In this case, however, because of the direct relevance and importance of these post-2012 evaluations, the PPI adjusted its methodology to include the countries in a way that did not punish the other 170 countries. Therefore, the above-mentioned 31 countries were able to obtain extra points (or suffer subtractions) on top of the 110 total possible points if they were evaluated as largely compliant or compliant (or non-compliant) with the new UN financial sanctions-related recommendation.

EXTRA CREDIT INDICATORS:

- **Compliant or largely compliant with FATF Recommendation 7 (2012)**[17]

FATF recommendation 7 (2012) refers to implementation of targeted financial sanctions related to proliferation. It states, "Countries should implement targeted financial sanctions to comply with United Nations

Security Council resolutions relating to the prevention, suppression and disruption of proliferation of weapons of mass destruction and its financing. These resolutions require countries to freeze without delay the funds or other assets of, and to ensure that no funds and other assets are made available, directly or indirectly, to or for the benefit of, any person or entity designated by, or under the authority of, the United Nations Security Council under Chapter VII of the Charter of the United Nations." A compliant or largely compliant score for R. 7 would allow a country to receive 10 additional points.

- **FATF Immediate Outcome (IO) 11: Proliferation financial sanctions**[18]

Immediate Outcome 11 states, "Persons and entities involved in the proliferation of weapons of mass destruction are prevented from raising, moving and using funds, consistent with the relevant UNSCRs." As such, IO 11 also refers to implementation of targeted financial sanctions related to proliferation. It assesses whether persons and entities involved in the proliferation of WMD are prevented from raising, moving, and using funds consistent with the relevant UNSCRs. IO 11 is measured in terms of a low, moderate, or substantial level of effectiveness, where a country only received points for "substantial." Examples of outcomes evaluated by the FATF are concrete actions that have been taken, including investigations and prosecutions relating to sanctions. A substantial rating for IO 11 allows a country to gain five points.

EXPERT JUDGMENT:

One final modification to the super criterion score resulted from extensive expert discussions. The PPI team considered the fact that there may be missing data relevant to the sub-criteria and experts often have the best, first-hand information about a country performing significantly better or worse than scored. In some cases, experts judged that a country had received too many or too few points based on real-world knowledge and information.

IMPACT AND FLOW CHART OF SUB-CRITERIA:

The PPI assigned a low to high impact for weighting each of the positive and negative sub-criteria. **Table 5.1** shows how each indicator was weighted in the evaluation and how much of an impact it therefore had on a country's score and rank within the super criteria. The steps of the process are indicated in the flow chart where negative indicators take away points, extra credit takes away or adds points, and expert judgment is factored in.

SCORING:

The Ability to Prevent Proliferation Financing super criterion incorporates 11 positive sub-criteria, five negative sub-criteria, two extra credit, case-by-case sub-criteria, and finally expert judgment, where countries could receive or lose additional points. The positive and negative sub-criteria are evaluated in terms of low, medium, or high impact. Of the 11 positive sub-criteria, two are considered low impact, seven are medium impact, and two are high impact. They are worth 5, 10, and 15 points, respectively. Of the five negative sub-criteria, four are medium impact and one is high impact. After extra credit and expert knowledge points, a country could receive a total of 110 points under this super criterion. This raw score is used later to arrive at a total, weighted score and rank for each country. It is also used to derive a ranking for the country under the Three Tiers.

The pie chart below (Figure 5.2) shows the fraction of countries that have scores exceeding fifty percent of the total, between fifty percent and twenty five percent of the total, less than 25 percent down to a score of 0, and below a score of 0. Only three countries received more than half of the available points. About one-third of all countries achieved negative scores.

OBSERVATIONS

Through the PPI research and consulting with experts, an overriding conclusion is that most countries do not do well on preventing proliferation financing. In the ranking of this super criterion, only two countries achieved two-thirds of the available points and only three received more

High Impact	Medium Impact	Low Impact
Positive indicators (points are added):		
FATF R. 2 (2012) 31 (2003) National Coordination	(Un)availability of trade finance	FATF R. 30 (2012) 27 (2003) Law Enforcement Responsibilities
FATF R. 40 (2012 and 2003) International Cooperation / Other Forms of Cooperation	FATF R. 10 (2012) 5 (2003) Customer Due Diligence	Lack of denied parties by US and EU
	FATF R. 13 (2012) 7 (2003) Correspondent Banking	
	FATF R. 26 (2012) 23 (2003) Regulation and Supervision	
	Low cumulative illicit financial outflows	
	FATF and Regional Body Membership	
	FATF Compliance Score	
Negative indicators (points are subtracted):		
Presence of denied parties by US and EU	2017 State Department List of countries posing money laundering/financial crime concern	
	Worldwide Biggest Black Markets ranking	
	Significant illicit financial outflows	
	Lack of influence of corruption	
Extra credit (points are added or subtracted on a case-by-case basis):		
Compliant or largely compliant with FATF R. 7 (2012) Substantial level in FATF Immediate Outcome 11		
Expert judgment (points are added or subtracted on a case-by-case basis)		

Table 5.1. Impact and point adjustment for Super Criterion Ability to Prevent Proliferation Financing.

than half the available points. Many of the usual "white knights" do poorly due to having excessive bank secrecy, providing tax havens, and being places where front companies find it easier to finance nefarious activities. Other countries simply lack regulations and effective institutions.

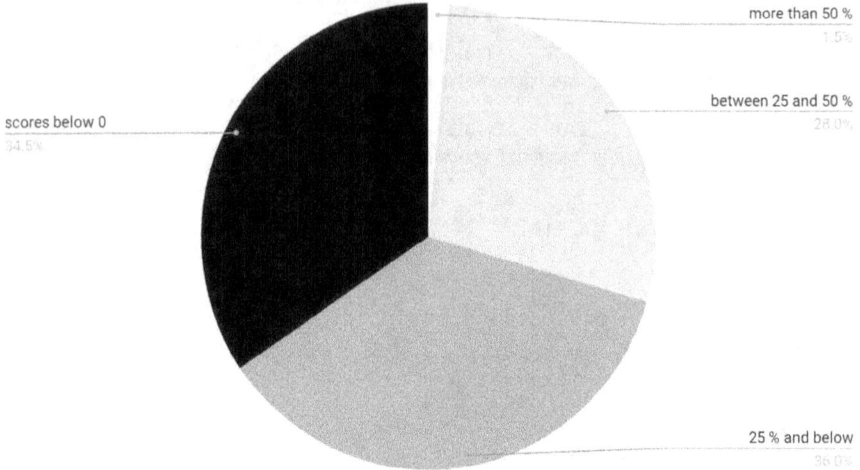

Figure 5.2. The pie chart shows the score distribution of countries in their Ability to Prevent Proliferation Financing. The majority of countries score less than 25 percent of the available points.

NOTES

1. Project staff considered an additional sub-criterion but were unable to find enough information, so it was not included in scoring: 1) Extent of training and knowledge of financial officials: Ideally, the PPI team would measure if a country has access to and participates in training and outreach programs relating to proliferation finance. However, information on this topic proved difficult to find. There does not seem to be much international assistance offered to countries wanting to improve proliferation financing prevention. Bilateral trainings to prevent financial crimes in general are conducted by the United States Federal Reserve System, Department of Homeland Security, Department of Justice, Federal Bureau of Investigation, Department of State, and Department of Treasury. The U.S. State Department has organized regional conferences and specific outreach events for countering financing of proliferation training, such as in South Korea and Qatar (2013) and Vienna (2015). The Asia-Pacific Group has also actively holds workshops for members.

2. These 31 countries are: Armenia, Australia, Austria, Bangladesh, Belgium, Bhutan, Canada, Costa Rica, Cuba, Ethiopia, Fiji, Guatemala, Honduras, Hungary, Italy, Jamaica, Malaysia, Norway, Samoa, Serbia, Singapore, Spain, Sri Lanka, Sweden, Switzerland, Trinidad and Tobago, Tunisia, Uganda, United States of America, Vanuatu, and Zimbabwe.

3. For the full text of recommendations see: FATF, *International Standards on Combating Money Laundering and the Financing of Terrorism and Proliferation–The FATF Recommendations*, Paris, France, published February 2012, updated October 2016, http://www.fatf-gafi.org/media/fatf/documents/recommendations/pdfs/FATF_ Recommendations.pdf

4. This formulation reflects the fact that Recommendation 2 in 2012 standards is the equivalent of Recommendation 31 in 2003 standards.

5. Jonathan Brewer, *Study of Typologies of Financing of WMD Proliferation, Interim Report* (London, United Kingdom: Project Alpha, King's College London, February 5, 2017), http://projectalpha.eu/wp-content/uploads/sites/21/2017/02/Study-of-Typologies-of-Financing-of-Proliferation-Interim-Report-5-Feb-2017.pdf

6. Global Financial Integrity, *Illicit Financial Outflows from Developing Countries, 2004-2013*, See Appendix Table 5, Illicit Hot Money Narrow Outflows (HMN), May 1, 2017, http://www.gfintegrity.org/report/ illicit-financial-flows-to-and-from-developing-countries-2005-2014/

7. FATF, *Countries*, 2017, http://www.fatf-gafi.org/countries/

8. Tax Justice Network, "Financial Secrecy Index–Country Reports," 2015, http://www. financialsecrecyindex.com/jurisdictions

9. Tax Justice Network, "Key Financial Secrecy Indicators," July 22, 2015, http://www. financialsecrecyindex.com/PDF/11-Anti-Money-Laundering.pdf

10. United States Department of the Treasury, Office of Foreign Assets Control, "SDN List by Country," https://www.treasury.gov/ofac/downloads/ctrylst.txt; United States Department of Commerce, Bureau of Industry and Security, "Supplement No. 4 to Part 744–ENTITY LIST," *Export Administration Regulations,* https://www.bis.doc.gov/index.php/forms-documents/regulations-docs/federal-register-notices/federal-register-2014/957-744-supp-4-1/file (Accessed Winter 2016); European Commission, "European Union - Restrictive measures (sanctions) in force," updated April 26, 2017, https://eeas.europa.eu/sites/eeas/files/restrictive_measures-2017-04-26-clean.pdf

11. See Organisation for Economic Co-operation and Development, Annex 2. A1, "A Note on FATF Data," in *Illicit Financial Flows from Developing Countries: Measuring OECD Responses,* 2014, https://www.oecd.org/corruption/Illicit_Financial_Flows_from_Developing_Countries.pdf

12. United States Department of the Treasury, Office of Foreign Assets Control, "SDN List by Country," https://www.treasury.gov/ofac/downloads/ctrylst.txt; United States Department of Commerce, Bureau of Industry and Security, "Supplement No. 4 to Part 744–ENTITY LIST," *Export Administration Regulations,* https://www.bis.doc.gov/index.php/forms-documents/regulations-docs/federal-register-notices/federal-register-2014/957-744-supp-4-1/file (Accessed Winter 2016); European Commission, "European Union–Restrictive measures (sanctions) in force," updated April 26, 2017, https://eeas.europa.eu/sites/eeas/files/restrictive_measures-2017-04-26-clean.pdf

13. United States Department of State, "International Narcotics Control Strategy Report–Money Laundering and Financial Crimes," Bureau for International Narcotics and Law Enforcement Affairs, Volume 2, March 2017, https://www.state.gov/documents/organization/268024.pdf

14. Havocscope Global Black Market Information, "Havocscope Country Risk Ranking," http://www.havocscope.com/country-profile/ (Accessed July 2017).

15. Dev Kar and Joseph Spanjers, "Appendix Table 5: Illicit Hot Money Narrow Outflows (HMN)," in *Illicit Financial Flows from Developing Countries: 2004-2013* (Washington, D.C.: Global Financial Integrity, 2015), http://www.gfintegrity.org/report/illicit-financial-flows-from-developing-countries-2004-2013/

16. Those countries or entities not included in the CPI but evaluated by the PPI are: Andorra, Antigua and Barbuda, Belize, Cook Islands, Equatorial Guinea, Fiji, Holy See, Kiribati, Liechtenstein, Marshall Islands, Micronesia, Monaco, Nauru, Niue, Palau, Palestine, Saint Kitts and Nevis, Samoa, San Marino, Swaziland, Tonga, and Tuvalu.

17. FATF, *International Standards on Combating Money Laundering and the Financing of Terrorism and Proliferation–The FATF Recommendations,* Paris, France, published February 2012, updated October 2016, http://www.fatf-gafi.org/media/fatf/documents/recommendations/pdfs/FATF_Recommendations.pdf

18. Financial Action Task Force, "An effective system to combat money laundering and terrorist financing," http://www.fatf-gafi.org/publications/mutualevaluations/documents/effectiveness.html (Accessed November 2017).

CHAPTER 6
SUPER CRITERION ADEQUACY OF ENFORCEMENT

Super Criterion Adequacy of Enforcement assesses the adequacy of a state's enforcement activities or efforts against strategic commodity trafficking and the control of strategic trade. It assesses a range of 19 sub-criteria, or national legal basis to act to penalize strategic commodity trafficking. The Enforcement super criterion assesses participation or lack thereof in applicable treaties, cooperation with countries that are strong on enforcement, and participation in foreign trainings and outreach. It also factors in issues that could inhibit enforcement, for example, high levels of national corruption. Of the 19 sub-criteria, four are considered low impact, nine are medium impact, and six are high impact. They are worth 5, 10, and 15 points, respectively. A country could receive a total of 200 points under this super criterion. This raw score is used later to arrive at a total, weighted score and rank for each country. It is also used to derive a ranking for the country under the Three Tiers.

To clearly highlight effectiveness rather than theoretical capabilities, this super criterion employs one negative sub-criterion, meaning countries lose points, if there is a significant number of real-world examples or a prevalence of expert opinions about government malfeasance or willful negligence in sound enforcement practices.

SUB-CRITERIA[1]:

- **Existence of legal basis or entity ensuring enforcement of the transit of nuclear weapons and related materials**

Data for this sub-criterion comes from matrices developed by the oversight committee of UN Security Council resolution 1540. The Committee provides information on the status of a country's implementation of this sub-criterion. Specifically, relevant data are from individual 1540 country matrices, namely Table OP 3 (c) and (d).[2] Just over half of all countries have reported to the Committee on this matter. Roughly 80 countries' reported enforcement mechanisms have been confirmed by the Committee.[3] This sub-criterion is judged as high impact.

- **Existence of legal basis or entity ensuring transshipment enforcement**

As above, these data are from the 1540 status of implementation matrix, namely Table OP 3 (c) and (d).[4] About 15 fewer countries have reported to the Committee in this sub-criterion than the above one, despite many countries referencing the same piece of legislation in both sub-criteria. Roughly half of all countries have reported some data to the Committee for this sub-criterion, and roughly 70 countries' reported enforcement mechanisms have been confirmed by the Committee. This sub-criterion is judged as high impact.

- **Participant in international legal assistance mechanisms[5]**

Countries that take advantage of existing international legal assistance mechanisms were awarded points. This is a high impact indicator, as certain international assistance agreements are considered especially effective by the PPI team.

- **National export control legislation includes a catch-all clause**

These data were obtained from the 1540 matrices and internet searches. Ideally, only points would be assigned to countries that not only have in place but also actively implement a catch-all clause. As this turned out to be infeasible to determine, points were assigned to all countries that have export control legislation containing a catch-all clause based on data collected under Super Criterion Legislation. It is a high impact sub-criterion.

• Has border seizure authority

Already collected under Super Criterion Legislation, this authority entails legal permission to investigate goods crossing borders. In most cases, it implies the legal authority to search and seize goods if necessary, which is why this sub-criterion was weighted as high impact. However, authorities vary depending on the point of entry (land border, airport, or sea port). Due to the lack of clear information on specific legal authorities and responsibilities across points of entry, the extent of the specific authority can only be inferred and not stated with certainty.

• Ability to conduct investigations

The World Justice Project scores countries' ability to conduct investigations, a critical process for successful enforcement of national and international law. The results are part of the annual publication of the Rule of Law Index for 2016. The score is extracted from each country's profile and can be found under Criminal Justice, indicator 8.1, "Effective investigations."[6] It is considered a high impact sub-criterion.

• Existence of a denied parties list[7]

This sub-criterion refers to a country using a list of sanctioned persons, entities, and groups that are denied exports. Many countries and the European Union have established their own nationally binding lists. However, all UN member states are subject to the Consolidated United Nations Security Council Sanctions List. The few countries or entities lacking a legally-based sanctions list are those that are not members of the United Nations, namely the Cook Islands, the Holy See, Kosovo, Niue, and Palestine. This sub-criterion is judged as medium impact.

• Party to the Arms Trade Treaty and brokering controls[8]

The Arms Trade Treaty acts to control international trade in conventional weapons. Unlike most treaties, it has brokering controls. It requires parties of the treaty to establish stringent systems to control and monitor the "export, import, transit, trans-shipment and brokering" of conventional arms, which, if implemented, would have an overarching positive effect on a country's general trade control. Although not specifically related to brokering for nuclear and other strategic items, these controls indirectly indicate the ability of a country to control brokering. About half of all countries have ratified the treaty. About 50 additional countries have brokering controls independent of the Arms Trade Treaty and received full points. The impact of this sub-criterion is medium.

- **Participates in foreign training and outreach on improving export control efforts**[9]

Combating illicit trade is an international effort. Many countries that have been identified as lacking sufficient trade controls reach out to the international community for training and assistance with the goal of improving their practices. Different forms of training and outreach exist, many of which are facilitated by the 1540 Committee. Trainings range from hour-long online courses to week-long, on-site drills and exercises. As there is not necessarily a direct correlation of amount of training received and enforcement effectiveness, points were only awarded for completion of specific sets of training programs. Points were awarded if a country participated in one or more key training programs that were deemed as the most effective and applicable to this sub-criterion. This sub-criterion had a medium impact in scoring.

- **Lack of influence of corruption**

Corruption can interfere significantly in the implementation of export controls and their enforcement. Companies engaged in exporting may think they can simply ignore any legal export requirements if they believe there is little likelihood of being investigated or prosecuted. Corruption would likely inhibit strong enforcement. In this sub-criterion, the 2016 Corruption Perceptions Index, or CPI, by Transparency International, is used.[10] This index was selected from a variety of corruption measures and indices, mainly because this index lists the most countries and is widely respected. The PPI team used the rank of a country in the CPI to assign points, rather than its score derived by Transparency International. The points in this sub-criterion were assigned in an inversely proportional way to their relative rank. If the country or entity did not appear on the CPI, it was not assigned points. This sub-criterion has a medium impact.

- **Enacts criminal penalties for illegal transportation of nuclear weapons by non-state actors**[11]

These data are from the 1540 status of implementation matrices for individual countries, in this case from the 1540 matrices, Table OP 2. The PPI team awarded points for having legislation enacting criminal penalties in place, because making the transport of a readily deployable nuclear weapon a crime is part of the bare minimum that any country can do to prevent the proliferation of nuclear weapons. A total of 113 countries or entities were individually confirmed by the PPI team to have this legislation. It is assigned a medium impact.

- **Enacts criminal penalties for illegal transfer of nuclear weapons by non-state actors[12]**

These data are from the 1540 status of implementation matrices for individual countries, and as above, from the 1540 matrices, Table OP 2. The PPI team awarded points for having legislation enacting criminal penalties in place, because making the transfer of a readily deployable nuclear weapon a crime is also part of a minimum that any country can do to prevent the proliferation of nuclear weapons. A total of 121 countries or entities were confirmed to have this legislation. It is assigned a medium impact.

- **Member of Interpol[13]**

Cross-border investigations are crucial to preventing, detecting, and dismantling commodity trafficking and activities of their procurement networks. Interpol aims to "facilitate international police cooperation even where diplomatic relations do not exist between particular countries." As such, being a member of Interpol is an indicator of a willingness and openness to prevent transnational crime such as import and export violations. As of October 2017, 192 countries had Interpol membership. It is a medium impact sub-criterion.

- **Legal authority in place to conduct undercover investigations[14]**

The legal authority to conduct undercover operations to sting those involved in illicit exports or to stop export control violations is important to enforcement efforts. This type of explicit legal authority to conduct undercover operations was found for only a fraction of countries (31). Authoritarian countries may also be able to conduct undercover operations under broad security laws but only countries with explicit legal authorities were awarded points in this sub-criterion. This is a medium impact sub-criterion.

• Lack of denied parties by the United States

Many countries have individuals or companies listed on the U.S. Commerce Department Bureau of Industry and Security or Treasury Department Office of Foreign Assets Control denied parties or sanctions designation lists. This sub-criterion awards points if a country does not appear on either list. When assigning points for this criterion, the number of entities was not taken into consideration, and points were only awarded if a country does not have a single entity on either sanctions list. Most countries have either no sanctioned entities or many. For example, both Russia and the United Arab Emirates have more than 100 entities on the 2017 BIS list alone, closely followed by China with 91.[15] Some countries may not have any proliferation-related denied parties but appear on the OFAC list because of terrorism, narcotics, or diamond trade violations. However, because of the difficulty of determining the cause of all the sanctions on particularly the OFAC list, the simplified approach of rewarding countries that do not appear on these lists was selected. This sub-criterion is measured as medium impact.

• Has an extradition treaty with the United States[16]

Extradition treaties with the United States, a strong export control enforcement state, require the signatory country to surrender U.S. nationals and can ask for the extradition of foreign nationals who are suspected of violating or have violated U.S. export control laws to be investigated and prosecuted in the United States. This serves not only as deterrent to foreign nationals who would violate U.S. export control laws, but also as deterrent for proliferators against setting up illegal procurement channels in the signatory country. Many countries, especially small or developing countries, have signed and ratified U.S. extradition treaties. Nevertheless, this sub-criterion is a judged as low-impact. First, this sub-criterion is limited only to extradition treaties with the United States. Second, there must be "dual criminality" for the treaty to be honored. The violation for which a person can be extradited must also be a violation in the signatory country. Some countries, such as Georgia, have not signed a U.S. extradition treaty but are known to extradite upon request.

• A low number of documents is required for exports[17]

A low number of documents needed for export is a suggestive yet indefinite indicator for efficient, transparent, and streamlined export control systems. This sub-criterion used the World Bank's "Ease of Doing Business" database. The number of documents needed in each country to export goods was taken as an average from World Bank research from 2005 to 2014. Of note, there appears to be a trend that corrupt countries as identified by Transparency International's CPI require a high number of documents, suggesting that to some extent corruption makes exporting less streamlined. This sub-criterion is judged as low impact.

• Utilizes voluntary tax disclosure procedures, as an indicator of voluntary WMD/dual-use proliferation disclosure procedures[18]

The PPI ideally sought to identify whether each country has a procedure for companies to voluntarily disclose to the government that an inadvertent or deliberate export of controlled or sensitive strategic goods had occurred.[19] However, no such information could be systematically found. As a result, another indicator, voluntary tax disclosure procedures, or self-disclosures of issues with tax filings, was identified as indirectly measuring the potential use or existence of voluntary disclosures for commodities. The assumption is that a country employing tax disclosure procedures increases the likelihood of there being a self-disclosure procedure involving commodities. Because of the assumption in deriving points in this sub-criterion, it is assigned a low impact.

• Legal commitment to enforce UN sanctions

Every UN member is required to enforce UN Security Council resolutions imposing sanctions on specific countries, including nuclear sanctions on North Korea and Iran. It was not feasible based on public information to determine which countries truly enforce UN Security Council sanctions. As a result, points were awarded to all UN members. Only few countries or entities are not UN members, including Cook Islands, Holy See, Hong Kong, Kosovo, Niue, Palestine (State of), and Taiwan. The impact is judged as low.

- ***Negative indicator:*** **Government interference with sound enforcement practices**

This is the only negative indicator applied under the Enforcement super criterion. Points were deducted for 44 countries based on several measures, including expert judgment and direct knowledge of a country's efforts to hinder enforcement, history of large-scale illicit procurements by state entities, and multiple, significant cases of illicit exports ignored by the state or known to be missed by the state. To help arrive at a conclusion about which states to include in this negative indicator, the project used a survey of about ten experts with specific knowledge of commodity trafficking in a wide range of countries. Seven known, failed states were also included in the survey. The number of points subtracted varied between 20 and 75. This affected known problem countries the most, such as Belarus, China, North Korea, Iran, Russia, Syria, and Turkey.

IMPACT OF SUB-CRITERIA:

The PPI assigned a high to low impact for weighting each of the sub-criteria. **Table 6.1** shows how each indicator was weighted in the evaluation and how much of an impact it therefore had on a country's score within the super criteria.

SCORING

Of the 19 sub-criteria, four are considered low impact, nine are medium impact, and six are high impact. They are worth 5, 10, and 15 points, respectively. A country could receive a total of 200 points under this super criterion. This raw score is used later to arrive at a total, weighted score and rank for each country. It is also used to derive a ranking for the country under the Three Tiers.

HIGH IMPACT	MEDIUM IMPACT	LOW IMPACT
Legal basis or entity ensuring transit enforcement of nuclear weapons, material	Denied parties list	Has extradition treaty with the U.S.
Legal basis or entity ensuring transshipment enforcement	Party to the Arms Trade Treaty and brokering controls	Large number of documents needed for export
International legal assistance mechanisms	Participates in foreign training and outreach	Uses voluntary tax disclosure procedures
Catch-all clause in legislation	Lack of influence of corruption	Legal commitment to enforce UN sanctions
Border seizure authority	Criminal penalties for illegal transport of nuclear weapons	
Ability to conduct investigations	Criminal penalties for illegal transfer of nuclear weapons	
	Interpol member	
	Legal authority to conduct undercover investigations	
	Lack of denied parties by the U.S.	
Negative indicator: Government interference and malfeasance		

Table 6.1. The impact of each sub-criterion and expert judgement on Super Criterion Adequacy of Enforcement.

NOTES

1. The project considered eight additional sub-criteria but was unable to find enough information, so these sub-criteria were not included in scoring:

1. Export controls are applied within FTZs: Unfortunately, this sub-criterion could not be measured systematically because of difficulties in determining how national export laws apply within countries' FTZs. Performance of countries with FTZs is analyzed in Section IV.

2. Licensing agency has authority within FTZs: No data were collected for this indicator, because a general lack of transparency, conformity, and regulations exist within FTZs and similar economic zones. To successfully prevent commodity trafficking, many countries need to drastically improve controls and regulations inside FTZs.

3. Has produced successful export control prosecutions: Successful prosecutions as an indicator of sound enforcement of export control systems were only considered on a case-by-case basis due to the difficulty of finding information for all countries. Only a few countries have specialized prosecution units for export control violations, such as Germany, Sweden, or the United States. Some countries, such as Japan, are known to have a high rate of successful prosecutions, while other countries, such as Malaysia, have a lower rate.

4. Has "technical reachback capacity," or access to expert knowledge on export control enforcement: This sub-criterion attempted to measure the ability of export control officials and companies to obtain technical information from the government or contractors about the potential misuse of goods. Not enough information could be found to assign points.

5. Country is known to act upon information from foreign intelligence sharing: This sub-criterion refers specifically to addressing export control cases. As it is difficult to determine the extent to which countries act upon foreign information for the clear majority of countries, no points were assigned for the PPI ranking. Nevertheless, it is an important aspect of combating strategic commodity trafficking. For some countries, such as South Korea, Germany, Britain, and Israel, cases of successful intelligence sharing and subsequent actions to thwart illegal activities are publicly known. In general, all Proliferation Security Initiative and North Atlantic Treaty Organization (NATO) members officially share intelligence among the members of these arrangements, nevertheless, the extent to which this is done in practice is unknown.

6. A country has sufficient criminal or civil penalties to deter export control violations. It is especially important to have criminal penalties in cases where the violation is willful and of a significant nature with respect to non-proliferation. Criminal or civil penalties for export control violations can serve as an effective deterrent for potential proliferators. Finding, comparing, and quantifying penal codes for all 200 countries was infeasible. Additionally, since not all countries have strategic trade control systems in place, many countries' penal codes for export control violations would not apply to strategic goods. Instead,

the PPI team looked for the countries with a trade control system in place, e.g. green legislation, where export control violations can lead to incarceration of convicted individuals. Prison sentences following export control violations were found for approximately a quarter of all countries. Some countries with otherwise strong export controls showed a trend of enacting relatively short prison sentences, often less than five years, or even less than one year, for export control violations. This trend in sentencing was strikingly apparent in Europe. Although these findings were not used as sub-criteria to assign points, they are discussed in Section IV, Chapter 17: Incarceration Penalties for Export Control Violations.

7. Uses information technology (IT) data system for licensing procedures: Ideally, when export license requests are submitted or granted, all information should be collected electronically. This not only helps investigators, but also allows for risk-based decision-making by licensing officials. The PPI team was unable to collect sufficient data on which countries collect licensing data electronically and which do not, therefore, no points were assigned.

8. Agency exists that investigates export control violations: The existence of such an authority was considered on a case-by-case basis. Only a few countries have a specialized criminal investigation unit for export control violations. In most countries, investigations are conducted by police or customs.

2. For example, see the 1540 Committee Matrix of Afghanistan, row 20, http://www. un.org/en/sc/1540/documents/Afghanistan%20revised%20matrix.pdf. In row 20 of a specific country's matrix, an "X" in the "Enforcement: civil/criminal penalties, and measures of implementation, etc" cell relating to NW (nuclear weapons) was taken as confirmation that sufficient enforcement mechanisms exist. A question mark was given partial credit. An empty cell received no points.

3. 1540 Committee Approved Matrices, Dated December 23, 2015, http://www.un.org/ en/sc/1540/national-implementation/1540-matrices/committee-approved-matrices. shtml

4. Ibid. In row 21, an "X" in the "Enforcement: civil/criminal penalties, and measures of implementation, etc" cell relating to NW (nuclear weapons) was taken as confirmation that sufficient enforcement mechanisms exist. A question mark was given partial credit. An empty cell received no points.

5. The international legal assistance mechanisms considered included:

1. Customs Mutual Assistance Agreements, a bilateral agreement with the United States: https://www.cbp.gov/border-security/international-initiatives/ international-agreements/cmaa;

2. *Nairobi Convention*, a WCO legally binding convention on customs assistance: http://www.wcoomd.org/~/media/wco/public/global/pdf/about-us/legal-in- struments/conventions-and-agreements/nairobi/ego019e1.pdf?la=en;

3. Program of measures, EU countries only. The full name of the program is Programme of Measures to Implement the Principle of Mutual Recognition

of Decisions in Criminal Matters. It supports judicial cooperation within the European Union, facilitating investigations and prosecutions: http://eur-lex.europa.eu/legal-content/EN/TXT/?uri=CELEX:32001Y0115%2802%29;

4. *Inter-American Convention on Mutual Assistance in Criminal Matters.* States agree to 'render to one another mutual assistance in investigations, prosecutions, and proceedings that pertain to crimes:' http://www.oas.org/juridico/english/treaties/a-55.html; and

5. *ASEAN Treaty on Mutual Assistance in Criminal Matters,* which is similar to the Inter-American Convention above: http://agreement.asean.org/media/download/20160901074559.pdf.

6. World Justice Project, Rule of Law Index Report, 2016, https://worldjusticeproject.org/our-work/publications/rule-law-index-reports/wjp-rule-law-index%C2%AE-2016-report

7. Examples of denied parties lists: Consolidated United Nations Security Council Sanctions List, updated April 18, 2017: https://scsanctions.un.org/fop/fop?xml=htdocs/resources/xml/en/consolidated.xml&xslt=htdocs/resources/xsl/en/consolidated.xsl; European Commission, European Union – Restrictive Measures (Sanctions) In Force, updated April 26, 2017: https://eeas.europa.eu/sites/eeas/files/restrictive_measures-2016-10-11-clean.pdf

8. United Nations, *The Arms Trade Treaty*, in force since December 24, 2014, https://unoda-web.s3.amazonaws.com/wp-content/uploads/2013/06/English7.pdf; Status of parties to the ATT is available here: https://s3.amazonaws.com/unoda-web/wp-content/uploads/2016/07/ATT-status-table-WebReport-30-June-2016.pdf

9. The trainings considered included:

1. The Export Control and Related Border Security (EXBS) Program, assisting countries to "develop and improve their strategic trade and related border control systems:" https://www.state.gov/t/isn/ecc/c27911.htm;

2. EU P2P (Partner-to-Partner) Dual-use Export Control Program, assisting countries to "enhance the effectiveness of export control systems of dual-use items:" https://export-control.jrc.ec.europa.eu/Home/Dual-use-trade-control;

3. International Criminal Investigative Training Assistance Program (ICITAP), assisting countries to "to develop professional and transparent law enforcement institution:" https://www.justice.gov/criminal-icitap;

4. WCO Columbus assistance program, which is the "largest and most comprehensive Customs Capacity Building initiative:" http://www.wcoomd.org/en/topics/capacity-building/activities-and-programmes/cb_columbus_programme_overview.aspx; and

5. Defense Threat Reduction Agency International Counterproliferation Program (DTRA ICP), providing education and equipment to countries' "police, border officials, investigators and national security executives:" http://www.dtra.mil/Missions/Partnering/ICP.aspx.

10. The countries or entities not included in the CPI but evaluated by the PPI are: Andorra, Antigua and Barbuda, Belize, Cook Islands, Equatorial Guinea, Fiji, Holy See, Kiribati, Liechtenstein, Marshall Islands, Micronesia, Monaco, Nauru, Niue, Palau, Palestine, Saint Kitts and Nevis, Samoa, San Marino, Swaziland, Tonga, and Tuvalu.

11. 1540 Committee Approved Matrices, Dated December 23, 2015, http://www. un.org/en/sc/1540/national-implementation/1540-matrices/committee-approved-matrices.shtml. For example, 1540 Committee Matrix for Afghanistan, in row 6 of Table OP 3 (c) and (d), http://www.un.org/en/sc/1540/documents/Afghanistan%20 revised%20matrix.pdf. An "X" in the "National legal framework" cell relating to NW (nuclear weapons) was taken as confirmation that sufficient enforcement mechanisms exist. For a question mark, legislation was individually confirmed to exist or not exist by PPI staff.

12. Ibid. For example, 1540 Committee Matrix for Afghanistan, in row 7 of Table OP 3 (c) and (d), http://www.un.org/en/sc/1540/documents/Afghanistan%20revised%20 matrix.pdf. An "X" in the "National legal framework" cell relating to NW (nuclear weapons) was taken as confirmation that sufficient enforcement mechanisms exist. For a question mark, legislation was individually confirmed to exist or not exist by PPI staff.

13. Non-members include the Cook Islands, North Korea, Kiribati, Kosovo, Micronesia, Niue, Palau, Taiwan, Tuvalu, and Vanuatu. See International Criminal Police Organization, "Overview – About Interpol," 2017, https://www.interpol.int/ About-INTERPOL/Overview

14. In the European Union, for example, entrapment is not allowed but undercover operations are permitted. See: Philip Gounev et al., "Part 3: Legal and Investigative Tools," Center on the Study of Democracy, https://ec.europa.eu/home-affairs/sites/homeaffairs/files/e-library/ docs/20150312_1_amoc_report_020315_0_220_part_2_en.pdf

15. U.S. Department of Commerce, Bureau of Industry and Security, "Supplement No. 4 to Part 744 – Entity List," *Export Administration Regulations*, September 25, 2017, https://www.bis.doc.gov/index.php/forms-documents/regulations-docs/ federal-register-notices/federal-register-2014/957-744-supp-4-1/file

16. Michael John Garcia and Charles Doyle, "Extradition to and from the United States: Overview of the Law and Recent Treaties" (Washington, D.C.: Congressional Research Service, March 17, 2010), see Appendix A: Countries with which the United States has a Bilateral Extradition Treaty, https://fas.org/sgp/crs/misc/98-958.pdf. Specifically, Chapter 209 "Extradition" of the U.S. Code, Title 18, "Crimes and Criminal Procedure," Paragraph 3181, reads: "The provisions of this chapter shall be construed to permit, in the exercise of comity, the surrender of persons […] who have committed crimes of violence against nationals of the United States in foreign countries […]." See: https:// www.law.cornell.edu/uscode/text/18/3181

17. The number of documents needed is found in the World Bank "Ease of Doing Business" database on a country-by-country case basis. Access to the database is available here: http://data.worldbank.org/indicator/IC.EXP. DOCS?end=2014&name_desc=false&start=2013

18. Organisation for Economic Co-operation and Development, "Update on Voluntary Disclosure Programmes: A pathway to tax compliance," August 2015, https://www. oecd.org/ctp/exchange-of-tax-information/Voluntary-Disclosure-Programmes-2015. pdf; World Customs Organization, "Voluntary Disclosure," Permanent Technical Committee 201st/202nd Sessions, Belgium, Brussels, November 4-8, 2013, http:// www.wcoomd.org/en/topics/facilitation/resources/permanent-technical-committee/~/ media/4C64301A393745989A29EAF535AE8D08.ashx

19. In the United States, for export control violations, a voluntary self-disclosure process is administered by the Department of Commerce's Bureau of Industry and Security. On its website, BIS provides an address and contact number and explains, "BIS encourages the submission of Voluntary Self Disclosures (VSDs) by parties who believe they may have violated the Export Administration Regulations (EAR)." In 2014, according to interviews conducted for a journal article on U.S. export control reform, BIS processed 225 VSDs. Typically, the majority of these cases result in settlements and civil penalties only, increasing the incentive for companies to make voluntary disclosures. See BIS, "Voluntary Self-Disclosure," https://www.bis.doc. gov/index.php/enforcement/oee/voluntary-self-disclosure; James E. Bartlett III and Jonathan C. Poling, "Defending the 'Higher Walls' – The Effects of U.S. Export Control Reform on Export Enforcement," *Santa Clara Journal of International Law*, Vol. 14, Issue 1, December 7, 2015, http://digitalcommons.law.scu.edu/cgi/viewcontent. cgi?article=1196&context=scujil

CHAPTER 7
TOTAL WEIGHTED SCORE AND RANK

A methodological question for the PPI team was how to combine the raw super criteria scores to derive final country scores, and subsequently the final PPI rank. We considered using simple addition of the raw super criteria scores (or scaling them, for example, where each super criterion score is scaled to 100 points and then added with the other super criteria scores) to achieve a total score. However, such an approach would imply that each super criterion is equal in value or weight. However, the project found that the Ability to Prevent Proliferation Financing and Adequacy of Enforcement super criteria are two of the most important due to their action-oriented nature; they are more important, for example, than the International Commitment or Legislation super criteria because the PPI measures the *implementation* of export controls. The PPI is different than other indices by focusing on tangible outcomes versus strictly capacities or theoretical outcomes. As a result, simply adding the raw super criteria scores, or even scaling each to 100 points and adding, would undermine the intent of the index.

WEIGHTING ARRANGEMENT

The project considered several weighting options for the super criteria. It decided to scale each super criteria score to 100 points and then apply a weighting factor. Based on discussions among experts, a favored weighting option emerged. In this option, the Ability to Prevent Proliferation

Financing and Adequacy of Enforcement super criteria each received double the scaled points of the Legislation and Ability to Monitor and Control Strategic Trade super criteria, which in turn received double the scaled points of the International Commitment super criterion. For International Commitment, Legislation, Ability to Monitor and Detect Strategic Trade, Ability to Prevent Proliferation Financing, and Adequacy of Enforcement, the weighting factors are, after scaling each to 100 points, 1, 2, 2, 4, and 4, respectively. The conversion of raw, possible super criteria scores from the earlier sections into scaled, weighted scores is summarized in Table 7.1.

	Int'l Commit-ment	Legislation	Ability to Monitor & Detect Strategic Trade	Ability to Prevent Prolif-eration Financing	Adequacy of Enforce-ment	PPI Total (Points)
Raw Points Possible	245 Points	130 Points	155 Points	110 Points	200 Points	850
Scaled, Weighted Points Possible	100 Points	200 Points	200 Points	400 Points	400 Points	1300
Scaled, Weighted Percentage	7.7	15.4	15.4	30.8	30.8	100

Table 7.1. Raw points are scaled and weighted for each super criterion before they are added to derive the final PPI scores and rank. Each scaled, weighted percentage is rounded, as is the percentage total.

Super Criterion International Commitment: The points received in International Commitment count toward **7.7 percent** of the total score. As discussed earlier, the International Commitment super criterion incorporates 22 sub-criteria—four are considered low impact, nine are medium impact, and nine are high impact, giving a total raw score of 245 points. This raw score was scaled to 100 and multiplied by its weight factor, in this case one, to contribute up to 100 points or 7.7 percent of the possible 1,300 points.

Super Criterion Legislation and **Super Criterion Ability to Monitor and Detect Strategic Trade: 15.4 percent each**

The Legislation super criterion incorporates 13 sub-criteria—four are considered low impact, five are medium impact, and four are high impact, with a total raw score of 130 points. This score was scaled to 100 and multiplied by its weight factor of two to contribute up to 200 points or 15.4 percent of the possible 1,300 points.

The Ability to Monitor and Detect Strategic Trade super criterion incorporates 15 sub-criteria—two are considered low impact, 10 are medium impact, and three are high impact sub-criteria, with a total raw score of 155 points. This score was scaled to 100 and multiplied by its weight factor of two to contribute up to 200 points or 15.4 percent of the possible 1,300 points.

Super Criterion Ability to Prevent Proliferation Financing and **Super Criterion Adequacy of Enforcement: 30.8 percent each,** the highest percentage of all super criteria.

The Ability to Prevent Proliferation Financing super criterion incorporates 11 sub-criteria—two are considered low impact, seven are medium impact, and two are high impact, for a total raw score of 110 points. This score was scaled to 100 and multiplied by its weight factor of four to contribute up to 400 points or 30.8 percent of the possible 1,300 points.

The Adequacy of Enforcement super criterion incorporates 19 sub-criteria—four are considered low impact, nine are medium impact, and six are high impact for a total raw score of 200 points. This score was scaled to 100 and multiplied by its weight factor of four to contribute up to 400 points or 30.8 percent of the possible 1,300 points.

TOTAL POINTS AND RANKINGS

The result of the weighting is a total point score and rank for each of the 200 countries, territories, and entities evaluated in the PPI. The scores vary widely, but no country received more than 80 percent of the total points (the highest score is 1,027 out of 1,300 points). Because points were deducted, scores below zero occurred. The lowest score is -349 points. Figure 7.1 shows a distribution of the scores. The median is 446 points, and the average is 486 points. The relatively low median suggests that overall countries did not score overly high. The average is somewhat greater than the median, suggesting a bimodal distribution, as can be seen in Figure 7.1.

Total PPI Point Distribution

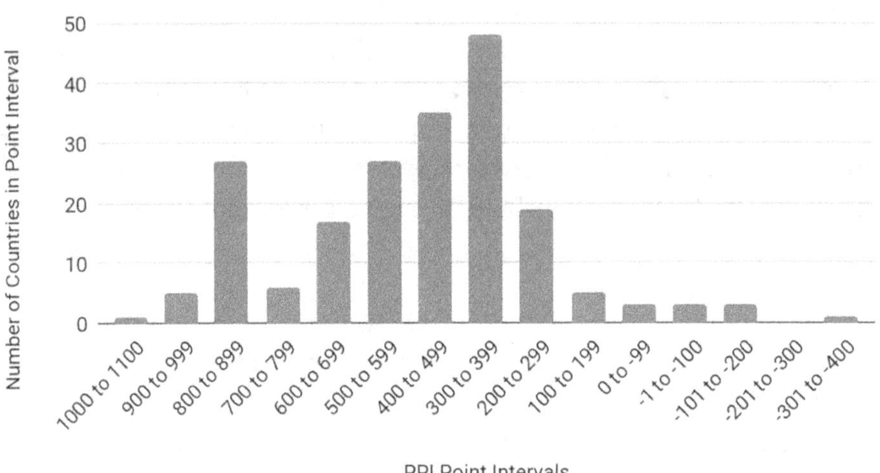

Figure 7.1. Distribution of total points in intervals of 100 points.

The annex contains the full PPI ranking, with total points for each country. However, this long list is less useful, because countries varied so widely on their need for strategic export controls and the nature of their economies. The project opted to discuss the most important results in terms of tiers of similar countries (see next two sections). In addition, the reader should not assign too high of a precision to each ranking because of uncertainties in determining the scores (see below and subsequent chapters for further discussion of uncertainties).

Several countries are difficult to rank because of their dependency on other countries or their non-state status. Monaco relies on France's export control system. Kosovo is a disputed territory. Palestine is under the authority of Israel. The Holy See is difficult to rank as well because of its small size and lack of any industrial capability or exports. Hong Kong is a special administrative region of China and many sub-criteria cannot be filled in. Taiwan's non-state status complicates developing a reliable rank for it. Oversea territories of countries, such as the British Virgin Islands and Aruba, were not evaluated and ranked individually, and in most cases the export control situation in an overseas territory was not considered in developing the rank of the state proper.

PERFORMANCE FRACTIONS

Although a country's total score is the fundamental measure of the effectiveness of its export control system, it is difficult to use it to prescribe a way for countries to improve. As a result, the "performance fraction" graph was developed in order to chart the extent to which countries have met the sub-criteria. For example, if the PPI team assigned 0, 5, or 10 points for a country's adherence to the Additional Protocol (0 would entail no signature or ratification, 5 would signify signature but not ratification, and 10 would be for full ratification), the performance fraction would assess those base points awarded to each country before subtracting any points from negative sub-criteria or deriving a weighted score. Performance fractions allow for a basic assessment of where points were not received and provide a straightforward roadmap for where countries can improve. In essence, performance fractions are calculated to locate omissions or deficiencies in a country's fulfillment of the PPI sub-criteria. Because of space limitations, we are not publishing individual country performance fractions in this report. They are available upon request.

Figure 7.2 is an example that shows that Afghanistan either fulfilled, partly fulfilled, or did not fulfill the sub-criteria in the International Commitment super criterion. Afghanistan, for example, received all ten points for being a party to the NPT after 1970 (it would receive zero points otherwise). It therefore has a performance fraction of 1 in the NPT sub-criterion. With respect to the IAEA Safeguards Conclusion for 2015, by contrast, Afghanistan received only five points out of a possible 10 points, and therefore its performance fraction is 0.5, because it only received the IAEA's "conclusion" instead of the more ideal "broader conclusion."

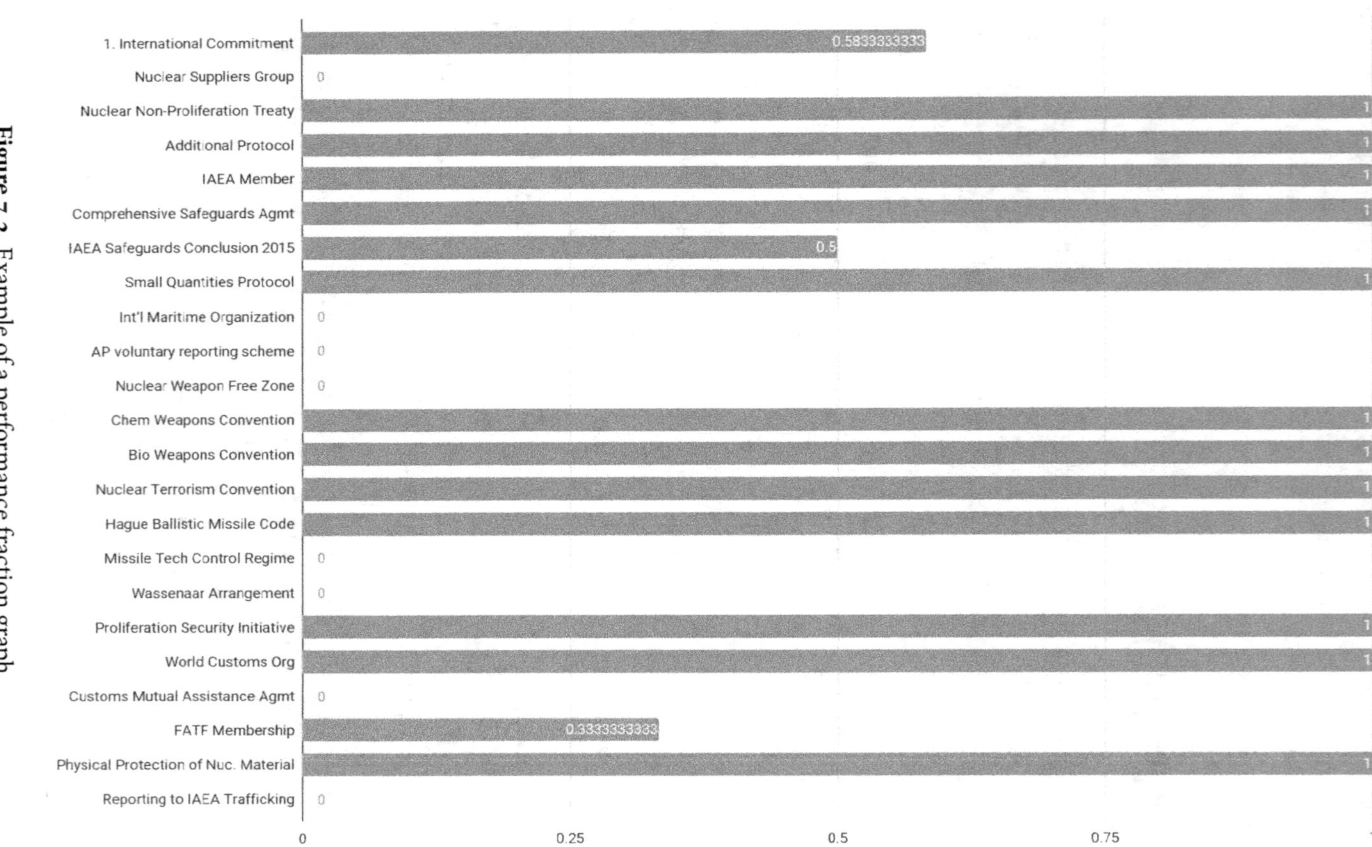

Figure 7.2. Example of a performance fraction graph.

UNCERTAINTIES IN THE PPI METHODOLOGY

The PPI has a number of uncertainties that affect the accuracy of the rankings. The largest uncertainty is created by lack of data. The project initially developed vastly more sub-criteria for each super criterion than staff could find data for, a particularly difficult endeavor when one must find data for the bulk of 200 countries before deciding to include the sub-criterion in the scoring system. In many cases, countries do not provide relevant information, or the 1540 Committee does not collect information in the 1540 matrices or other data sources. In other cases, countries do not publish relevant information and thus receive zero points on that sub-criterion. As a result, the project encourages countries to complete fully the 1540 matrices and submit them to the 1540 Committee. Reports should include full explanation of entries and reference to or copies of relevant legislation and appropriate explanation, and they should be updated as needed to maintain their currency.[1] Another recommendation is that countries should fulfill the additional sub-criteria footnoted in the super criteria sections which were not used by the PPI to derive a total score.

Another uncertainty involves the difficulty of determining specific, measurable criteria to evaluate the effectiveness of export controls. The process is ongoing with an eye toward future PPI versions.

The project depended on expert judgements in the adding and subtracting of points in the Ability to Prevent Proliferation Financing super criterion and to subtract points in the Adequacy of Enforcement super criterion. Although a wide variety of experts were consulted, this approach in the end entails some subjectivity. On balance, the use of experts was viewed as making the PPI sounder and more credible.

Despite the difficulties in finding all the desired data and other uncertainties, the staff on the project believe they collected enough data involving 88 sub-criteria to rank the 200 countries, territories, or entities in the PPI. However, the total scores, and thus the ranks, should not be considered without caution about the uncertainties. Overall, a variation in the total PPI point score of up to plus or minus 50 points is not viewed as significant. This equates to a percent uncertainty of roughly six percent, given that the total possible point range is -400 to 1,300 points.

SENSITIVITY APPLIED TO ADEQUACY OF ENFORCEMENT SUPER CRITERION

Because the PPI emphasizes the effectiveness of the enforcement and implementation of export control laws, not just the creation of those laws, a test of the effect of enforcement on the rankings was performed. In this test, the enforcement super criterion was more heavily weighted in deriving each country's final score and rank; the Enforcement super criterion was weighed at 50 percent of the final score. The resulting rank was compared to another case where the countries' ranks are derived by weighting the super criteria equally (with the exception of the International Commitment super criterion). The equal weighting of the super criteria in the second case was done to further magnify the effect of enforcement. The result shows the difference or change in a country's rank from the first test case to the case where the super criteria are weighted equally. By looking at the differences, it is evident that many countries experience a shift in their ranking relative to the case of equal weights (the graph was too large to include in this report but is available on the Institute's PPI report page, www.isis-online.org/ppi). A shift with a negative number means that the country's rank decreased (worsened) by that amount, a positive number means that its ranking increased (improved), and zero means the rank did not change. Significantly, several states with strong, balanced export control systems tended not to fluctuate much in the rankings, e.g. by more than plus or minus 10-15 places. An example is the United States, where its overall score is generally independent of a variation of weights, because its score is high in all five of the super criteria. Similarly, if a country performed poorly in all the super criteria, the weightings would have little effect in shifting the rank significantly.

By contrast, the countries that experienced a significantly worsened rank (e.g. more than 15 places) included those that have had trouble enforcing their export control laws or in general did poorly on the Enforcement super criterion, such as China, Russia, and Turkey, but in general do reasonably well on Legislation or the other super criteria. In general, the states that most experience a drop in rank by emphasizing enforcement are countries that one would expect to drop in rank.

The significance of the positive increase in relative rank is more difficult to judge. Several countries underwent a great increase in rank because they did somewhat well in Enforcement but poorly in other super criteria, such as Legislation or Ability to Prevent Proliferation Financing.

SENSITIVITY APPLIED TO ABILITY TO PREVENT PROLIFERATION FINANCING SUPER CRITERION

The ranking of a country in the Ability to Prevent Proliferation Financing super criterion is affected significantly by negative sub-criteria, such as having significant black markets, being on sanctions lists, or experiencing substantial corruption. A negative indicator results in the subtraction of points and was used to create a more realistic ranking (see Chapter 5). To better understand the effect of negative indicators on the rankings in the Ability to Prevent Proliferation Financing super criterion, this super criterion is evaluated here without any negative indicators, resulting in a new ranking of countries. This new ranking is compared to the existing one, resulting in a difference in the country's ranking. A shift with a negative number means that the country's rank decreased (worsened) by that amount and a positive number means that its ranking increased (improved) from the existing ranking to the hypothetical ranking, without considering negative indicators. The shift in the rankings can be dramatic, meaning that a substantial amount of points are subtracted from some countries' scores. (The graph was too large to include in this report but is available on the Institute's PPI report page, www.isis-online.org/ppi).

The average reduction of points is about 30, and almost all countries had points subtracted by negative sub-criteria. About one-tenth of all countries also had points returned based on expert analysis and judgment. However, overall, many states experience significant subtractions of points due to the negative sub-criteria considered in this super criterion.

Those countries that have a substantial increase in their rank are in general ones with a high theoretical capacity to stop financial crimes but have large black markets, are on sanctions lists, or have high levels of corruption.

The decrease in rank is less significant, similar to the case of enforcement discussed above. Many countries decreased in rank simply because many other countries rose in rank. This phenomenon is in part a result of the relative poor overall performance on positive and negative indicators in this super criterion.

NOTE

1. In UN Security Council resolution 2235 (2016), the Security Council encouraged all states that have submitted reports to provide additional information to the Committee on their implementation of Resolution 1540 (2004), including, voluntarily, on their laws and regulations and on effective practices and to prepare on a voluntary basis national implementation action plans mapping out their priorities and plans for implementing the key provisions of Resolution 1540 (2004), and to submit these plans to the Committee.

SECTION II
THREE FUNDAMENTAL TIERS

CHAPTER 8
DEFINING THE THREE TIERS

The PPI generates a score for each of the 200 countries, territories, and entities to measure the effectiveness of export control systems. However, not all countries face the same challenges and priorities in creating and implementing export control systems. Resources available for doing so also vary. As a result, the PPI project presents its findings in terms of tiers of similar countries with respect to export control challenges and requirements. This tiering approach is unique in its categorization of countries compared to other indexes. Instead of assessing countries only by a full ranking and comparing them against one another – for example, regardless of whether they are small island nations without significant international trade or a major world economy – the project separates countries into three basic, mutually exclusive tiers. This manner of evaluating countries acknowledges that smaller countries and countries that trade less, and that have fewer resources to devote to export controls, cannot realistically be expected to match the performance of major world export economies. The tiering system allows for a fairer ranking and allows a more relevant comparison of countries' ranks among peers in their potential to prevent the illicit trade in nuclear, nuclear-related, missile-related, and other WMD-related commodities. It also serves to create a more transparent method to improve export controls among peer countries.

The three tiers are defined in broad terms as:

Tier One: Major suppliers of, or capability to supply, nuclear facilities and components, nuclear-related commodities, and other ballistic missile, WMD, and related strategic commodities.

Tier Two: Potential nuclear, missile, WMD, and related strategic commodity transshipment countries. These countries may have limited capabilities to manufacture dual-use items, or they may have limited nuclear infrastructure in place, such as nuclear research or power reactors or uranium mines.

Tier Three: All other countries.

TIER ONE COUNTRIES:

Tier One is comprised of 57 countries, namely the countries known to possess nuclear weapons, other countries or entities that are members or adherents of the Nuclear Suppliers Group, and a few additional countries with otherwise extensive nuclear capabilities. NSG membership is considered under Tier One because membership requires that a country be a supplier of at least some goods on the NSG nuclear direct- and dual-use lists. This tier includes countries with past, alleged nuclear weapons programs or extensive nuclear research, such as Egypt and Taiwan. As a group, Tier One countries pose the greatest risk of being suppliers of sensitive commodities.

Countries in Tier One include the following:

Argentina, Australia, Austria, Belarus, Belgium, Brazil, Bulgaria, Canada, China, Croatia, Cyprus, Czech Republic, Denmark, DPRK, Egypt, Estonia, Finland, France, Germany, Greece, Hungary, Iceland, India, Iran, Ireland, Israel, Italy, Japan, Kazakhstan, Latvia, Liechtenstein, Lithuania, Luxembourg, Malta, Mexico, Monaco, Netherlands, New Zealand, Norway, Pakistan, Poland, Portugal, Republic of Korea, Romania, Russia, Serbia, Slovakia, Slovenia, South Africa, Spain, Sweden, Switzerland, Taiwan, Turkey, Ukraine, the United Kingdom, and the United States.

Monaco and Liechtenstein are considered part of Tier One because of their close legal association with France and Switzerland, respectively. Although Taiwan is included, its special international status makes it is difficult to obtain a thorough ranking.

TIER TWO COUNTRIES:

Tier Two is comprised of 57 countries that are broadly defined as potential strategic commodity transshipment countries. They do not have extensive nuclear capabilities and are not members of the Nuclear Suppliers Group, but nevertheless pose a risk of illicit or unauthorized supply, facilitation, or transfer of sensitive commodities. Tier Two countries include those that: are major traffic locations for land, sea, and air containers; are major financial hubs; possess significant manufacturing capabilities; have nuclear facilities under safeguards but are not in Tier One; or are exporters of uranium.[1] Many Tier One countries would also meet these conditions, such as Canada and the United States, but they are excluded from this tier.

The financial hubs in were determined by amounts of countries' illicit money outflows.

Based on these conditions, the 57 countries in Tier Two are the following alphabetically:

Afghanistan, Albania, Algeria, Armenia, Azerbaijan, Bahamas, Bangladesh, Bosnia and Herzegovina, Brunei Darussalam, Chile, Colombia, Costa Rica, Dominican Republic, Ecuador, Ethiopia, Georgia, Hong Kong, Indonesia, Iraq, Jamaica, Kuwait, Kyrgyzstan, Lao People's Democratic Republic, Lebanon, Libya, Madagascar, Malawi, Malaysia, Moldova (Rep of the), Mongolia, Morocco, Namibia, Nicaragua, Niger, Nigeria, Oman, Panama, Paraguay, Peru, Philippines, Qatar, Saudi Arabia, Singapore, Sri Lanka, Syrian Arab Republic, Tajikistan, Tanzania (United Rep of), Thailand, Tunisia, Uganda, United Arab Emirates, Uzbekistan, Vanuatu, Venezuela (Bolivarian Republic of), Viet Nam, and Zambia.

TIER THREE COUNTRIES:

This tier encapsulates all the remaining countries that are not included in Tiers One or Two.

The 86 countries in Tier Three are the following:

Andorra, Angola, Antigua and Barbuda, Bahrain, Barbados, Belize, Benin, Bhutan, Bolivia, Botswana, Burkina Faso, Burundi, Cambodia, Cameroon, Cape Verde, Central African Republic, Chad, Comoros, Congo (Dem Rep of the), Congo (Rep of the), Cook Islands, Côte d'Ivoire, Cuba, Djibouti, Dominica, El Salvador, Equatorial Guinea, Eritrea,

Fiji, Gabon, Gambia, Grenada, Guatemala, Guinea-Bissau, Guyana, Haiti, Holy See, Honduras, Jordan, Kenya, Kiribati, Kosovo, Lesotho, Liberia, Macedonia, Maldives, Mali, Marshall Islands, Mauritania, Mauritius, Micronesia (Federation of), Montenegro, Mozambique, Myanmar, Nauru, Nepal, Niue, Palau, Palestine (State of), Papua New Guinea, Rwanda, Saint Kitts and Nevis, Saint Lucia, Saint Vincent and the Grenadines, Samoa, San Marino, Sao Tome and Principe, Senegal, Seychelles, Sierra Leone, Solomon Islands, Somalia, South Sudan, Sudan, Suriname, Swaziland, Timor-Leste, Togo, Tonga, Trinidad and Tobago, Turkmenistan, Tuvalu, Uruguay, Yemen, and Zimbabwe.

DISTRIBUTION OF TIERS' AVERAGE AND MEDIAN SCORES

The results for each tier are in the next three chapters. Here, it is useful to summarize the tiers' average and median scores (Figure 8.1). As can be seen, Tier One did considerably better than Tiers Two and Three.

Average and Median Scores

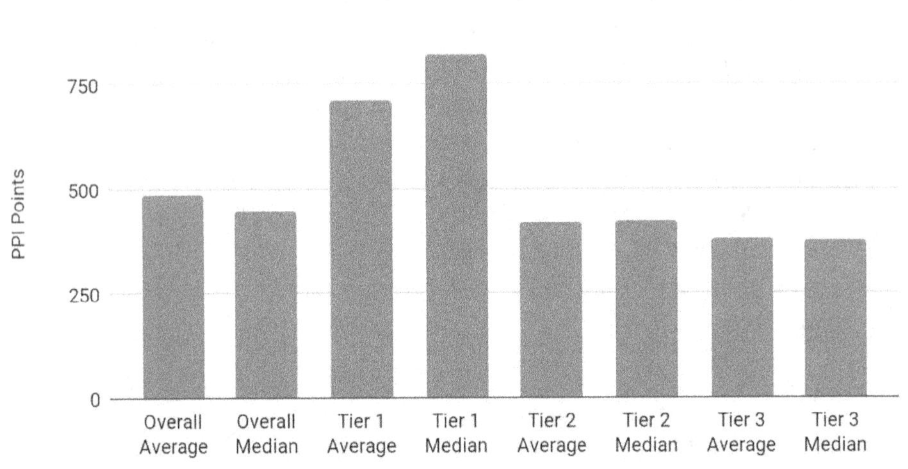

Figure 8.1. Average and median scores for total scores and the Three Tiers. The overall average is 486 points and the overall median is 446 points.

NOTE

1. The major land and air transshipment locations were measured in terms of freight in metric tonnes, and the top sea locations were measured in terms of twenty-foot equivalent units (TEU). The top twenty to thirty entries were selected from each list. Many countries were in the top of two or more of the lists or in Tier One, further narrowing the Tier Two list. The major financial hubs were determined by picking the countries with the largest amount of illicit money outflows. Sources: International Union of Railways, "Railway Statistics," Paris, France, 2014, http://www.uic.org/IMG/pdf/synopsis_2014.pdf; World Shipping Council, "Top 50 World Container Ports," 2015, http://www.worldshipping.org/about-the-industry/global-trade/top-50-world-container-ports; Airports Council International, "International Freight Traffic Monthly Ranking," December 2015, updated April 2016, http://www.aci.aero/Data-Centre/Monthly-Traffic-Data/International-Freight-Traffic/Monthly; Dev Kar and Joseph Spanjers, "Appendix Table 5. Illicit Hot Money Narrow Outflows (HMN)," in *Illicit Financial Flows from Developing Countries: 2004-2013* (Washington, D.C.: Global Financial Integrity, 2015), http://www.gfintegrity.org/report/illicit-financial-flows-from-developing-countries-2004-2013/; United Nations Industrial Development Organization, "Industrial Development Report 2016–The Role of Technology and Innovation in Inclusive and Sustainable Industrial Development," United Nations Publications, http://www.keepeek.com/Digital-Asset-Management/oecd/economic-and-social-development/industrial-development-report-2016_a1cf26ea-en#.WTcW72jyuUk#page1; United States Department of the Interior and United States Geological Survey, "Mineral Commodity Summaries 2016," U.S. Geological Survey, Reston, Virginia, 2016, https://minerals.usgs.gov/minerals/pubs/mcs/2015/mcs2015.pdf; Organisation for Economic Co-operation and Development and Nuclear Energy Agency, "Uranium 2014: Resources, Production and Demand," 2014, https://www.oecd-nea.org/ndd/pubs/2014/7209-uranium-2014.pdf

CHAPTER 9
TIER ONE RANKING

Tier One is composed of 57 countries capable of supplying countries with goods needed to create the wherewithal to build nuclear weapons, other WMD, and ballistic missiles:

Argentina, Australia, Austria, Belarus, Belgium, Brazil, Bulgaria, Canada, China, Croatia, Cyprus, Czech Republic, Denmark, DPRK, Egypt, Estonia, Finland, France, Germany, Greece, Hungary, Iceland, India, Iran, Ireland, Israel, Italy, Japan, Kazakhstan, Latvia, Liechtenstein, Lithuania, Luxembourg, Malta, Mexico, Monaco, Netherlands, New Zealand, Norway, Pakistan, Poland, Portugal, Republic of Korea, Romania, Russia, Serbia, Slovakia, Slovenia, South Africa, Spain, Sweden, Switzerland, Taiwan, Turkey, Ukraine, the United Kingdom, and the United States.

Table 9.1 (and Figure 9.1) show the rankings of the countries in Tier One. The average score in Tier One is 710 points out of a possible 1,300 points. The median is 822. The difference between the average and median scores reflects the large range of points achieved by members of the tier.

The reader is cautioned not to assign too much precision to close rankings between countries in the table. Countries ranked close to one another do not differ substantially in the effectiveness of their export control systems.

It is large differences in total points in the Tier One ranking that matter. A score that achieved at least two-thirds of the total points, or about 870 points out of the total 1,300 possible points, is viewed in this tier as a country having a sufficient export control system (20 countries), although improvements are always necessary. A score below 50 percent of the total points means that these countries need to do considerable work to improve their export control systems (19 countries). Those in between need to take significant steps to improve their controls (18 countries). Figure 9.2 shows the number of countries in each of these percentage ranges.

Out of a total possible score of 1,300 points, the highest scorer in Tier One (and also in the full ranking of all 200 countries) was the United States with 1,027 points.[1] It received 79 percent of the total possible points. Top scorers were mostly Western countries.

TIER ONE IN THE OVERALL RANKING

Forty-one of the 57 countries in Tier One rank in the top 25 percent of the total PPI ranking. The full ranking of all 200 countries is included in Annex I of this report. The top 18 countries in the overall PPI ranking are identical to the Tier One ranking. This result shows that Tier One countries have, in general, the most developed export controls of the 200 countries, territories, or entities. However, eight countries only achieved a ranking between 51 and 100 in their placement, and eight ranked below 100 in the total ranking.

Tier One countries that ranked in the bottom half of the overall ranking included, from higher to lower ranking: Pakistan, Ukraine, Russia, Belarus, Egypt, Iran, and the DPRK. Taiwan also did poorly, partially due to its special status which, for example, makes it impossible for it to receive points under the International Commitment super criterion.

Iran and North Korea each received a negative score. These scores reflect their lack of export control systems meeting international standards and wide-scale illicit procurements.

TIER 1 PERFORMANCE FRACTIONS–
HOW COUNTRIES CAN IMPROVE

Although a country's total score is the fundamental measure of the effectiveness of its export control system, it is difficult to use it to prescribe a way for countries to improve. As a result, the performance fraction charts the extent to which countries have met the sub-criteria. For example, if the PPI team assigned 0, 5, or 10 points for a country's adherence to the Additional Protocol (0 would entail no signature or ratification, 5 would signify signature but not ratification, and 10 would be points for full ratification), the performance fractions would assess those base points awarded to each country before weighting as low, medium, or high impact. It does not factor in any negative indicators. Performance fractions, in fact, allow for a basic assessment of where points were *not* received. Please refer back to Chapter 7: Total Weighted Score and Rank for a longer discussion of performance fractions.

The performance fraction can also be tabulated for the entire tier. Given that two out of the 57 countries in Tier One are countries under international sanctions for proliferation-related activities (the DPRK and Iran), one hundred percent performance by the countries in this tier is not possible. These two countries account for 0.04 in the performance fraction, meaning in Figures 9.3-9.8, Tier One countries can maximally achieve a performance fraction of 0.96. Nevertheless, as seen in Figure 9.3, near-perfect performance is not achieved in any case by Tier One under any super criterion. The Legislation super criterion comes the closest, with 85 percent fulfillment of its sub-criteria. Tier One countries barely reached 75 percent of the sub-criteria requirements under two super criteria, namely International Commitment and Adequacy of Enforcement. Ability to Monitor and Detect Strategic Trade did not reach 75 percent but exceeded the 50 percent mark, while Ability to Prevent Proliferation Financing fell short of even that.

Individual country performance fractions are not included in this report but are available upon request.

SCORE AND PERFORMANCE BY SUPER CRITERIA

The Tier One countries varied in their scores under each super criterion.

INTERNATIONAL COMMITMENT

Tier One countries are in general committed to international conventions, bodies, and regimes relating to non-proliferation. Forty-six of the 57 countries achieved two-thirds or higher of the possible points in this super criterion.[2] Three countries received half of the possible points. Several of the countries that received less than half of the possible points were Pakistan, Iran, Egypt, and the DPRK.

The performance fractions show that under the International Commitment super criterion, near-perfect performance is achieved in three sub-criteria (see Figure 9.4). Based on sub-criteria that are fewer than 75 percent fulfilled, there is room to add to the tier's memberships to the Wassenaar Arrangement and the Missile Technology Control Regime.

LEGISLATION

Overall, countries in Tier One did well on their enactment of export control-relevant legislation, with 43 of the 57 countries receiving 90 percent or more of the possible points in this super criterion. All except three countries have export control legislation that put them in the most developed category, namely Dark Green. Egypt, Iran, and the DPRK were categorized as red, which indicates an absence of robust export control legislation. Those that received less than two-thirds of the possible points are Egypt, Monaco, Iran, and the DPRK. As discussed in Chapter 7, Monaco is subject to French export control laws and regulations and thus in effect should score similarly to France; however, since it does not have its own legislation, it cannot achieve a high score. As expected, Figure 9.5 shows that the performance fraction exceeds 0.75 or 75 percent in all but one sub-criterion.

ABILITY TO MONITOR AND DETECT STRATEGIC TRADE

Tier One did not perform as well under this super criterion compared to Super Criterion International Commitment and Super Criterion Legislation. Here, the top country received 74 percent of the possible points in the Ability to Monitor and Detect Strategic Trade super criterion. Only 16 out of 57 countries achieved at least two-thirds of the possible points in this super criterion. The next 28 countries in the ranking garnered at least half of the possible points but did not reach the two-thirds threshold. The remaining 13 countries scored less than half of the possible points in this super criterion. This suggests that while Tier One countries generally have the legislative basis for export controls, many lack the ability to effectively monitor and detect illicit trade.

In terms of performance fractions, Figure 9.6 shows that only one third of all sub-criteria (5 out of 15) reached or exceeded a fraction of 75 percent. Examples of sub-criteria that need improvement across the tier are physical inspections of cargo; transparency of doing business, especially starting a business; and efficiency of customs clearance processes, including having better training and more sophisticated equipment for those processes.

ABILITY TO PREVENT PROLIFERATION FINANCING

Countries scored the worst in their Ability to Prevent Proliferation Financing. The top country received only 55 percent of the possible points in this criterion, with the second country achieving 54 percent of the possible points. The third-place country, followed by the remaining 54 countries, achieved less than half of the possible points in this super criterion. The bottom twelve countries had negative scores and included, listed from higher to lower ranking India, China, Argentina, South Africa, Pakistan, Egypt, Russia, Serbia, Belarus, Ukraine, the DPRK, and Iran. Similar to Super Criterion Ability to Monitor and Detect Strategic Trade, while countries appear to have the legislative basis to prevent illicit trade, many lack the ability to prevent the flow of money that finances it.

The performance fraction of countries is lowest in the prevention of proliferation financing. Figure 9.7 shows that Tier One countries fulfilled none of the sub-criteria to 75 percent. A general observation is that Tier One countries need to work more closely with the FATF and its regional bodies on proliferation financing, and that they need to work to improve compliance with proliferation financing-relevant FATF recommendations.

ADEQUACY OF ENFORCEMENT

Generally, the data show that Tier One countries have the capacity and willingness to enforce export control regimes. Thirty-nine of the 57 countries garnered at least two-thirds of the possible points in this super criterion with the top five countries achieving 90 percent or higher. Eight countries received at least half of the points, while not achieving two-thirds in this super criterion. The bottom ten countries, which achieved less than 50 percent of the total points in this super criterion are, listed from higher to lower ranking, Pakistan, Monaco, Taiwan, Turkey, China, Belarus, Russia, Egypt, Iran, and the DPRK. Excluding Taiwan and Monaco, for reasons discussed above, these poorly performing countries appear to lack either the will or capacity to enforce their export control regimes, which is particularly concerning given their potential for proliferating nuclear-related goods.

The performance fraction for the Adequacy of Enforcement super criterion shows the majority of sub-criteria are fulfilled to more than 0.75 (see Figure 9.8). Two examples of areas where countries need to improve are putting in place better voluntary disclosure procedures for export control violations and developing better abilities to conduct investigations.

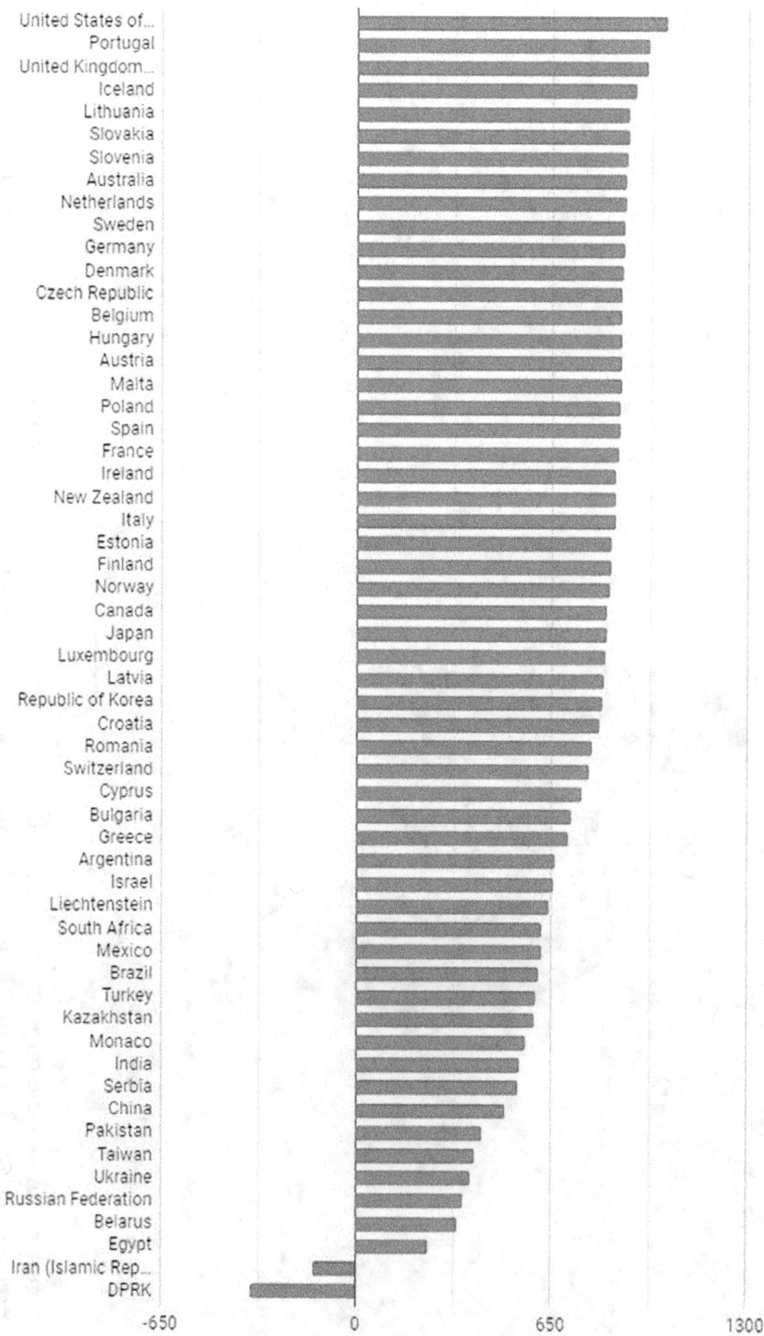

Figure 9.1. Total points received by each country in relation to the total possible points (1,300). The vertical line at 650 represents the 50 percent marker.

Scores of Tier One Countries

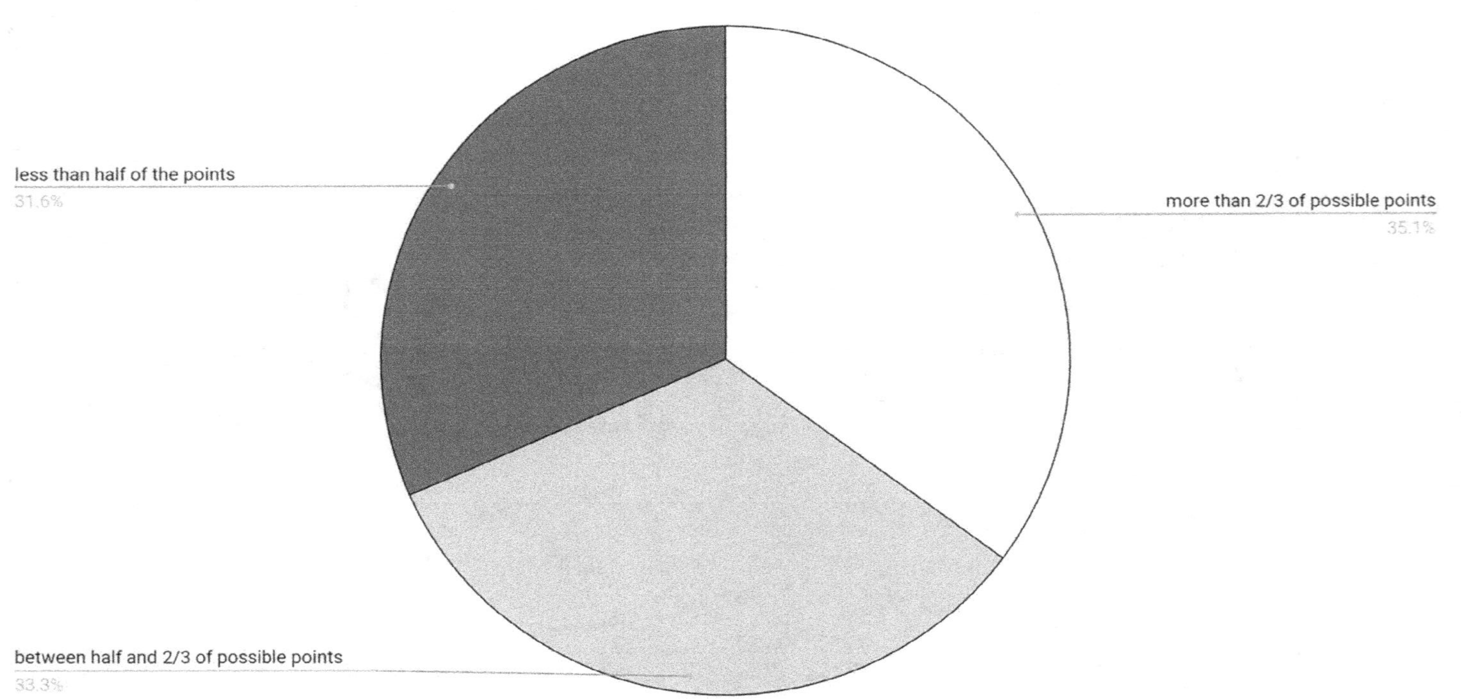

Figure 9.2. About one-third of Tier One countries need significant work on their export controls, while an additional third needs some work. A score that achieved at least two-thirds of the total points, or about 870 points, is viewed in this tier as a country having a sufficient adequate export control system (20 countries), although improvements may be necessary.

Figure 9.3. Extent to which the super criteria were fulfilled by Tier One as a group.

Figure 9.4. Extent to which sub-criteria making up the International Commitment super criterion were fulfilled by Tier One as a group.

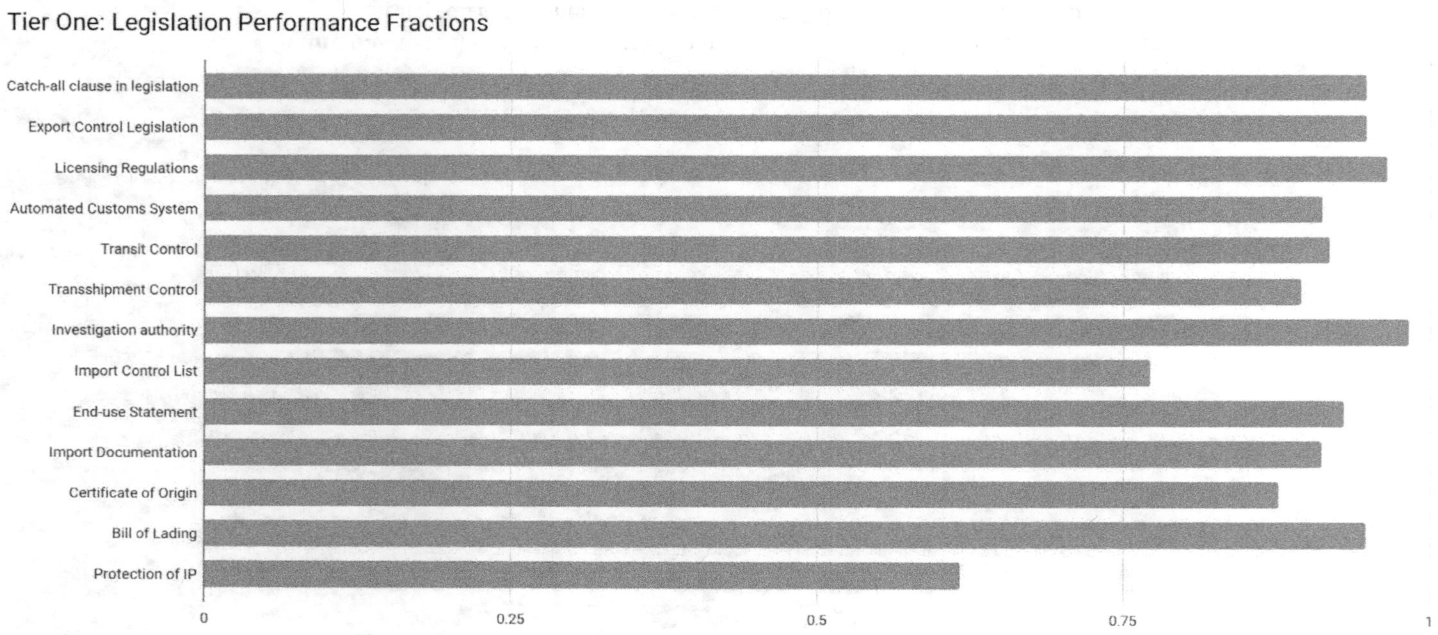

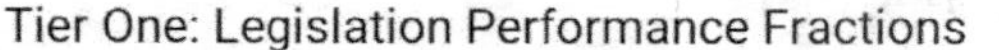

Figure 9.5. Extent to which sub-criteria making up the Legislation super criterion were fulfilled by Tier One as a group.

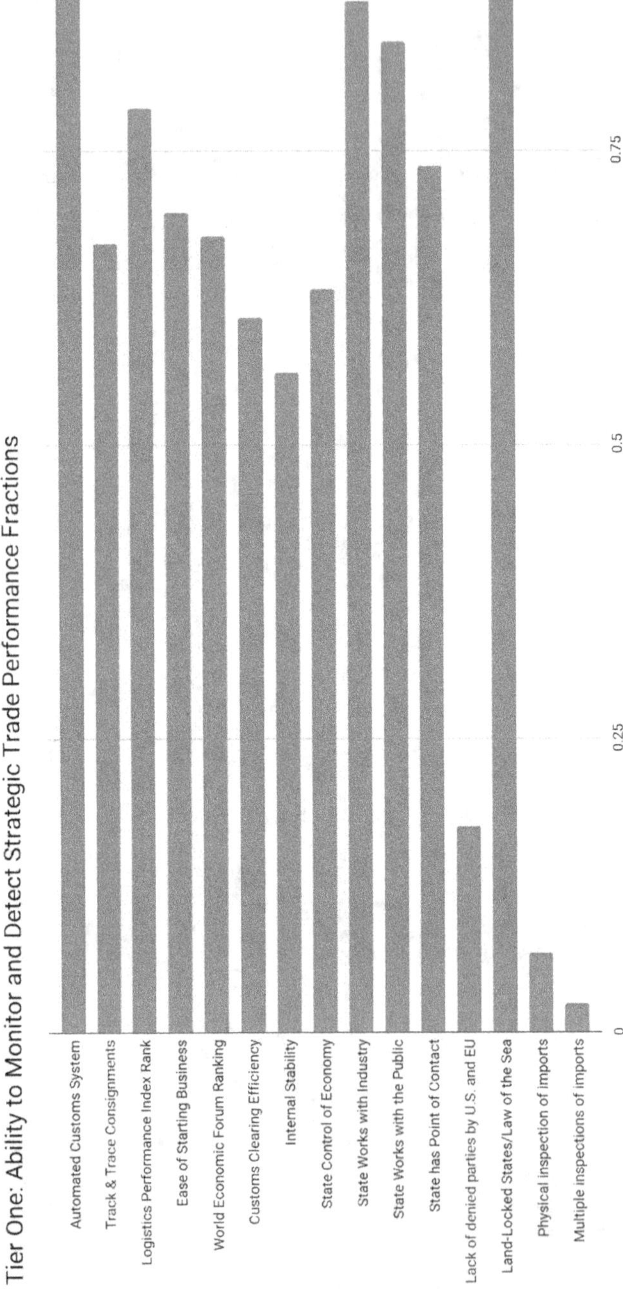

Figure 9.6. Extent to which sub-criteria making up the Ability to Monitor and Detect Strategic Trade super criterion were fulfilled by Tier One as a group.

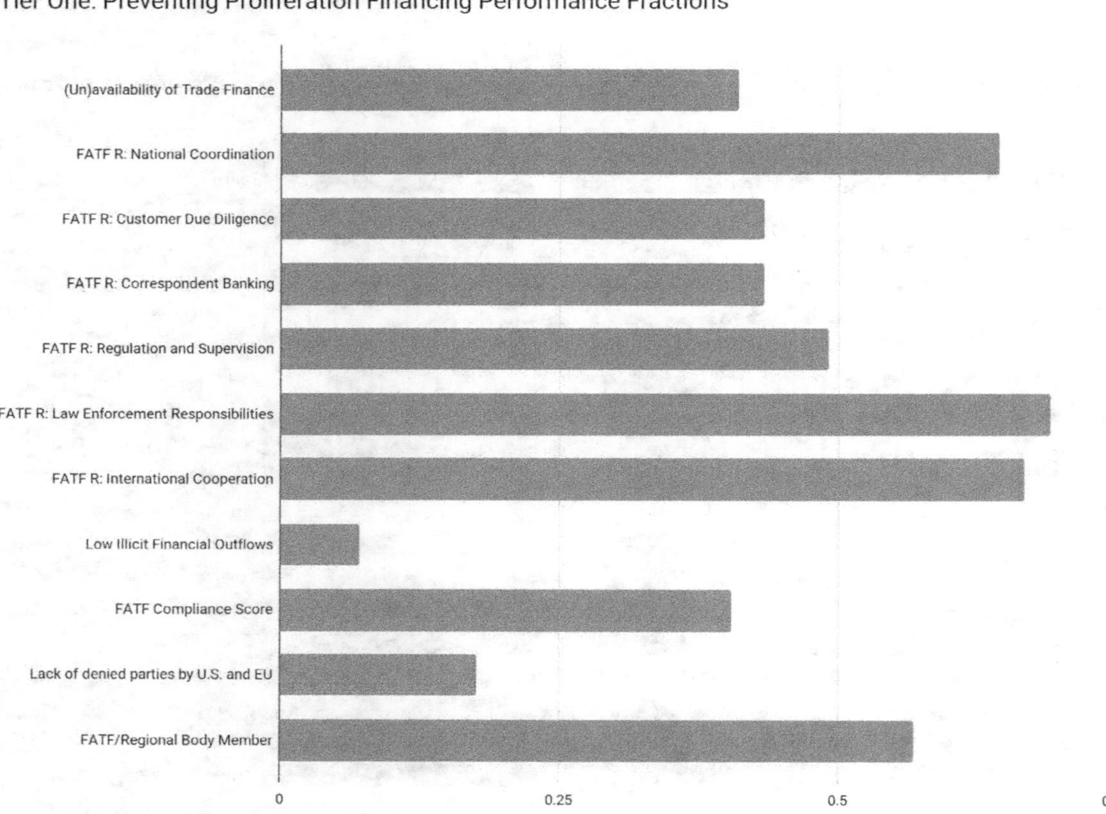

Figure 9.7. Extent to which sub-criteria making up the Ability to Prevent Proliferation Financing super criterion were fulfilled by Tier One as a group.

Figure 9.8. Extent to which sub-criteria making up the Adequacy of Enforcement super criterion were fulfilled by Tier One as a group.

TIER RANK	COUNTRY	TOTAL POINTS
1	United States of America	1027
2	Portugal	970
3	UK (Great Britain & Northern Ireland)	962
4	Iceland	927
5	Lithuania	901
6	Slovakia	901
7	Slovenia	897
8	Australia	893
9	Netherlands	890
10	Sweden	887
11	Germany	886
12	Denmark	884
13	Czech Republic	878
14	Belgium	877
15	Hungary	876
16	Austria	876
17	Malta	875
18	Poland	875
19	Spain	872
20	France	869
21	Ireland	858
22	New Zealand	858
23	Italy	856
24	Estonia	843
25	Finland	842
26	Norway	838
27	Canada	829
28	Japan	827
29	Luxembourg	822
30	Latvia	817
31	Republic of Korea	812
32	Croatia	807
33	Romania	782
34	Switzerland	769
35	Cyprus	749
36	Bulgaria	713
37	Greece	701
38	Argentina	661
39	Israel	655
40	Liechtenstein	647
41	South Africa	642
42	Mexico	616
43	Brazil	614
44	Turkey	607
45	Kazakhstan	598
46	Monaco	593
47	India	562
48	Serbia	541
49	China	493
50	Pakistan	420
51	Taiwan	395
52	Ukraine	381
53	Russian Federation	356
54	Belarus	335
55	Egypt	238
56	Iran (Islamic Republic of)	-141
57	DPRK	-349

Table 9.1. Rank of Tier One countries, including total points received.

NOTES

1. We note that as a U.S.-based organization, our ranking of the United States as first in Tier One and in the overall rankings is awkward, as we strive to determine rankings without bias toward our national system. However, this result is not surprising given the United States' strong focus on proliferation financing and enforcement, and given the PPI's own strong focus on proliferation financing and enforcement in determining rankings. The United States' score is high particularly on enforcement of export controls. However, it is important to point out that the U.S. export control system overall is not ideal by any means as the total score also shows, and even the top scorer can improve its system. For a set of recommendations on ways in which the United States can improve its export control system, particularly in light of a recent reform process, see: Stricker with Albright, *U.S. Export Control Reform: Impacts and Implications for Controlling the Export of Proliferation-Sensitive Goods and Technologies: A Policy Document for the New President and Congress,* Institute for Science and International Security, May 17, 2017, http://isis-online.org/isis-reports/detail/u.s.-export-control-reform-impacts-and-implications/20

2. As noted above, in general, it is not feasible for an entity or country to achieve 100 percent of available points under this super criterion. For example, membership in export control arrangements such as the Nuclear Suppliers Group is by invitation. In addition, some countries with even small amounts of nuclear material or small nuclear facilities cannot have an IAEA Small Quantities Protocol.

CHAPTER 10
TIER TWO RANKING

Tier Two is composed of 57 transshipment countries that pose a risk of illicit or unauthorized supply, facilitation, or transfer of sensitive commodities:

Afghanistan, Albania, Algeria, Armenia, Azerbaijan, Bahamas, Bangladesh, Bosnia and Herzegovina, Brunei Darussalam, Chile, Colombia, Costa Rica, Dominican Republic, Ecuador, Ethiopia, Georgia, Hong Kong, Indonesia, Iraq, Jamaica, Kuwait, Kyrgyzstan, Lao People's Democratic Republic, Lebanon, Libya, Madagascar, Malawi, Malaysia, Moldova (Rep of the), Mongolia, Morocco, Namibia, Nicaragua, Niger, Nigeria, Oman, Panama, Paraguay, Peru, Philippines, Qatar, Saudi Arabia, Singapore, Sri Lanka, Syrian Arab Republic, Tajikistan, Tanzania (United Rep of), Thailand, Tunisia, Uganda, United Arab Emirates, Uzbekistan, Vanuatu, Venezuela (Bolivarian Republic of), Viet Nam, and Zambia.

Table 10.1 (and Figure 10.1) show the rankings of the countries in Tier Two. The average score in Tier Two is 420 points. The median is 422. The scores are more clustered than in Tier One (see Chapter 9).

As with Tier One countries, the reader is cautioned not to assign too much precision to close rankings between countries in Table 10.1. It is the large differences in total points between Tier Two countries that matter, not a country's particular numerical rank.

Tier Two countries by their nature have not developed as extensive of export control systems as countries in Tier One. This is reflected in the overall scores. However, Tier Two countries cannot be expected to develop as robust of export controls as Tier One countries. As a result, in this tier, countries that achieved a score of at least half of the total points (650 points out of a total possible 1,300 points), are viewed as having sufficient export control systems (which accounts for only three countries). It should be noted that having sufficient export controls does not mean that improvements are not needed. A score below one third of the total possible points indicates that these countries need to do considerable work to improve their export control systems (33 countries). Those in between need to improve their systems somewhat (21 countries). This is shown by the pie chart in Figure 10.2.

Although a country's total score is the fundamental measure of the effectiveness of its export control system, it is difficult to use it to prescribe a way for countries to improve. As a result, the performance fraction charts the extent to which countries have met the sub-criteria. For example, if the PPI team assigned 0, 5, or 10 points for a country's adherence to the Additional Protocol (0 would entail no signature or ratification, 5 would signify signature but not ratification, and 10 would be points for full ratification), the performance fractions would assess those base points awarded to each country before weighting as low, medium, or high impact. It does not factor in any negative indicators. Performance fractions, in fact, allow for a basic assessment of where points were *not* received. Please refer back to Chapter 7: Total Weighted Score and Rank for a longer discussion of performance fractions.

TIER TWO IN THE OVERALL RANKING

Tier Two countries did not do as well as Tier One countries in the overall PPI ranking. Only five countries ranked among the top 50 countries. Eighteen countries ranked between 50 and 100. The remaining 34 of the 57 countries were in the bottom half of all 200 countries.

The highest ranked Tier Two country was Singapore which ranked 19th overall and achieved 67 percent of the possible points. The second highest rank in Tier Two in terms of the overall rank, 41st overall (Malaysia), achieved only 52 percent of the possible points.

The performance fractions confirm that collective Tier Two performance has considerable room for improvement (Figure 10.3). As described below, there are many easy fixes that Tier Two countries can make. Top performing countries like Singapore and Malaysia could play a role in assisting their peers in this tier.

SCORE AND PERFORMANCE BY SUPER CRITERIA

INTERNATIONAL COMMITMENT

Six of the 57 countries received two-thirds of the total possible points in this super criterion. Forty countries received more than half but less than two-thirds of the points. The bottom 11 countries receiving less than 50 percent of achievable points were, listed from higher to lower ranking: Thailand, Niger, Lebanon, Brunei Darussalam, Oman, Sri Lanka, Venezuela, Ethiopia, Laos, Syria, and Hong Kong.

The performance fractions show that satisfactory performance was achieved in ten sub-criteria (Figure 10.4). However, stronger commitment can be shown by participating more actively in organizations such as FATF, by joining initiatives such as the Proliferation Security Initiative, and by having bilateral agreements in place such as the Customs Mutual Assistance Agreement with the United States. Many of these countries offer trade benefits to major global economies, including cheap and fast transshipment opportunities. Therefore, Tier Two countries should not hesitate to take advantage of international organizations and assistance mechanisms. In fact, Tier Two's major global trade partners, including the United States, should demand more participation and visible commitment to preventing commodity trafficking from Tier Two countries.

LEGISLATION

Overall, Tier Two countries were nearly equal in distribution among doing well, less than adequate, and poorly at having in place export control-relevant legislation. Nineteen countries received more than two-thirds of the points, and 21 received half but less than two-thirds of the points. The remaining 17 countries did not receive half of the possible points. In terms of the quality of export control legislation, Tier Two countries were relatively mixed. Fifteen countries are Dark Green, six are Light Green, 14 are Yellow, 16 are Orange, and six are Red (see Chapter 3, Table 3.2, for a full list of countries' legislative categories). The following countries in Tier Two have Orange color-coded Legislation, listed from higher to lower ranking: Malawi, Zambia, Mongolia, Panama, Ethiopia, Costa Rica, Niger, Saudi Arabia, Vanuatu, Dominican Republic, Laos, Ecuador, Viet Nam, Kuwait, Paraguay, and Syria. Those with Red legislation include: the Bahamas, Madagascar, Tunisia, Colombia, Oman, and Afghanistan. Non-Green categorized countries in this tier should improve their legal basis for export controls and thereby enable more effective implementation and enforcement. Sixty three percent (if we include Yellow countries) of Tier Two transshipment countries lack relevant and adequate dual-use and nuclear-related export controls, which is related to their poor performance in the remaining super criteria.

The performance fractions show that these countries need to significantly strengthen their export control laws and lists (Figure 10.5). Only a small fraction of Tier Two countries includes a catch-all clause in their export control legislation. Moreover, legislative controls on transit and transshipment of nuclear-related goods were only found for only half of Tier Two countries. Additionally, the Tier Two countries with nuclear infrastructure in place especially should protect intellectual property better to ensure that nuclear-related knowledge and information are not proliferated (see Chapter 3 on Legislation).

ABILITY TO MONITOR AND DETECT STRATEGIC TRADE

Tier Two countries did poorly in their Ability to Monitor and Detect Strategic Trade, a significant deficiency since this tier is comprised of transshipment countries. The highest scoring country achieved 59 percent of the available points. The next nine countries scored more than 50 percent, while the following 47 countries did not receive half of the possible points. Indeed, the majority of Tier Two countries are unable to achieve half of the possible points, lacking the capacity, knowledge, or willingness to monitor and detect strategic trade.

The performance fractions show that only two sub-criteria were fulfilled to 75 percent: Using an automated customs system, and being a party to the UN Convention on the Law of the Sea (see Figure 10.6). Both initiatives are supported and promoted by the United Nations. For example, the UN ran a global campaign to implement the ASYCUDA automated customs software, showing that international organizations can help individual countries to increase their ability to monitor and control trade. All other sub-criteria are not fulfilled to even 50 percent. While it may take a long time to move up the ranks in a World Bank ranking, countries can improve their performance under some sub-criteria rather quickly, such as providing a point of contact for Resolution 1540 implementation, or working with the public and the industry to increase awareness of export-controlled items and often-used illicit trade schemes.

ABILITY TO PREVENT PROLIFERATION FINANCING

Like Tier One countries, Tier Two countries performed the worst on Preventing Proliferation Financing. The top-ranking country received 42 percent of the possible points, the top three countries received at least one-third of possible points, and the remaining 54 countries scored under 33 percent. Two countries received between a quarter and a third of the total possible points and 23 countries scored between zero and 25 percent of possible points. The remaining 28 countries, or roughly half of Tier Two, received negative points and included the following, listed from higher to lower ranking: Ethiopia, Peru, Costa Rica, Tunisia, Ghana, Bosnia and Herzegovina, Algeria, Tanzania, Kuwait, Nicaragua, Philippines, Ecuador, Laos, Dominican Republic, Tajikistan, Indonesia, Viet Nam, Nigeria, Uganda, Sri Lanka, Paraguay, Morocco, Syria, Thailand, Afghanistan, Libya, Lebanon, and Iraq.

Considering that many of these countries ranked toward the bottom of the Corruption Perceptions Index, it is particularly concerning that these transshipment states lack the ability to prevent proliferation financing. Since the availability or ease of illicit financing facilitates strategic commodity trafficking, it is significant that a majority of Tier Two countries perform so poorly in general under Super Criterion Ability to Prevent Proliferation Financing, coupled with poor performance in Super Criterion Ability to Monitor and Detect Strategic Trade.

The performance fractions reveal why Tier Two countries performed worst in preventing proliferation financing. Only one of the sub-criteria passed the 50 percent marker (see Figure 10.7). FATF compliance overall and compliance with the selected recommendations is very poor. All Tier Two countries need to work more closely with FATF and its regional bodies to implement the FATF recommendations, especially the six recommendations judged as most relevant to preventing proliferation financing.

ADEQUACY OF ENFORCEMENT

Only three countries achieved at least two-thirds of the total possible points, while the next 19 countries scored above 50 percent but failed to reach the two-thirds mark. The next 29 countries achieved 25-50 percent of the total points. The remaining seven countries received less than 25 percent of the total points, and included the following (listed from higher to lower ranking): Venezuela, Viet Nam, Afghanistan, Iraq, Libya, and Syria (the only Tier Two state to receive a negative score). Such frequent, poor performance among transshipment countries and their apparent lack of capacity or willingness to enforce export controls, while simultaneously tending to rank poorly in the Corruption Perceptions Index, needs to be seen as collectively hindering of their non-proliferation efforts.

The performance fractions show that satisfactory performance across the entire tier was achieved in four sub-criteria: Having a denied parties list, being a member of the UN and legally-bound to enforce UNSC sanctions, being a member of Interpol, and having a border seizure authority (see Figure 10.8.) Five further sub-criteria were fulfilled to 50 percent, including two that are very important for this tier: making use of training and outreach and of international legal assistance mechanisms. Nevertheless, having transit and transshipment controls, which are arguably the most important mechanisms in terms of sub-criteria for Tier Two countries, are not fulfilled to 50 percent.

Tier Two Rank

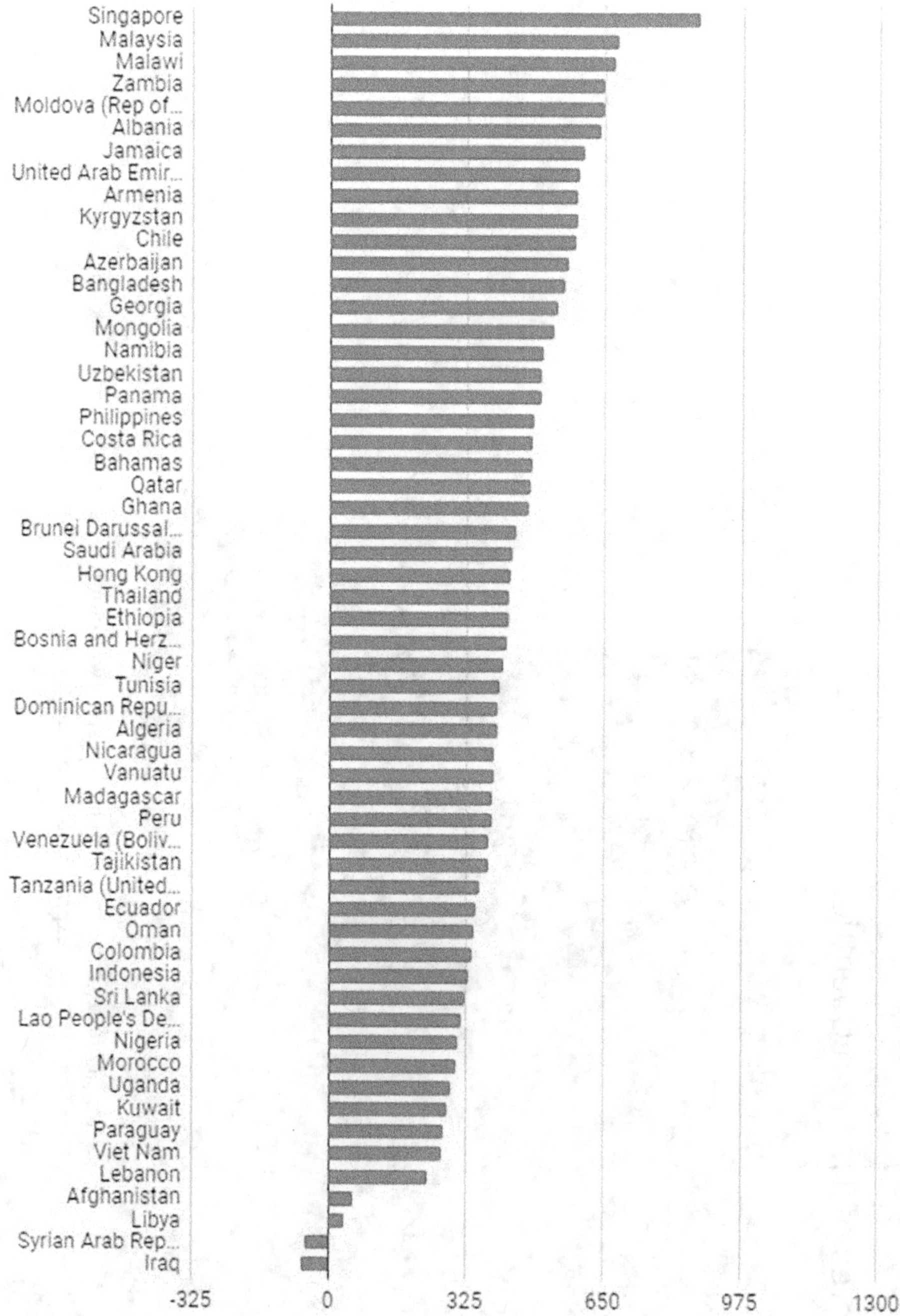

Figure 10.1. Total points received by each country in relation to the total possible points. The points result in the rank.

Scores of Tier Two Countries

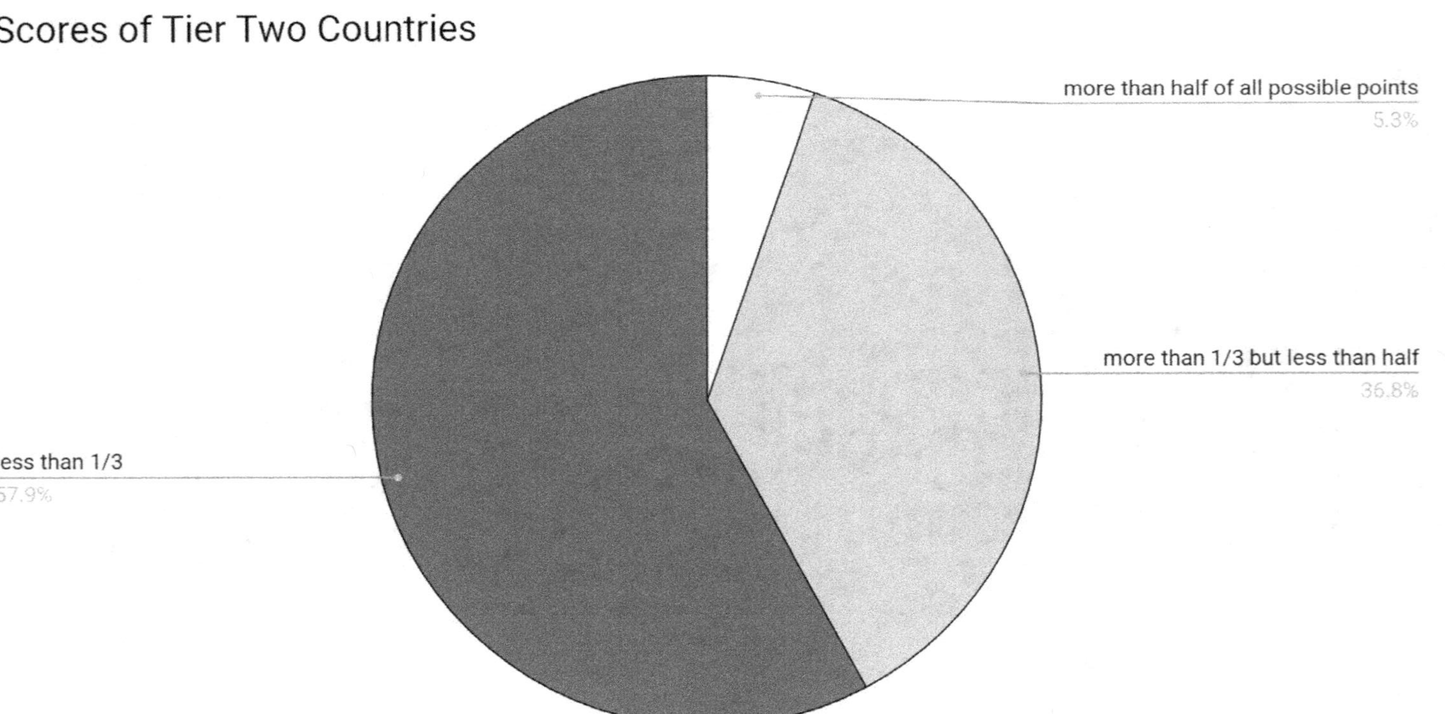

Figure 10.2. More than half of Tier Two countries need significant work on their export controls and an additional third need some work.

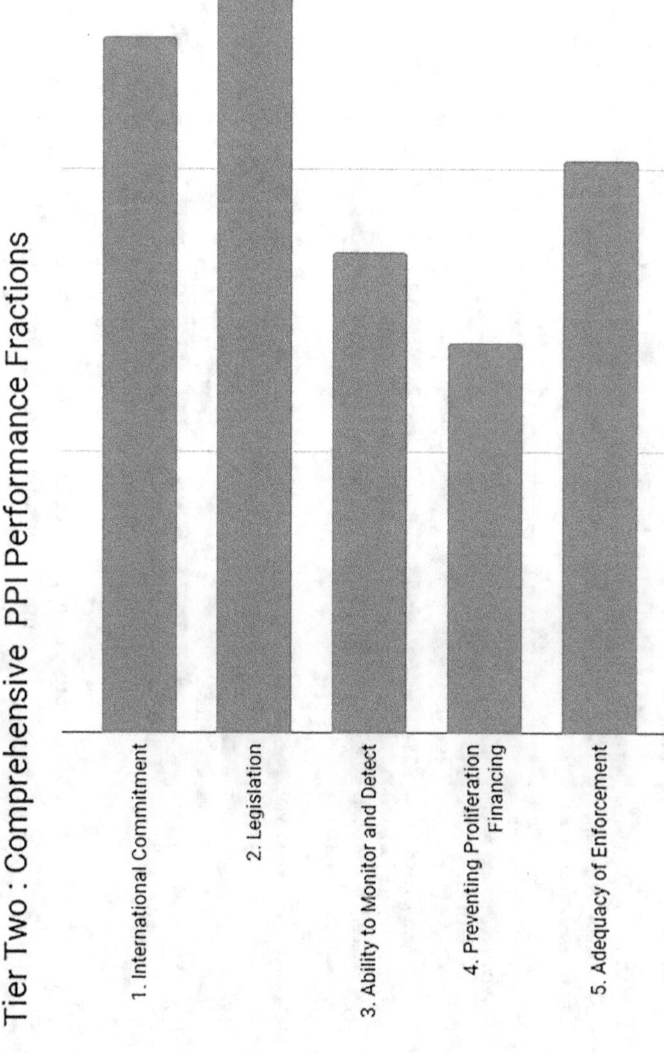

Figure 10.3. The extent to which the super criteria were fulfilled by Tier Two as a group.

Figure 10.4. The extent to which sub-criteria making up the International Commitment super criterion were fulfilled by Tier Two as a group.

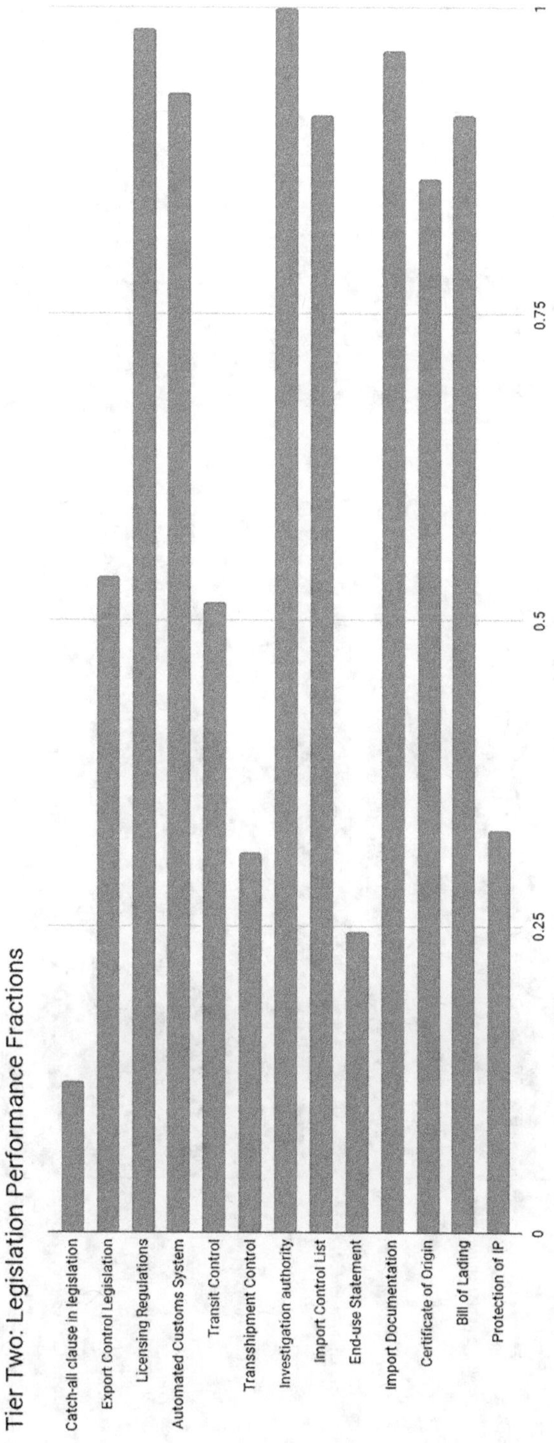

Figure 10.5. The extent to which sub-criteria making up the Legislation super criterion were fulfilled by Tier Two as a group.

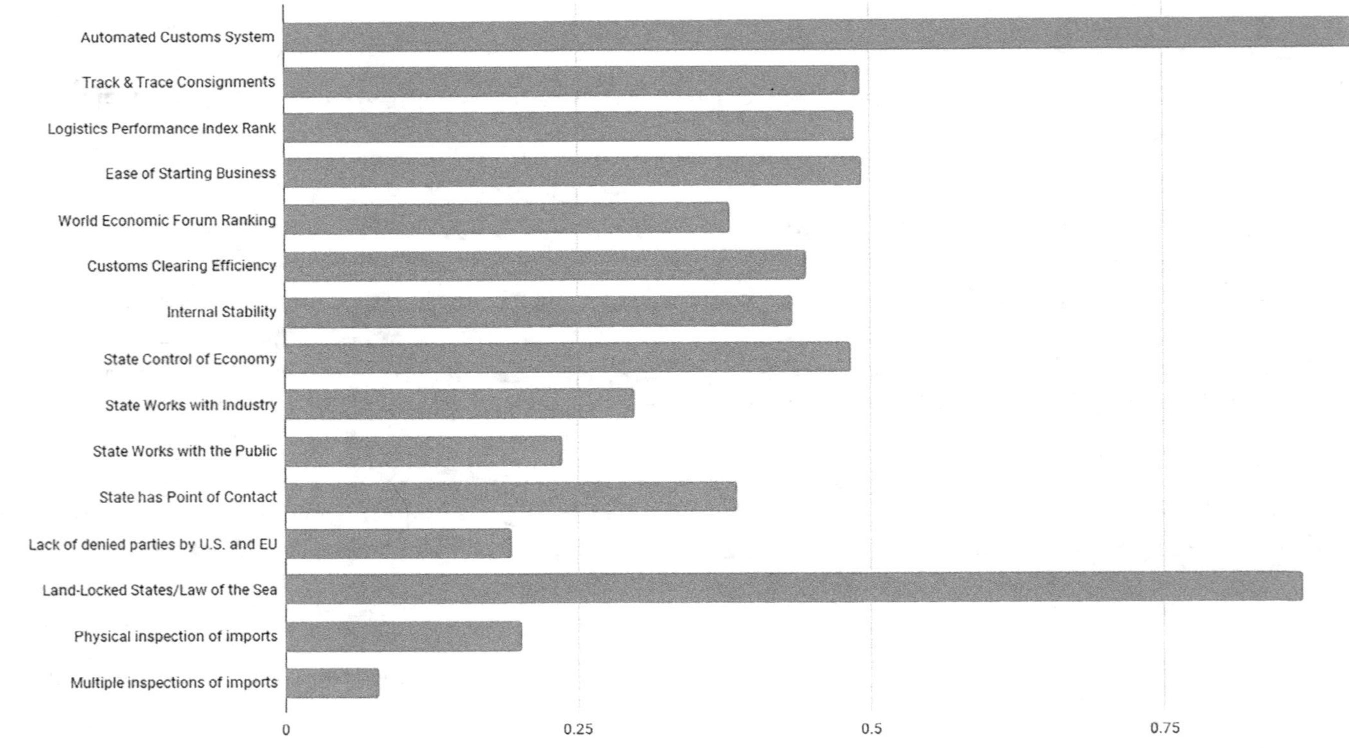

Figure 10.6. The extent to which sub-criteria making up the Ability to Monitor and Detect Strategic Trade super criterion were fulfilled by Tier Two as a group.

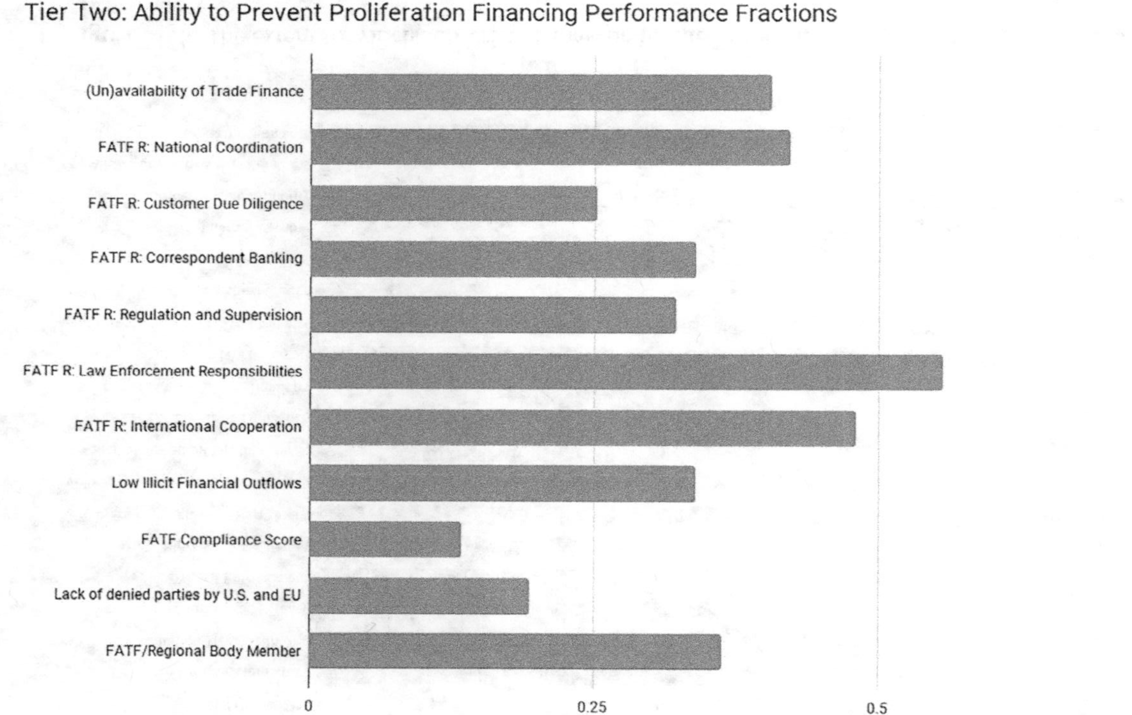

Figure 10.7. The extent to which sub-criteria making up the Ability to Prevent Proliferation Financing super criterion were fulfilled by Tier Two as a group.

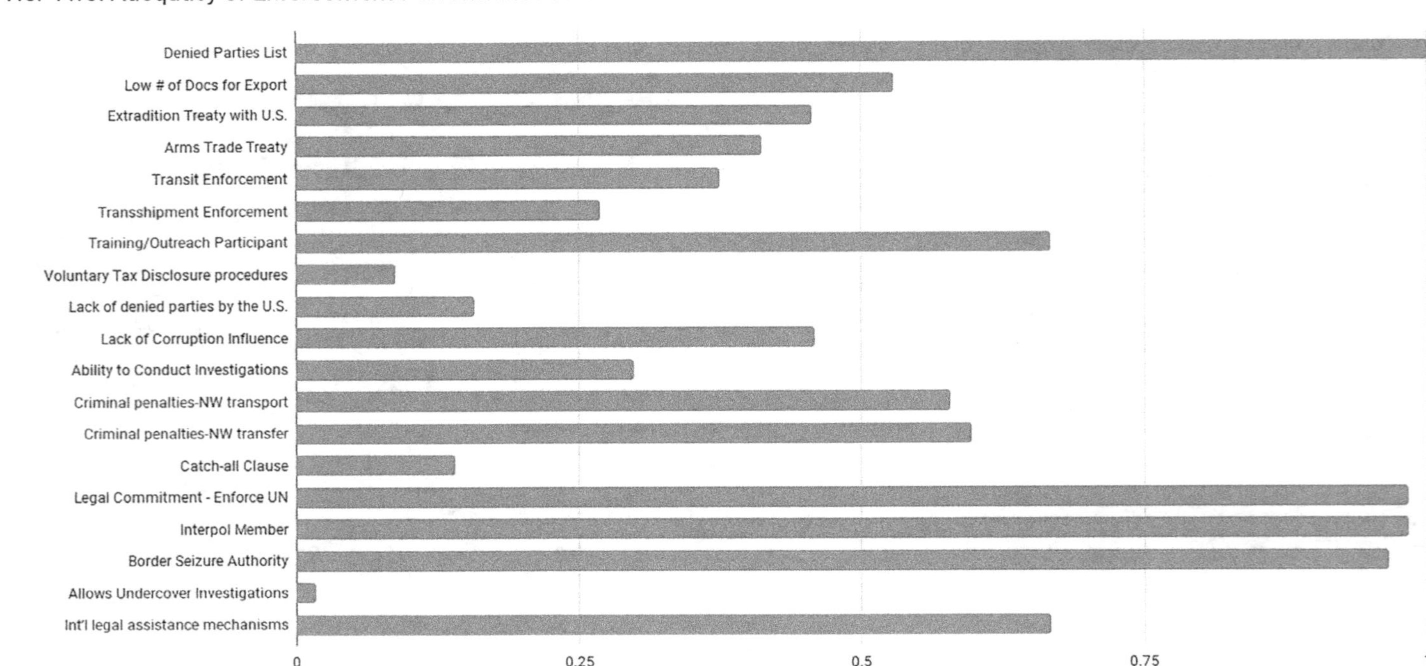

Figure 10.8. The extent to which sub-criteria making up the Enforcement super criterion were fulfilled by Tier Two as a group.

TIER RANK	COUNTRY	TOTAL POINTS		TIER RANK	COUNTRY	TOTAL POINTS
1	Singapore	872		30	Niger	411
2	Malaysia	681		31	Tunisia	404
3	Malawi	671		32	Dominican Republic	400
4	Zambia	645		33	Algeria	397
5	Moldova (Rep of the)	645		34	Nicaragua	391
6	Albania	639		35	Vanuatu	391
7	Jamaica	598		36	Madagascar	388
8	United Arab Emirates	589		37	Peru	387
9	Armenia	584		38	Venezuela (Bolivarian Republic of)	379
10	Kyrgyzstan	584		39	Tajikistan	376
11	Chile	581		40	Tanzania (United Republic of)	356
12	Azerbaijan	562		41	Ecuador	350
13	Bangladesh	553		42	Oman	342
14	Georgia	536		43	Colombia	341
15	Mongolia	528		44	Indonesia	331
16	Namibia	504		45	Sri Lanka	322
17	Uzbekistan	500		46	Lao People's Democratic Republic	313
18	Panama	500		47	Nigeria	308
19	Philippines	484		48	Morocco	301
20	Costa Rica	479		49	Uganda	288
21	Bahamas	478		50	Kuwait	281
22	Qatar	475		51	Paraguay	273
23	Ghana	469		52	Viet Nam	268
24	Brunei Darussalam	441		53	Lebanon	235
25	Saudi Arabia	431		54	Afghanistan	57
26	Hong Kong	428		55	Libya	39
27	Thailand	424		56	Syrian Arab Republic	-56
28	Ethiopia	423		57	Iraq	-62
29	Bosnia and Herzegovina	422				

Table 10.1. Rank of Tier Two countries, including total points received.

CHAPTER 11
TIER THREE RANKING

Tier Three is composed of 86 countries:

Andorra, Angola, Antigua and Barbuda, Bahrain, Barbados, Belize, Benin, Bhutan, Bolivia, Botswana, Burkina Faso, Burundi, Cambodia, Cameroon, Cape Verde, Central African Republic, Chad, Comoros, Congo (Dem Rep of the), Congo (Rep of the), Cook Islands, Côte d'Ivoire, Cuba, Djibouti, Dominica, El Salvador, Equatorial Guinea, Eritrea, Fiji, Gabon, Gambia, Grenada, Guatemala, Guinea-Bissau, Guyana, Haiti, Holy See, Honduras, Jordan, Kenya, Kiribati, Kosovo, Lesotho, Liberia, Macedonia, Maldives, Mali, Marshall Islands, Mauritania, Mauritius, Micronesia (Federation of), Montenegro, Mozambique, Myanmar, Nauru, Nepal, Niue, Palau, Palestine (State of), Papua New Guinea, Rwanda, Saint Kitts and Nevis, Saint Lucia, Saint Vincent and the Grenadines, Samoa, San Marino, Sao Tome and Principe, Senegal, Seychelles, Sierra Leone, Solomon Islands, Somalia, South Sudan, Sudan, Suriname, Swaziland, Timor-Leste, Togo, Tonga, Trinidad and Tobago, Turkmenistan, Tuvalu, Uruguay, Yemen, and Zimbabwe.

Table 11.1 (and Figure 11.1) show the rankings of the countries in Tier Three. The average score in Tier Three is 380 points. The median is 377.

While the requirements or expectations for non-supplier and non-transshipment countries may not be as high with regard to strategic export controls, Tier Three still performed poorly overall. The results suggest that for these countries, which comprise almost 45 percent of all countries, export controls are a low priority. In general, Tier Three countries lack a commitment to international conventions and legislation from which to enforce export controls.

Moreover, they lack capacity, resources, and possibly the will to combat proliferation and enforce trade controls. This is especially true given the prevalence of corruption in these countries and the related ease with which illicit funds can be used to support trafficking in strategic commodities. Tier Three countries could potentially be used by unscrupulous "middlemen" or facilitators to finance and procure commodities from supplier countries. As a result, the same sufficiency standards are used for Tier Three as for Tier Two. A score that achieved at least half of the total points (650 points), is viewed as sufficient (4 countries), and a score below one third of the total possible points means that these countries need to do considerable work to improve their export control systems (54 countries). Those in between need to improve their systems (28 countries). This is visualized in the pie chart in Figure 11.2.

Although a country's total score is the fundamental measure of the effectiveness of its export control system, it is difficult to use it to prescribe a way for countries to improve. As a result, the performance fraction charts the extent to which countries have met the sub-criteria. For example, if the PPI team assigned 0, 5, or 10 points for a country's adherence to the Additional Protocol (0 would entail no signature or ratification, 5 would signify signature but not ratification, and 10 would be points for full ratification), the performance fractions would assess those base points awarded to each country before weighting as low, medium, or high impact. It does not factor in any negative indicators. Performance fractions, in fact, allow for a basic assessment of where points were *not* received. Please refer back to Chapter 7: Total Weighted Score and Rank, for a longer discussion of performance fractions.

The performance fractions for Tier Three show that their low scores stem from these countries having taken little to no action to meet the criteria. Only one super criterion was fulfilled to more than 50 percent (see Figure 11.3).

TIER THREE IN THE OVERALL RANK

In general, Tier Three did not perform as well in all sub-criteria, and overall compared to Tiers One and Two. Only four of the 86 countries were in the top 25 percent of all 200 countries. Twenty-Four Tier Three countries fell between the top 25 and 50 percent; the remaining 58 countries ranked in the bottom half of all 200 countries.

One observation is that many of the countries in Tier Three have *not* been used as transshipment countries by proliferant states as these states illegally procure goods or move funds illegally. Overall, these countries appear to pose a generally a lower risk of being caught up in illicit trading schemes. However, this could change as countries develop or illicit trading networks look to exploit additional states with weak controls.

INTERNATIONAL COMMITMENT

No Tier Three country was able to achieve two-thirds of the total possible points in this super criterion; the highest scorer received 63 percent of possible points. Thirty-five countries, however, did receive at least half of the possible points. Forty-three countries received between 25 and 50 percent of possible points while the remaining nine countries received less than 25 percent.

The performance fractions in this super criterion suggest a lack of commitment to adopting international agreements and conventions (see Figure 11.4). While the great majority of Tier Three countries are parties to the three major WMD Treaties (NPT, CWC, and BWC), membership in other important conventions such as the Convention for the Suppression of Acts of Nuclear Terrorism, the Convention on the Physical Protection of Nuclear Materials, and the Proliferation Security Initiative, fall short of 50 percent. There is room for improvement regarding IAEA cooperation. Of all the tiers, Tier Three countries have the highest rate of participation in regional Nuclear Weapon Free Zone treaties, implying an important commitment to preventing the spread of nuclear weapons in their regions. This should not be taken as an indication that countries in Tiers One and Two lack commitment to non-proliferation. It more likely reflects the fact that, for many countries in Tiers One and Two, NWFZ treaties have not been established in their regions, for example, in Europe and the Middle East.

LEGISLATION

Ten countries received more than two-thirds of the possible points in this super criterion, with the highest achieving 96 percent of possible points. The next 24 countries received at least half but less than two-thirds of the points in this super criterion, while the remaining 52, with the exception of the bottom three ranking countries (Marshall Islands, Cook Islands, and Holy See), received less than half but more than 25 percent of possible points. Overall, the quality of export control legislation is poor as only 10 percent of countries were in the Dark or Light Green category of legislation and the overwhelming majority, or 81 percent, of countries have legislation in the Red or Orange categories.

The following lists countries by the quality of their commitment to export control legislation, listed from higher to lower ranking:

Dark Green (6): San Marino, Macedonia, Andorra, Montenegro, Jordan, Holy See

Light Green (3): Cambodia, Myanmar, Kosovo

Yellow (8): Botswana, Guatemala, Uruguay, Sierra Leone, Cape Verde, Cuba, Rwanda, Niue

Orange (25): Solomon Islands, Burkina Faso, Timor-Leste, Lesotho, Gabon, Fiji, Samoa, Nauru, Grenada, Trinidad and Tobago, Bhutan, Mauritania, Palau, Barbados, Seychelles, Gambia, Suriname, El Salvador, Turkmenistan, Bolivia, Côte d'Ivoire, Senegal, Saint Kitts and Nevis, Tuvalu, and Benin

Red (44): Mauritius, Cameroon, Antigua and Barbuda, Bahrain, Tonga, Saint Lucia, Swaziland, Mali, Maldives, Togo, Djibouti, Nepal, Congo (Rep of the), Dominica, Sao Tome and Principe, Guinea, Saint Vincent and Grenadine, Liberia, Papua New Guinea, Congo (Dem Rep of the), Angola, Chad, Mozambique, Comoros, Zimbabwe, Marshall Islands, Honduras, Yemen, Kenya, Kiribati, Haiti, Micronesia, Guinea-Bissau, Guyana, Equatorial Guinea, Cook Islands, Belize, Central African Republic, Burundi, Eritrea, Palestine, Sudan, Somalia, and South Sudan

The performance fractions show that some trade legislation exists that could support potential future nuclear commodity export control laws (see Figure 11.5). As of 2017, relevant nuclear commodity control lists are missing in all but a handful of Tier Three countries. Several sub-criteria such as having export licensing regulations, using automated customs systems, having an investigative authority, and requiring a certain set of documents for imports are fulfilled to more than 75 percent, but since relevant control lists are missing, these laws and authorities do not apply to many nuclear- or dual-use items. For the other six sub-criteria, countries fall far short of 50 percent, with four of the sub-criteria not reaching 25 percent.

ABILITY TO MONITOR AND DETECT STRATEGIC TRADE

Similar to Tier One and Tier Two countries, Tier Three countries do not perform well overall on Ability to Monitor and Detect Strategic Trade. The highest-ranking country received 55 percent of possible points; only the top three countries achieved more than 50 percent of the possible points. The next 63 countries received at least 25 percent of possible points while the remaining 20 countries did not achieve 25 percent.

Performance fractions show that only two sub-criteria were fulfilled to more than 75 percent (see Figure 11.6): Using automated customs systems and being a party to the UN Convention on the Law of the Sea or on Transit of Land-locked States. As such, the performance fraction profile of Tier Three looks similar to that of Tier Two. Both initiatives are supported and promoted by the United Nations, as discussed in the Tier Two section, showing that international organizations can help individual countries increase their ability to monitor and detect strategic trade. All other sub-criteria are fulfilled less than 50 percent. While it may take a long time to move up the ranks in, for example, a World Bank ranking, other sub-criteria can be met quickly, such as providing a governmental point of contact for Resolution 1540 implementation or working with the public and industry to increase awareness of export-controlled items and often-used illicit trading schemes. Tier Three countries do perform better in their lack of having sanctioned entities. Almost half of the countries do not have a single sanctioned entity on the United States' several sanctions lists. This suggests that these countries have so far not been targeted by illicit trade networks. Moreover, it also could reflect that Tier Three countries do not participate as much in global trade to the level that Tier Two countries do.

ABILITY TO PREVENT PROLIFERATION FINANCING

Tier Three countries performed the worst in preventing the financing of proliferation with the highest ranking country is this super criterion receiving only 45 percent of the possible points. The top 21 countries only achieved 25 percent of possible points while the next 37 countries received between zero and 25 percent of possible points. The remaining 28 countries received negative scores and include the following, listed from higher to lower ranking: Mali, Jordan, Congo (Rep of the), Rwanda, Sierra Leone, Djibouti, Tuvalu, Zimbabwe, Micronesia, Montenegro, Congo (Dem Rep of the), El Salvador, Haiti, Belize, Kosovo, Guinea-Bissau, Palestine, Kenya, Guyana, Bolivia, Cambodia, Central African Republic, Eritrea, Sudan, Burundi, Myanmar, Somalia, and South Sudan.

The performance fractions show that significant improvement can be made in preventing proliferation financing in Tier Three. Only one of the sub-criteria exceeds the 50 percent fulfillment marker (see Figure 11.7).

It should be noted, however, that for many countries in Tier Three the sub-criterion's *overall FATF compliance score* was not available from a data source used in the PPI ranking. If data were available, the performance fraction would likely be higher, but would still fit the trend set by the other sub-criteria. Six of the sub-criteria are based on specific FATF recommendations, and would be part of the overall FATF compliance score. These six sub-criteria were generally low, namely below fifty percent (see Figure 11.7). Given these low scores, the overall FATF compliance score would be expected to be comparable to these scores or at least not significantly greater than those sub-criteria scores.

ADEQUACY OF ENFORCEMENT

Tier Three countries in general lack the capacity to enforce export controls. Only the top two countries achieved two-thirds of possible points in this super criterion, and the next 13 countries in the ranking received between 50 and 67 percent of possible points. The next 65 countries received less than 50 percent but more than 25 percent of the points, and the remaining six countries received less than 25 percent (two countries) or negative scores (four countries) in this super criterion.

Again, the enforcement performance fraction profile for Tier Three looks similar to the one for Tier Two. Satisfactory performance was achieved in four sub-criteria: having a denied parties list, being a member of the UN and legally-bound to enforce UNSC sanctions, being a member of Interpol, and having a border seizure authority (see Figure 11.8). For the remaining 15 sub-criteria, countries reached around 50 percent of the points. Tier Two countries perform significantly better in participating in training and outreach and international legal assistance mechanisms, which Tier Three countries would greatly benefit from.

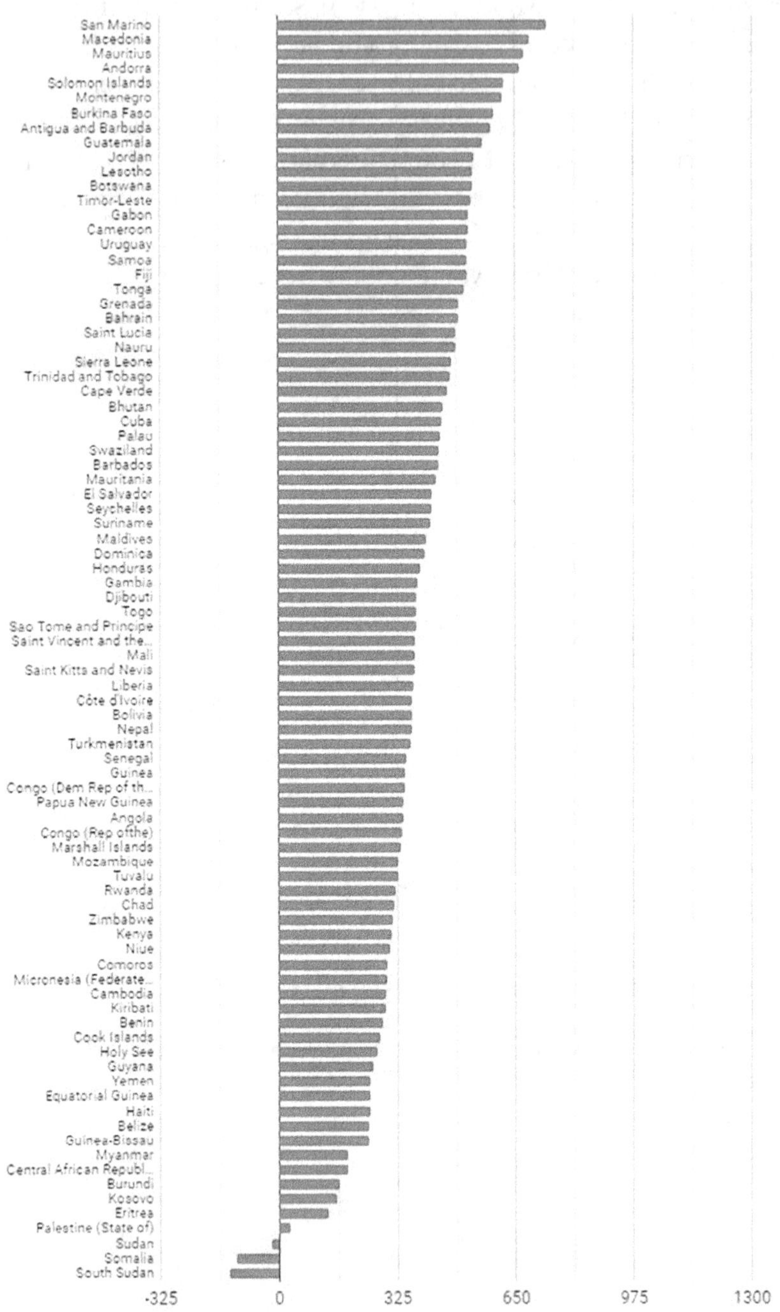

Figure 11.1. Visualization of the total points received by each country in relation to the total possible points (1,300). The scores lead to the rank. The vertical line at 650 represents the 50 percent marker, and the vertical line at 325 is the 25 percent marker.

Scores of Tier Three Countries

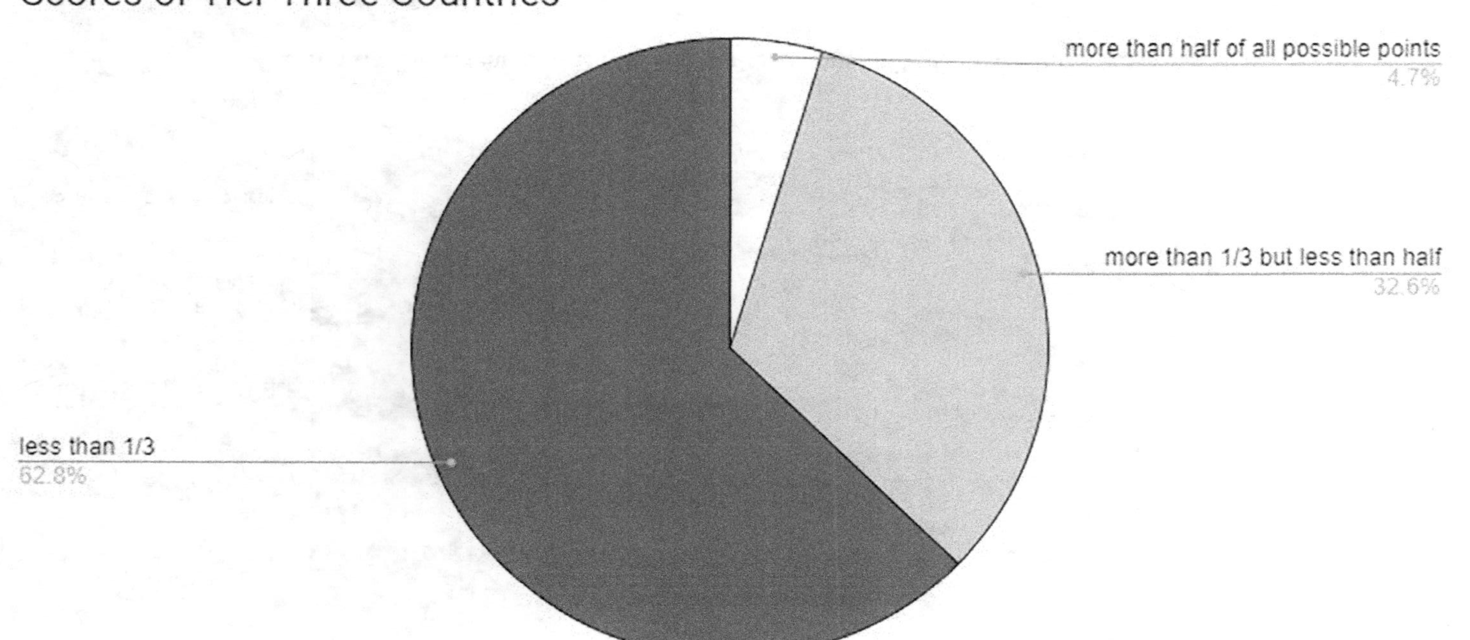

Figure 11.2. The pie chart looks similar to Tier Two. More than half of Tier Three countries need significant work on their export controls. As Tier Three includes more countries than Tier Two, half of Tier Three represents a greater number of countries.

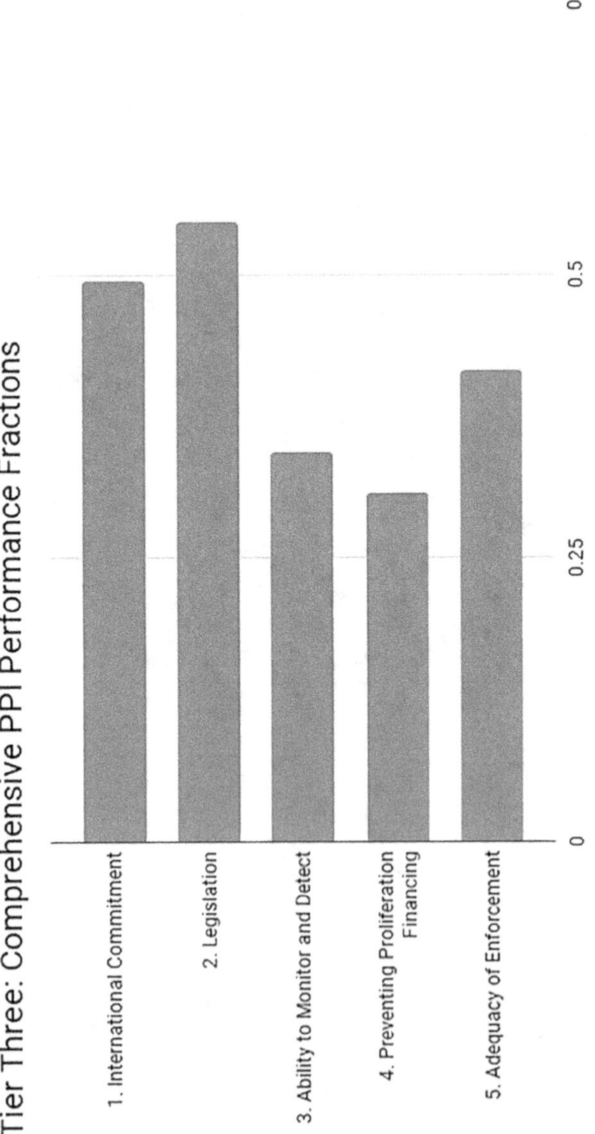

Figure 11.3. The extent to which the super criteria were fulfilled by Tier Three as a group.

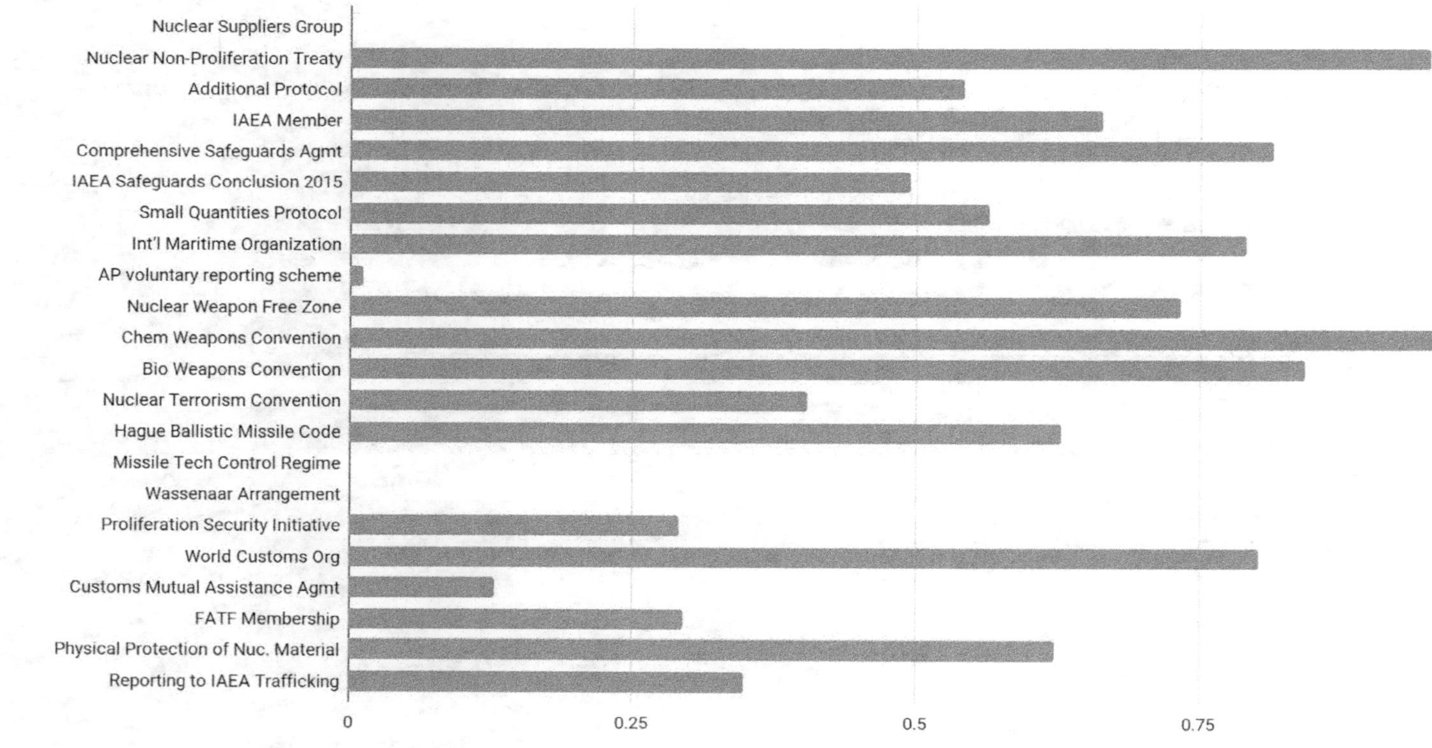

Figure 11.4. The extent to which sub-criteria making up the International Commitment super criterion were fulfilled by Tier Three as a group.

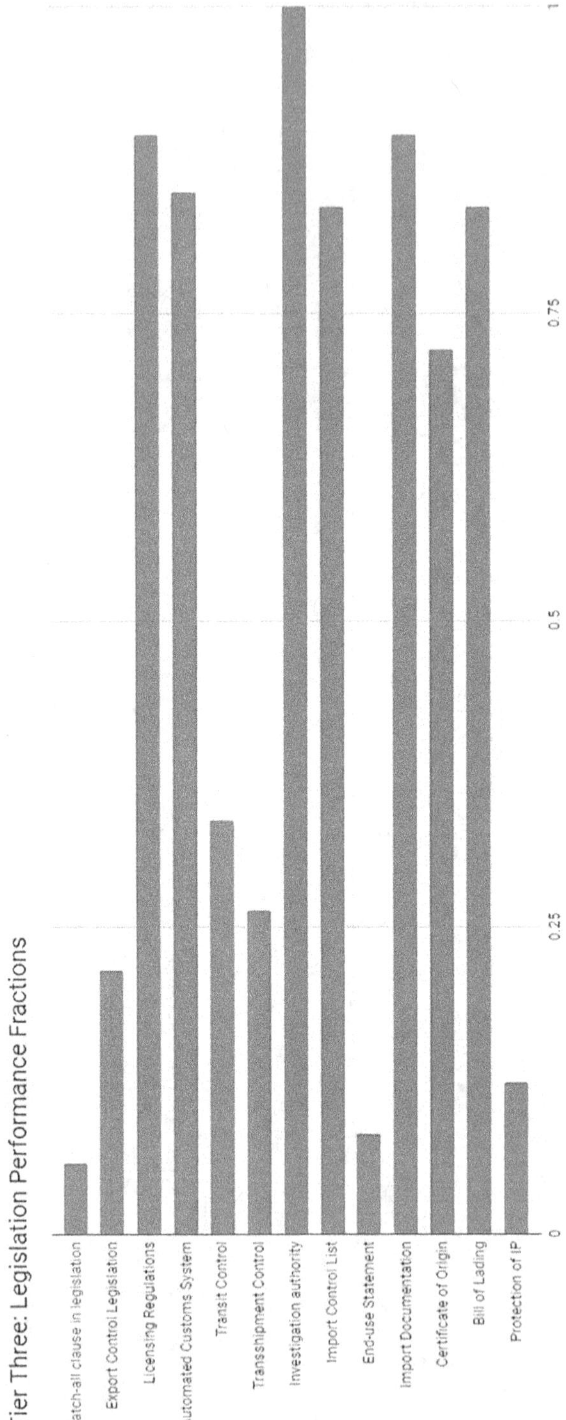

Figure 11.5. The extent to which sub-criteria making up the Legislation super criterion were fulfilled by Tier Three as a group.

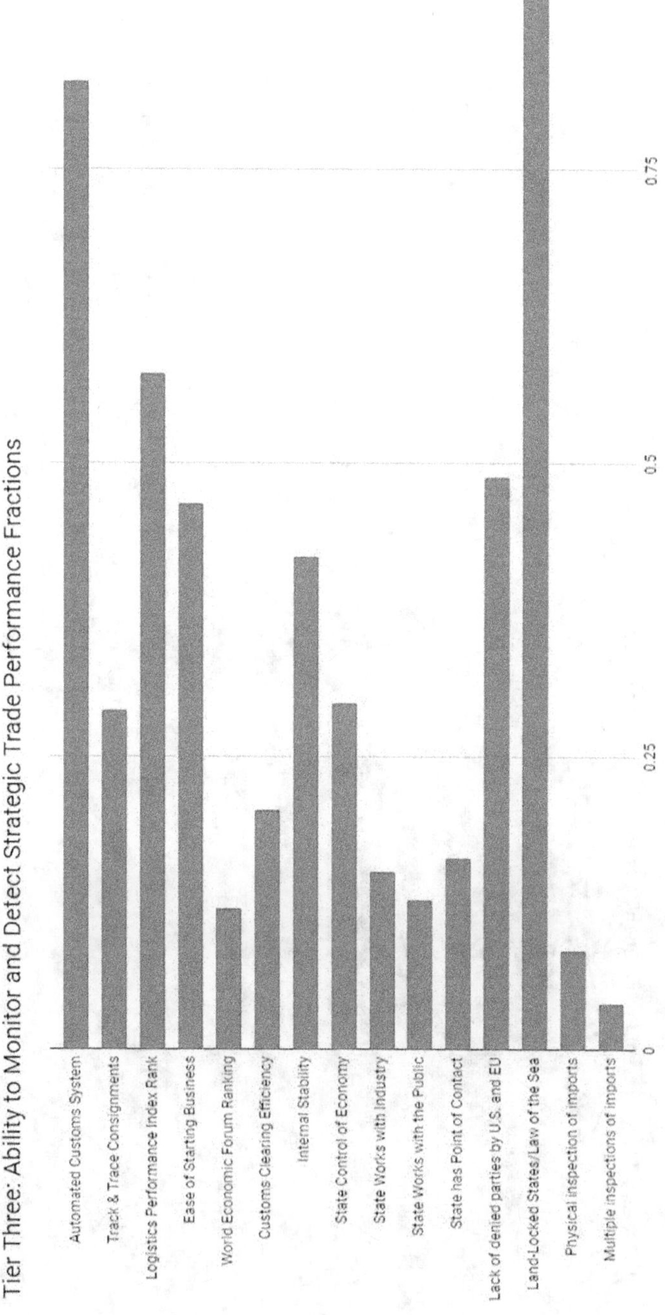

Figure 11.6. The extent to which sub-criteria making up the Ability to Monitor and Detect Strategic Trade super criterion were fulfilled by Tier Three as a group.

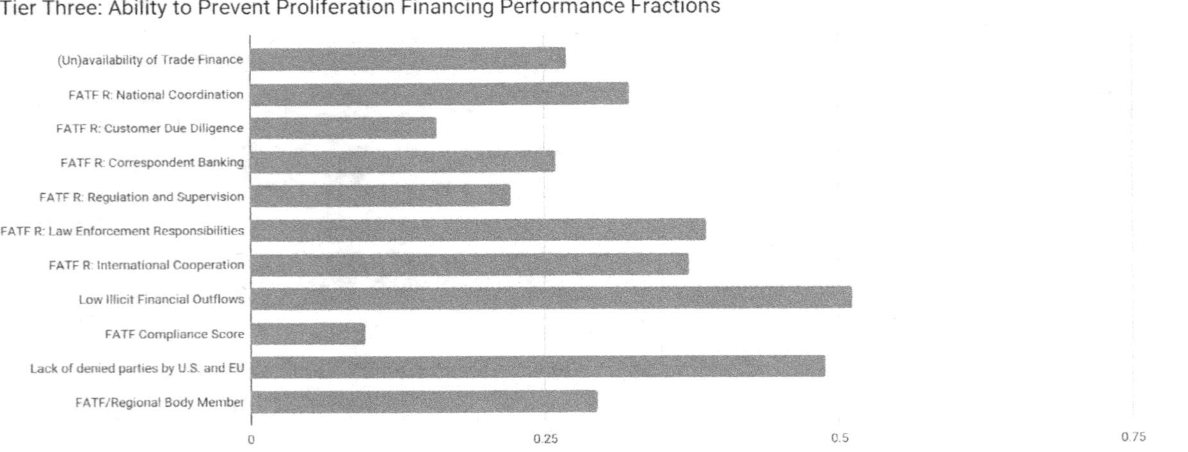

Figure 11.7. The extent to which sub-criteria making up the Ability to Prevent Proliferation Financing super criterion were fulfilled by Tier Three as a group.

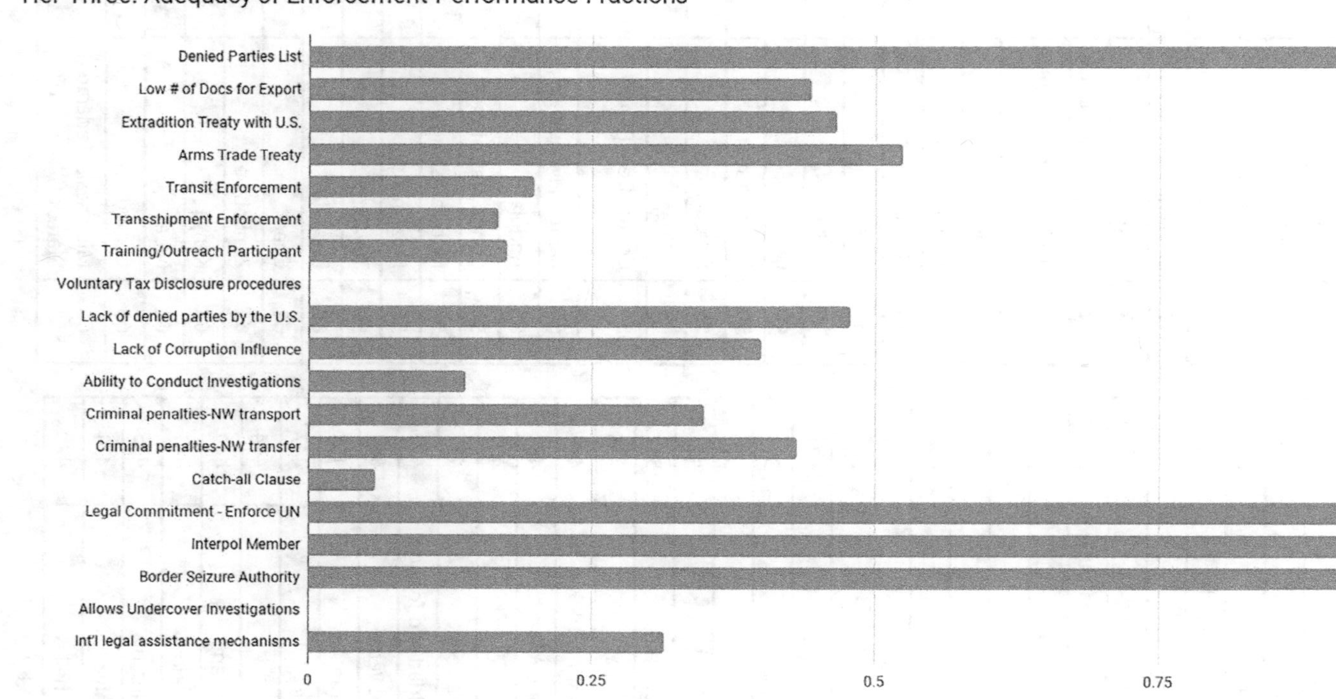

Figure 11.8. The extent to which sub-criteria making up the Adequacy of Enforcement super criterion were fulfilled by Tier Three as a group.

TIER RANK	COUNTRY	TOTAL POINTS
1	San Marino	736
2	Macedonia	688
3	Mauritius	674
4	Andorra	663
5	Solomon Islands	620
6	Montenegro	615
7	Burkina Faso	593
8	Antigua and Barbuda	584
9	Guatemala	560
10	Jordan*	538
11	Lesotho	536
12	Botswana	536
13	Timor-Leste	532
14	Gabon	522
15	Cameroon	521
16	Uruguay	519
17	Samoa	519
18	Fiji	518
19	Tonga	512
20	Grenada	495
21	Bahrain	494
22	Saint Lucia	488
23	Nauru	487
24	Sierra Leone	477
25	Trinidad and Tobago	472
26	Cape Verde	464
27	Bhutan	453
28	Cuba	447
29	Palau	444
30	Swaziland	442
31	Barbados	441
32	Mauritania	435
33	El Salvador	421
34	Seychelles	420
35	Suriname	418
36	Maldives	406
37	Dominica	402
38	Honduras	390
39	Gambia	384
40	Djibouti	379
41	Togo	379
42	Sao Tome and Principe	377
43	Saint Vincent and the Grenadines	377
44	Mali	376
45	Saint Kitts and Nevis	374
46	Liberia	373
47	Côte d'Ivoire	369
48	Bolivia	368
49	Nepal	367
50	Turkmenistan	363
51	Senegal	350
52	Guinea	348
53	Congo (Dem Rep of the)	346
54	Papua New Guinea	344
55	Angola	342
56	Congo (Rep of the)	341
57	Marshall Islands	337
58	Mozambique	329
59	Tuvalu	328
60	Rwanda	320
61	Chad	316
62	Zimbabwe	312
63	Kenya	311
64	Niue	305
65	Comoros	299
66	Micronesia (Federated States of)	297

TIER RANK	COUNTRY	TOTAL POINTS
67	Cambodia	294
68	Kiribati	293
69	Benin	286
70	Cook Islands	278
71	Holy See**	269
72	Guyana	260
73	Yemen	252
74	Equatorial Guinea	251
75	Haiti	250
76	Belize	246
77	Guinea-Bissau	245
78	Myanmar	190
79	Central African Republic	190
80	Burundi	165
81	Kosovo**	156
82	Eritrea	135
83	Palestine** (State of)	30
84	Sudan	-20
85	Somalia	-118
86	South Sudan	-136

Table 11.1. Rank of Tier Three countries, including total points received.

Notes for Table 11.1:

* Jordan started a small research reactor in mid-2017. In future revisions or versions of the PPI, Jordan may be more suitable for Tier Two. See also Chapter 13: Countries with their First Nuclear Power Reactors Proposed, Planned, or Under Construction.

** The Holy See, Kosovo, and Palestine are difficult to rank because of their relatively small size and special international status.

SECTION III
FINDINGS AND RECOMMENDATIONS

CHAPTER 12
PPI GENERAL FINDINGS AND RECOMMENDATIONS

The PPI measures the effectiveness of strategic export controls using a set of criteria relating to a country's existing laws, regulations, procedures, practices, international obligations, and actions. Its fundamental purpose is to identify in a measurable manner the relative strengths and weaknesses of national export control systems throughout the world. We recognize that with currently available information, the PPI can only be a rough measure of these strengths and weaknesses. In addition, we have weighted various factors to construct an overall index and recognize that different observers may chooses different weights.

A central recommendation of this project is that countries should seek to improve their PPI scores and be more transparent about their strategic export controls systems. The performance fractions serve as the most direct way to determine whether sub-criteria are fulfilled. Although we decided not to publish individual country performance fractions in this report mainly because of space limitations, if a country is interested in improving its ranking, we would be happy to provide that country's performance fraction, ranking, and information that led to it and the country's ranking and consult with relevant representatives for a follow-up report. We encourage interested countries to contact us. We also welcome comments and reactions to the rankings.

Beyond the specific recommendations implicit in many of the super criteria and their sub-criteria, several more general recommendations emerged in the course of creating the PPI. This chapter focuses on those recommendations and certain major findings, including recommendations specific to each tier. Section IV: Additional Groupings and Applications contains several applications of the PPI, and those chapters comprise additional recommendations relevant to the chapter topic.

THE THREE TIERS

Rather than opting to rank all countries in a list, the PPI focuses on tiers of similar countries. As expected, Tier One did substantially better than Tiers Two and Three. Figure 12.1 shows the average and median scores by tier.

The average for Tier One is 710 points out of 1,300 points. This reflects the participation of Tier One countries in the major export control arrangements, such as the Nuclear Suppliers Group, as well as their adherence to the major international nonproliferation treaties, conventions, and other relevant instruments. The NSG demonstrates the value of such groups of suppliers in advancing shared values and in creating, improving, and promoting effective strategic export controls. Non-member countries in Tier One that seek to adhere to regime guidelines help contribute to the advancement of these values and of the effective systems of control that normally accompany them.

Tiers Two and Three have averages of 420 and 380 points, respectively. These averages are approximately 300 points lower than Tier One's average. Moreover, the averages and medians of Tiers Two and Three fall below 50 percent of the maximum points possible.

The differences in the tiers can be seen in Figure 12.1, which was first presented in Chapter 7. It indicates that global implementation of export controls is bimodal. One peak illustrates that about one quarter of countries have fairly robust strategic export controls, e.g. comprehensive legislation and effective implementation, and the other shows that about three quarters of countries have far less effective systems.

Figures 12.1 and 12.2 showcase an underlying problem in the global effort to combat strategic commodity trafficking. For developed countries, controlling trade is a matter of national security to which they accordingly dedicate resources. For many other countries, however, trade is mainly regulated for economic reasons, and, compared to Tier One countries,

Tier Two and Tier Three countries generally have fewer available financial and technical resources available. Items crossing borders are controlled to collect tariffs. For example, in many developing economies, import controls are in place while export controls are minimized in order to increase income and decrease trade deficits.

To an extent, lower scores in Tiers Two and Three result from those countries' lack of perceived need for substantial export control systems and fewer resources available to adopt and implement such controls. Nonetheless, a general recommendation is that countries in Tiers Two and Three should create or improve viable strategic trade control systems by adopting both the legislation necessary to control the export, transit, transshipment and re-export of strategic goods and the appropriate control lists (see below for further discussion on this issue).

No country received more than 80 percent of the total points and seven countries received negative scores. The former indicates that even those states with sufficient strategic export controls can improve the effectiveness of their controls. For those countries that received negative scores—such as Iran, Iraq, Somalia, South Sudan, Sudan, Syria, and North Korea, responsible suppliers and transshipment countries should exercise extreme caution when trading with them.

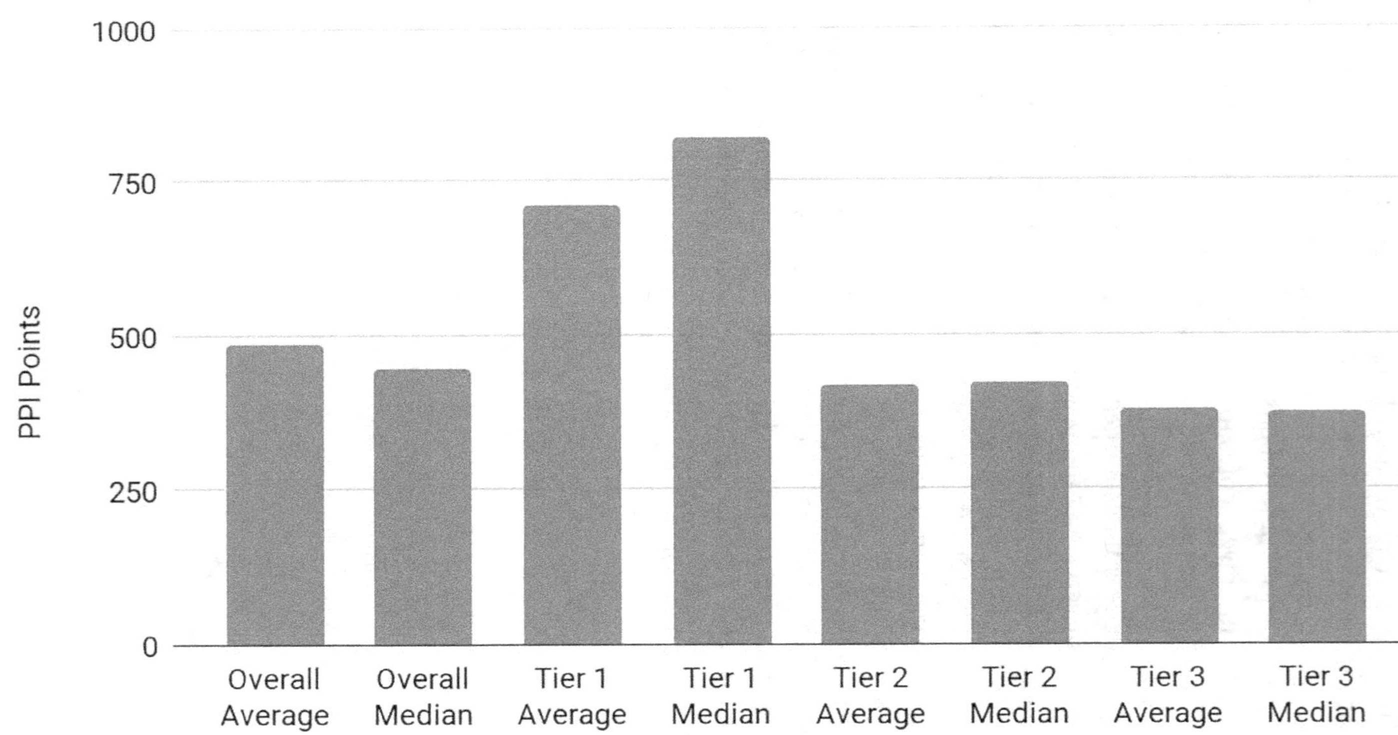

Figure 12.1. Average and median scores (from left to right) for: all countries in the PPI, Tier One, Tier Two, and Tier Three. A total of 1,300 points are possible across all five super criteria.

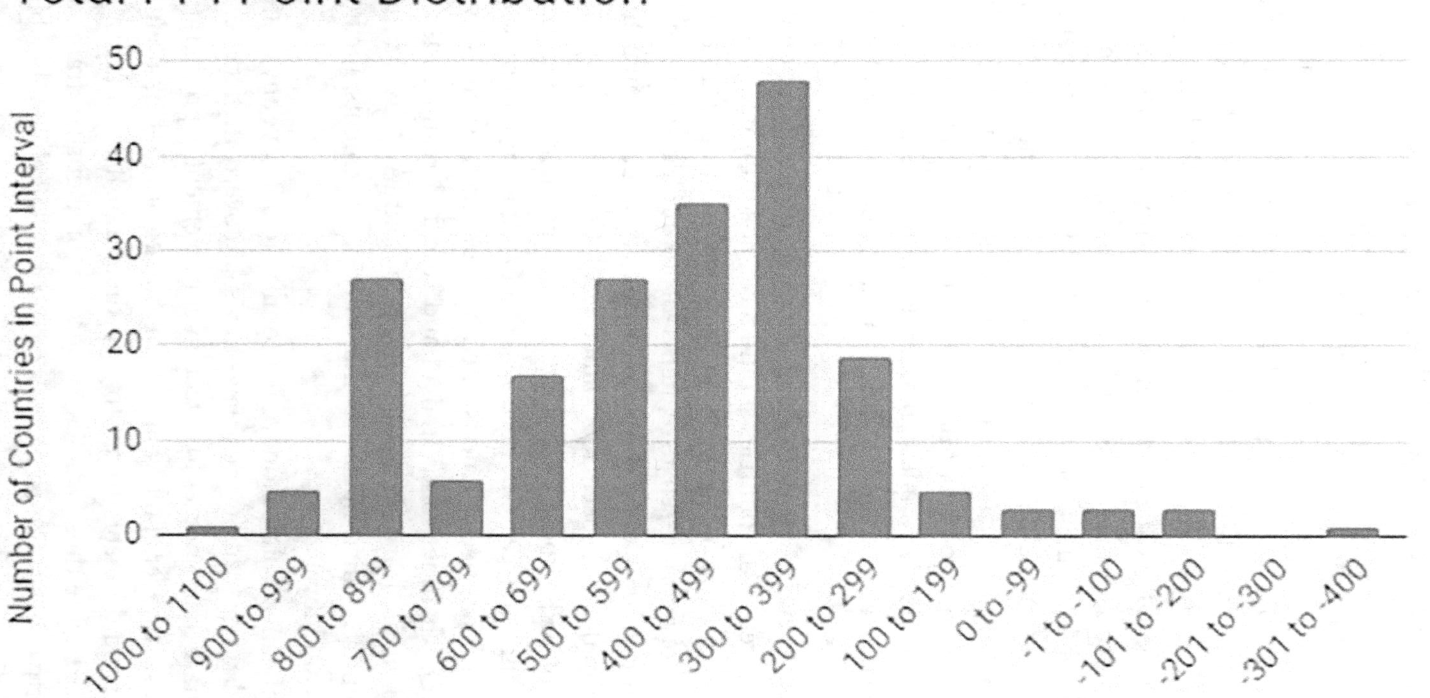

Figure 12.2. Distribution of total PPI scores in intervals of 100 points.

NEED FOR ALL COUNTRIES TO HAVE MINIMAL STRATEGIC EXPORT CONTROLS FOR THEIR PARTICULAR TIER

Based on data collected on the Legislation super criterion, strategic export controls are not universally applied, but they should be. This finding is separate from the question of full implementation of controls, including cases where a country does have strategic export control legislation.

As was tabulated in Chapter 3, almost 120 countries do not have strategic export controls, despite UN Security Council resolution 1540 (2004) requiring the establishment, development, review, and maintenance of "appropriate effective national export and transshipment controls with appropriate control lists."[1] In general, the majority of countries neither have sufficient export controls nor do they appear committed to their development and effective implementation. Moreover, there is great variation among countries in their specific export and import control systems and arrangements.

At issue, finally, is that strategic commodity trafficking should not have any safe havens. All countries should have, at a minimum, the legal authority necessary to control the export, re-export, transit and transshipment of proliferation-sensitive items or to proliferation-sensitive end-users. All countries should also have the capability to implement sanctions required by UN Security Council resolutions.

The lack of such export control laws, as well as their ineffective implementation and enforcement, pose a risk to national and international security. This risk has been demonstrated in many cases, such as by the rise of the A.Q. Khan network,[2] Iranian and North Korean efforts to illicitly outfit their nuclear and missile programs, and IAEA exposures of a range of countries' illicit nuclear commodity procurements, including those by Iraq and Libya.

It is simply unacceptable today for a country to not have any strategic trade control laws or to allow those laws to remain overly ineffective. Not all countries have the resources to detect illicit movement of proliferation-sensitive goods; however, if relevant information comes to their attention, all countries should be able to act to stop their transit or to arrest and prosecute or extradite those who carry out, aid, or abet such trafficking. Without effective legislation in place, a country will likely not be able to take appropriate enforcement or compliance action.

Creating robust export control systems can be difficult and resource-intensive. The PPI's findings show that when the United Nations and other international organizations spearhead measures to improve trade controls, or when there are active regional champions, countries are more likely to take part in these efforts. There are many groups and countries that can offer assistance on strategic trade control legislation and its implementation, such as the European Union, Japan, Australia, the United States, Organization for Security Cooperation in Europe (OSCE), the 1540 Committee, World Customs Organization, Organization for the Prohibition of Chemical Weapons, United Nations Office on Drugs and Crime (UNODC), International Atomic Energy Agency, and a variety of NGOs.

Assistance should also be tailored to the specific level or capability of each state, such as the tiering system used in the PPI. For example, states differ in their need for export control legislation. As will be discussed more below, guides, handbooks, and other assistance should become more tailored to the economic development of states, particularly several of the less developed states in Tier Two and the states in Tier Three. The first step should be the establishment of adequate legislation and control lists. Even where resources are scant, the direct costs of adopting legislation and control lists is modest and should be attempted as a first step.

Nonetheless, as required by Resolution 1540, a global goal should be for all states to have comprehensive strategic export controls. In terms of the PPI, all states should strive to have legislation in the dark green category together with robust control lists. This is a first step and should be accepted by all as a basic objective, even if implementation of a full-fledged, comprehensive export control system might remain a long-term goal.

Achieving this objective carries distinct benefits. In addition to allowing all state to participate in efforts to prevent illicit trafficking, it can facilitate foreign investment and increase domestic companies' global competitiveness. In order to create more positive incentives, the United States should seek other methods to incentivize countries to establish quality export control legislation, such as giving preferential treatment on import tariffs for goods entering the United States.

The United States and other major suppliers also need to increase pressure on countries to create export control systems. For example, a country that lacks strategic export controls and does poorly on the PPI should have its imports from the United States subjected to greater scrutiny in order to ensure that goods are not misused or transshipped to pariah countries or terrorist groups, or sent onward into weaker systems of control where the goods can be diverted again to these illegitimate end-users.

RECOMMENDATIONS FOR THE 1540 COMMITTEE AND UN MEMBER STATES ON STRENGTHENING RESOLUTION 1540

The strengthening of Resolution 1540 and its implementation should be a priority for all countries that seek to prevent the spread of strategic and nuclear-related commodities. However, there are obstacles within the Security Council to efforts to strengthen 1540 provisions and its mandates. It has not been possible to achieve significant strengthening of the resolution's provisions at 1540 comprehensive reviews. These reviews occur every five years; the last one was in 2016. The United States and its allies should nevertheless continue to work to improve 1540 implementation and pressure Russia (and gain China's support) on strengthening the resolution.

The PPI project identified several recommendations to improve the work of the 1540 Committee:

- Even though some U.N. Security Council members have blocked a stronger mandate for the Committee and its Group of Experts, the United States and other countries should provide more resources to the 1540 Committee and its Group of Experts to support the deepening of activities allowed under their current mandate.

- Review of the process by which the 1540 Committee assesses submitted state information about export control systems. The PPI project found that states have difficulty in filling out matrix information or understanding what is being asked for. The project encountered one state in Tier One that stated that although it submitted relevant information, the 1540 Committee was unable to glean from the reporting that several of its 1540 matrix criteria are fulfilled. The country ultimately felt that the process was too burdensome on its limited staff to devote effort to ensuring that its matrix was filled out correctly, and ultimately lost points in the PPI because of it. Pursuant to

Committee interaction with non-governmental think tanks and academics, an interested party such as the United States should retain a non-governmental organization to publish a set of recommended guidelines for the completion of the indices, focusing on common terms and definitions, so as to ease the process of completing the submissions and to make them more easily compared one to the next. This would be an important step forward, since the Committee itself is not empowered to establish standards except to note those instances in which countries report the adoption of similar practices. Establishing a common vocabulary for 1540 submissions should therefore become a priority for those seeking to strengthen Resolution 1540's implementation.

- Encouragement for states to increase reporting to the 1540 Committee and update their information as appropriate, particularly for those states that fail to report or do not fully report required information used in the development of matrices. States should pay more attention to filling out the matrices accurately and seek out NGO or partner government support in doing so, if needed. For example, the PPI project found reporting on the matrices that is not truly reflective of export control laws and their implementation.

- Clear timetables and targeted assistance plans by the 1540 Committee and its Group of Experts for countries in adopting and implementing best export control systems and practices (more on this below). To that end, countries should specifically request from the Committee's Group of Experts support in developing a targeted assistance plan, which includes steps towards implementing best trade control practices.

- Full cooperation by all countries with the 1540 Committee to create and advance their voluntary national implementation action plans.

- Pressing of states to ratify international conventions relevant to improved export controls. The 1540 Committee provides a list of 19 international legal instruments relevant to its work. Of those, the following are most relevant to the PPI's purpose of strengthening export controls: ratification of the International Convention for the Suppression of Acts of Nuclear Terrorism, the Convention for the Suppression of Unlawful Acts Against Civil Aviation, the Convention for the Suppression of Unlawful Acts Against Maritime Navigation and associated protocol, and the Convention on the Physical

Protection of Nuclear Materials. States should consider joining the Proliferation Security Initiative.

- Encouragement to member states that the 1540 Committee be granted the resources to employ or contract a roster of experts who could provide regular assistance to the Committee and it Group of Experts. The Committee should have assistance from member states in identifying such experts.

- A model adequate strategic trade control system handbook created by the 1540 Committee and associated member state experts on how to improve the creation, implementation, and enforcement of export controls. The models and handbook should contain specific information including step-by-step guidance geared to the general level of industrial and nuclear development of different types of states. The World Customs Organization has produced a useful handbook, titled *Strategic Trade Control Enforcement (STCE): Implementation Guide,*[3] which could serve as a model and be drawn on by the Committee. As part of this effort, the 1540 Committee should devise a basic "starter kit" for Tier Three countries that matches the resources these countries can muster in the short term for strategic export control creation and implementation, focusing initially on basic legislative language and adoption of regulations and control lists. This should be accompanied, when appropriate, by staffing expectations, and a budget (see also below on recommendations specific to Tier Three). The starter kit should be available in local languages as well as in English.

ENTITY TO EVALUATE NATIONAL EXPORT CONTROLS

Although UNSC resolution 1540 mandates the development and implementation of strategic export controls in all countries, the 1540 Committee does not currently have the ability to review overall whether national systems are effective or sufficient. Moreover, the implementation of the resolution depends extensively on states self-reporting critical information about their national systems to the 1540 Committee.

Toward that end, and failing any effort by the UN to strengthen the mandate of the 1540 Committee to do so, states could separately provide a mandate to an organization or organizations to conduct export control evaluations that states could participate in on a voluntary basis. This body could:

- Develop model adequate strategic trade control systems and a handbook on how to improve the implementation and enforcement of export controls. The models and handbook should contain specific information geared to the general level of industrial and nuclear development of different states.

- Have adequate resources to conduct in-country visits upon request by teams of export control experts to assess the state of export control implementation and provide confidential feedback to states on status, areas that need improvement, and best practices. Team visits would allow for the collection of information on what needs to be improved in each country. Teams could conduct follow-up visits and send relevant individual experts to provide targeted assistance, or, at the request of the participating government, recommend which national or multilateral assistance programs are best positioned to provide this assistance.

- The development of a team outreach effort could evolve into the body conducting mutual evaluation reports, similar to those done by FATF, on the status of countries' export control systems. Such reports could make judgments about the sufficiency or status of states' compliance with best export control practices.

- The WCO itself should also be mandated to support broader export control evaluations and provided more resources to organize country visits in order to conduct diagnoses of the maturity of customs in implementing strategic trade control laws. The WCO combines a mission of improving customs with trade facilitation, offers both economic and political incentives to many countries to work with it, and is therefore a welcomed partner by many countries. It receives self-reported information from many countries on gaps and deficiencies in their customs systems. In line with its *Strategic Trade Control Enforcement* handbook, the WCO assigns levels of STCE "maturity,"[4] which can provide all interested parties, including the WCO member state being assessed, with a standardized means to determine the level and kind of assistance that is needed to remedy identified export control system gaps.

SPECIAL ROLE OF HARMONIZED SYSTEM CODES

Information analysis and sharing is greatly facilitated by countries using international nomenclature for product classification. The most widely used codes are the **Harmonized System (HS) codes**, which are customs classification codes developed by the WCO. For non-proliferation purposes, however, they need further development, especially in the strategic commodity category. The codes are too broad and leave too much room for misinterpretations and mischaracterizations of goods.[5] Gaining concrete information on dual-use goods trade from these broad categories is very difficult, if not impossible, in many cases. It is also a challenge for customs agencies or personnel, since many countries cannot use the HS codes to then identify specific controlled items. Many states have gone through lengthy efforts to correlate HS codes and control lists in so-called Correlation Tables.[6] Ideally, critical goods listed on multinational control lists should have their own specific code. The United States could modify its Export Commodity Classification Numbers (ECCNs) in a similar manner.

"REACHBACK" CAPABILITIES

STRENGTHENING AND FORMALIZING TECHNICAL "REACHBACK" CAPABILITIES FOR TIER TWO AND THREE COUNTRIES

Enforcement of strategic trade controls depends on customs and other enforcement agencies being able to identify controlled or sensitive goods moving illegally through their countries. However, many dual-use goods are often difficult for government officials to reliably identify. For many countries, particularly those in Tiers Two and Three, they simply lack the technical resources to identify strategic goods. The PPI research found that many countries lack the capability to conduct basic training in WMD commodity awareness, and even if such capabilities exist or have been provided, by the WCO for example, countries do not have the resources or knowledge needed to provide domestic technical expertise or "reachback" when suspect goods are detected and require analysis as to their purpose and potential misuse. In light of the technical scope and complexity of strategic controls, creating sufficient cadres of technical experts needed to provide technical reachback for enforcement (as well as licensing) is prohibitively expensive and, when successful, can need years of outside technical assistance.

In addressing global needs, the PPI recommends finding meaningful ways to meet these needs that are graded to match resources available for implementation. For customs and other enforcement agencies, this means ensuring access to expertise as needed, both for the assessment of suspect goods, and for the assessment of suspect shipment destinations and end-users. With adequate technical "reachback" of this kind, countries can also survey their own ability to manufacture sensitive goods. The development of technical reachback capabilities and the ways they might be put to best use in Tier Two and Three countries are assessed below. While reachback is also required in Tier One countries, many of them have far more developed technical resources and histories of bilateral or multilateral cooperation among suppliers on this issue.

An alternative way to meet the needs of these countries while in parallel developing longer-term national capacities is to provide access to outside technical reachback that can identify specific strategic or otherwise sensitive commodities, in order to ensure that goods are not illegally imported, exported, re-exported, or transshipped. Toward that goal, there is a need for organizations to bilaterally, regionally, or multilaterally assist reachback for Tier Two and Three states, as well as some in Tier One.

Developing other means for Tier Two and Three countries to obtain reachback support is not as challenging as it used to be. It has become more feasible due to modern communications technology and the ability to send photos and descriptions of detained shipments. This process can be as simple as officials texting photos of goods, handbooks or technical literature found with the goods, brand names, and customs documents using a smartphone. It is critical that answers are generated within hours or a few days. The information should be encrypted, and privacy laws respected, and controls could be put in place to protect commercial and proprietary information.

The United States and other Security Council members could initiate the creation of such organizations in support of the UNSCR 1540 Committee, which already has the mandate to process suspect transfers when reported by member states. For example, countries interested in ensuring that Tier Two and Three countries receive rapid responses to reachback requests could work with regional bodies, such as CARICOM or the African Union. They could also work within existing national organizations or multinational organizations like the European Union to establish which entities might, in collaboration with one another and multilateral organizations, create a coalition of technical reachback organizations with the prioritization of nuclear, missile, and related dual-use goods. One approach would be to then link these assets to the WCO, under its communications network, as described below.

Use of WCO and other multilateral trade and security organizations to this end is important for another reason: even if countries lacking the internal resources receive effective reachback support, this support cannot always contain information related to illegitimate end-users. In other words, sound technical assessments as to the control parameters of a suspect shipment will usually avoid political sensitivities by making reference exclusively to the good's technical specifications rather than making what is bound to be seen as a subjective judgement about a given end-user's intentions or non-proliferation *bona fides*. In assessing what action to take with regard to interdicted items, countries may therefore need to assess on their own whether or not an item's intended destination combined with the control parameters of an item, might warrant detaining a suspect shipment.

To answer these kinds of questions, any country can make reference to lists of destinations – countries, companies and individuals – contained on the U.S. denied parties list, as well as on other such lists as maintained by Japan and others. Even with these resources, however, questions about specific end-users and shippers can be especially difficult to discover. One way to help resolve this is for countries to make more complete use of the WCO's Customs Enforcement Network (CEN).[7] The system is meant to 'assist the Customs enforcement community in gathering data and information for intelligence purposes.'

To achieve this objective, CEN has its own communications platform known as CENcomm. CENcomm provides a secure, online platform for instant messaging and other forms of communication so that national customs administrations can make requests of other customs administrations in attempts to check the bona fides of parties to a suspect transaction. CENcomm also serves as a 'database of seizures and offences including photos, required for the analysis of illicit trafficking," which may enable countries to better assess whether or not an entity involved in a suspect shipment might have a prior track record in illicit commodity transactions.

The WCO Information Intelligence Center (I2C) already uses CEN-comm to this end on a limited basis by brokering inquiries to reachback experts. This organization cannot on its own assess all illegitimate end users; however, it is connected to a wide range of advanced customs administrations that are ready to provide assistance to WCO. This center could therefore benefit from more resources in order to staff the center full-time and the development and cataloguing of willing technical reachback specialists. I2C could function as an effective hub for brokering technical requests if a coalition of member states were to provide the financial resources, expertise, and leadership in the identification of technical resource assets.

Finally, and most fundamentally, customs and border officials need the authority to hold seized, potentially controlled goods long enough to benefit from a reachback system. For example, if reachback to experts takes a week, customs and border officials need legal authority to keep the goods for a week, but in many countries, no such authorities exist. Worse, officers who detain goods may be subject to legal penalties. As a result, the problem should be confronted at multiple ends. National authorities must strengthen so-called "indemnity" protections for their officers when shipments are delayed, while adding rapid response capabilities for technical reachback requests.

An additional, effective use of technical reachback assets for Tier Two and Three countries would be for these countries to ask available outside experts to collaboratively review multilateral export control lists with their national authorities to identify those few goods on the lists that are manufactured or used in those countries, which by definition, do not manufacture large numbers of strategic goods. Ideally, reachback experts would have support of national authorities to identify enterprises with the means to manufacture goods controlled under the multilateral export control regimes. This step can be taken even in advance of the adoption of export control laws or related export control licensing authorities.[8]

Under this scenario, when enterprises with relevant capabilities are identified and Tier Two and Three governmental officials are informed of the potential WMD uses of these capabilities, already existing agencies like customs or other governmental authorities could then conduct basic outreach to them. This outreach can ensure that relevant enterprises are supplied with an understanding of these potential WMD uses and a government point of contact for these enterprises if they need help reviewing a request for the export of a controlled item. These points of contact could also be on call if suspect actors approached companies and company managers wished to report this information. In many Tier Two and Tier Three countries, it is anticipated that the number of items on the export control lists relevant to domestic production would be small, as would be the number of companies. Therefore, within a relatively short period using existing agencies and authorities, meaningful sensitive goods monitoring could be put in place at a cost well below the requirements of a full implementation of a complete export control system.

Such an approach also fills a gap often overlooked in Tier One countries since most exporters of sensitive goods conduct outreach to exporters only. And yet, proliferators will often target manufacturers of sensitive goods who do not export, hoping that the targeted company personnel will be unaware of national or multilateral export control laws associated with their goods. Having Tier Two and Three countries examine those manufacturers who possess sensitive goods for domestic use only would effectively jump ahead of an industry outreach process that would normally happen much later in the export control system development process, if at all. This process would enable these Tier Two and Three countries to defeat one of the proliferation networks' most time-tested procurement techniques.

If national leaders in Tier Two and Three countries adopt the steps outlined in this section, proliferation networks will be less able than is currently the case to exploit Tier Two and Three countries as safe havens. This is partially what allowed the A.Q. Khan network to operate for years beyond the reach of national authorities or international attention.

STRENGTHENED CUSTOMS

Customs and border security services are critical not only to facilitate legitimate trade but also to implement strategic export controls and protect against commodity trafficking. Countries should strengthen their customs services, including, as previously discussed in the section on recommendations for the 1540 Committee, implementing the WCO recommendations for strategic export control enforcement. They should also increase the transparency and efficiency of their customs regulatory processes so that companies are more aware of regulations and how to comply with them. Countries should seek training for customs officials and establish the technical capabilities to detect illicit shipments moving across their borders.

As noted above, reachback capabilities should be made available to customs officials to amplify the effectiveness of on-site reviews and inspections.

Close cooperation between customs and licensing agencies is critical. Licensing entities should routinely provide information on exports to the customs and border security entities. This sharing enables customs and border officials to be more knowledgeable about that country's exports and industries. In turn, this knowledge can improve these agencies' abilities to detect illicit exports and imports that are outside the licensing process.

DOMESTIC INTELLIGENCE CAPABILITY ON STRATEGIC COMMODITY TRAFFICKING

Countries, particularly those in Tier One, should have domestic intelligence capabilities that devote resources and expertise to knowing their own supply potential and understanding the strategic commodity trafficking networks and agents targeting them. Most of this latter activity involves individuals and trading companies that are unlikely to seek a license for their illegal exports. Groups like MI5 in Britain, the FBI, Bureau of Industry and Security's Office of Export Enforcement, and Homeland Security Investigations, in the United States, and the Bundesnachrichtendienst and Bundesverfassungsschutz in Germany, have become successful, critical repositories of domestic information on supply potential and illicit trade and have developed multiple ways to detect and thwart strategic commodity trafficking. Critical information sources are collaborations and sharing programs with industry and academia (for more on this, see section below on Corporate Vigilance and Internal Compliance Programs).

ROBUST PROSECUTIONS

A number of countries prioritize the criminal enforcement of strategic trade controls. However, for many countries, enforcement lags significantly. Countries should make it a national priority to prosecute crimes of illicit nuclear, missile, and WMD trafficking. They should establish trained units within investigatory agencies to further this purpose. Several countries, including Germany, Sweden, and the United Kingdom, have established federal prosecution units for major strategic export related cases.[9] Because of the technical complexity of many strategic export cases, countries should also consider establishing a specialized court responsible for national security cases rather than having primarily local courts take on cases. These recommendations are more relevant to Tiers One and Two countries, but Tier Three countries should gradually develop some expertise as well.

Countries should consider extending mandatory minimum sentencing guidelines to make violations of export control requirements, especially those related to WMD, worthy of longer sentences. This is especially important in single markets, such as the European Single Market, so that exporters intending to violate export controls cannot knowingly violate laws in countries with the mildest penalties. Sentences of more than five years in prison and fines appear to better deter violators (see Chapter 17).

Countries should cooperate more on prosecuting strategic commodity traffickers. They should seek cooperation with other countries and set up procedures to exchange sensitive law enforcement information on illicit trade attempts. This would increase the chances that officials could stop sensitive goods in transit before they leave the country.

UNDERCOVER OPERATIONS AGAINST STRATEGIC COMMODITY TRAFFICKING

The United States effectively uses undercover, or "sting" operations, to detect and prosecute illicit procurement agents and networks whether operating within or outside the United States. Agents at U.S. enforcement agencies set up front companies that appear to supply sensitive goods but whose purpose is to catch illicit agents attempting to commit illegal acts. They often receive tips from supplier companies suspicious of potential customers, who then pass the customer on to the U.S. government front company. Other countries could significantly improve their enforcement of strategic trade controls by developing their own programs to create and utilize front companies in sting operations. It should be noted, however, that some countries' laws prohibit the enactment of such undercover operations. They should consider re-evaluating these laws. Countries should also establish points of contact for the general public, including officials at companies, to submit tips to about potential export control related crimes (see also below section on Corporate Vigilance and ICPs).

As part of undercover or sting operations, the United States sometimes lures egregious violators of its export controls to U.S. territories where they are arrested, or to friendly countries where they can be arrested and extradited to the United States. More countries should cooperate with the United States or others in these efforts via treaties, legal agreements, or policy. Underlying such cooperation is for both countries to have the same laws outlawing a wide range of strategic commodity trafficking so as to allow extradition. Countries should also conclude similar extradition treaties with other countries besides the United States.

FATF AND PROLIFERATION FINANCING

A general observation is that all countries should become parties to the International Convention for the Suppression of the Financing of Terrorism.

In addition, all countries need to work closely with the Financial Action Task Force and its regional bodies to improve their efforts to prevent proliferation financing. They need to work also to improve compliance with proliferation financing-relevant FATF recommendations. All countries should join FATF, if they have not already done so, and work closely with it to improve the integrity of their national financial controls against proliferation financing and other financial crimes. Israel is an example of a country that has prioritized joining FATF and is involved in a process of reviews. It expects to finish and join in the next year.

Membership and cooperation with FATF would not only reduce the chances that states' financial institutions will be used for the financing of proliferation, but also reduce illicit outflows, the rise and permeability of black markets, and other nefarious business that could be taking place.

Doing so would enhance the potential to attract foreign investment and trade.

Improvement in many of the sub-criteria under the Ability to Prevent Proliferation Financing super criterion, particularly a country's performance in many of the negative indicators, would flow from strengthened financial controls overall. Countries should apply to have a mutual evaluation performed following coordination and assistance in bringing their controls into line with FATF-recognized best practices.

The FATF should add recommendations that more specifically focus on improving countries' capabilities to prevent and detect financing of proliferation. For example, it could integrate its 2008 "indicators of possible proliferation financing" into recommendations. In this way, countries' actions on preventing proliferation financing could be evaluated.

Developed countries should encourage and provide resources to the FATF to increase the speed at which they conduct follow-up mutual evaluation reports. This would reduce current lag times between countries self-reporting on their performance following a mutual evaluation report and FATF verifying that self-reporting.

FATF should expand the number of categories it uses to evaluate countries with regard to proliferation financing and financial crime. For example, countries that actively improve their financial controls often remain in the partially compliant category, which may not encourage further improvements.

FATF should standardize between regional bodies the way that the bodies evaluate countries in their regions. It should seek to diminish disparities in levels of stringency utilized in the evaluations in order to bring about improved understanding of where countries stand in the FATF mutual evaluations and compliance categories.

Countries should implement financial transaction monitoring systems that help to identify and freeze transactions by sanctioned entities and individuals. For this reason, it is important for countries to either have their own denied parties lists in place or to use those created by other countries that are strong on listing such parties.

Advanced countries in this area should establish outreach programs that provide training and share best practices with countries seeking to improve financial controls. The PPI team was unable to locate many such programs outside of FATF. Most such programs appear to be led by the United States.

ACTIONS TO COUNTER ILLICIT PROCUREMENT EFFORTS

Certain countries continue to pursue illicit procurement of and/or trafficking in nuclear, WMD, missile, and conventional military commodities. Their actions should be recognized as fundamentally inconsistent with international efforts to enact effective export controls. The highly negative total scores of Iran, North Korea, and Syria, for example, reflect their failures to respect international non-proliferation norms. Pakistan and perhaps India still reportedly conduct limited illicit nuclear commodity procurements and their actions undermine the credibility of their export control systems. At the very least, all countries and their exporters should view such countries as posing a high risk of violating their export control laws. Countries should implement the following policies:

- Fully implement UNSC sanctions.
- Commit resources to ensure that, where confidence is lacking, countries, their entities, and their agents world-wide are detected and fully prosecuted when they seek to export without a license or to prohibited end-users or end-uses, goods for WMD and their means of delivery. Countries should consider adopting or enacting their own unilateral sanctions against proliferant state actors and their illicit programs to the extent that certain entities and individuals are discovered to be violating their export controls or known violators do not appear on UNSC sanctions lists.
- In the case of North Korea, countries should severely limit or curtail non-humanitarian-essential trade and fully enforce UN sanctions.
- Fully enforce the Joint Comprehensive Plan of Action (JCPOA) on Iran and related UNSC resolution 2231, including ensuring that all nuclear and nuclear-related exports to Iran are approved by the JCPOA Procurement Working Group (PWG) and subject to regular end-use checks in Iran. If end-use checks cannot be guaranteed and scheduled, the PWG should not approve the export to Iran.
- Work in the UN Security Council and UN General Assembly (UNGA) to hold countries to obligations under Resolution 2231 and

national sanctions laws not to sell Iran military or missile-related goods.

- Work in the UN Security Council, as well as strengthened work within the JCPOA Joint Commission and PWG, to urge Iran to develop and implement an internationally acceptable export control system, which entails ending its illicit nuclear, missile, and military commodity procurements.

- The FATF should re-impose its counter-measures against Iran's money laundering and terrorist financing activities, which were suspended in June 2016. It should ask banks and governments to re-implement bans on transacting with Iran since Iran is unlikely to reform its practices under its FATF Action Plan.[10]

CORPORATE VIGILANCE AND INTERNAL COMPLIANCE PROGRAMS (ICPS)

Industry is the first line of defense against strategic commodity trafficking. Those who seek goods for WMD programs and the means to deliver them must ultimately finds ways to obtain goods from legitimate suppliers, who by nature are not part of a criminal culture.

Despite its importance and multiple efforts, the PPI had difficulty measuring industry effectiveness in detecting and preventing strategic commodity trafficking. Nonetheless, certain findings and recommendations emerged during the research.

All countries should increase or start government outreach programs to companies (including trading companies and freight forwarders), research institutes, and academic communities, as well as establish and publicize points of contact relevant to strategic trade control matters. Companies should also be encouraged to cooperate with regional groupings that seek to improve industry implementation of strategic export and financial controls. It is, however, proven difficult to reach out to small and medium size companies. Enlisting chambers of commerce and industry federations in outreach could be helpful to reach these smaller enterprises in all countries, but especially in Tier Two and Three countries, where these organizations may be the only institutional means by which companies that manufacture potentially sensitive goods might be recognized.

Particularly for Tiers One and major Two countries, companies should be well informed about trade controls and have a regular means of finding out information about laws and controls, as well as updates or modifications to controls. Government officials should be easily accessible to companies on questions about trade controls, such as licensing, shipping, and reasonable assistance on checking the *bona fides* of end users, such as if an internal due diligence process fails to uncover nefarious actors but there remain reasons for suspicion about the declared end-user. Companies should have in place a regular mechanism for asking the government for assistance on determining the *bona fides* of customers of concern.

To the best of their ability, governments should provide tips to companies about the illicit procurement schemes targeting their sectors and explain how industry compliance officials can avoid accidentally making sales to such entities.

More countries should develop systems that encourage or require companies to provide information to their government on suspicious approaches by customers for price quotations or other types of enquiries. Governments need to establish official, easy to find points of contact where companies can provide this information confidentially to their national authorities.

More countries should encourage or require companies to come forward and voluntary disclose to the government information about inadvertent exports to potential illicit procurement networks. While coming forward would not absolve them of responsibility in the case of an inadvertent export, it could be considered as a mitigating factor if penalties are assigned for inadvertent exports. Voluntarily disclosing intentional exports by a poorly trained associate or a bad actor within a company could also serve to mitigate penalties. Penalty mitigation absent a long history of company export control lapses is a frequent practice in the United States.[11]

Countries should close down companies on their territories that are egregious violators of other countries' export control laws and which land these entities and associated individuals on prominent sanctions lists.

In practice, many supplier companies have found that it is necessary to establish **Internal Compliance Programs** within their companies to ensure that their exports are legal and do not damage the companies' reputation or pose an undue risk to the company. Such a company program, whose size varies proportionately to the company's size and number of exports of controlled or sensitive goods, can also lead to receiving an export license more quickly and with less paperwork.

Lack of data prevented the PPI project from evaluating individual countries' ICP programs requirements, status, and effectiveness. Nonetheless, the project found that many governments require companies that export controlled goods to establish an ICP. Moreover, supplier states tend to recommend a company establish an ICP, and many companies in fact do so, particularly larger companies. Small and medium size companies often do not.

Increasingly, as a way to induce the adoption of ICPs, supplier states are making an ICP a requirement to receive a general export license or to be considered an "Authorized Economic Operator (AEO)" or an entity eligible to trade internationally. By itself, having an ICP in place is rarely enough to receive an export license; they cannot (and should not) replace thorough due diligence by companies and government licensing officials.

To add to the effectiveness of ICPs, some, but from the PPI's point of view, not enough governments hold top level company officials legally responsible for violations. Making the company CEO or another top manager who must be a member of the legal entity's executive body responsible for an illegal violation has worked to ensure that an ICP is developed and followed by all company officials.

In general, ICP programs should be established by all exporters, regardless of the size of the company. For larger companies, a staff may be necessary. For smaller companies, the ICP may involve compliance with a manual and a person who is responsible for these functions within the company in addition to other responsibilities.

Companies vary dramatically, so there is no "one size fits all" guide or manual for all companies. However, an ICP typically has a set of common elements, including to name a few:[12]

- An ICP manual tailored to the company's products and practices;
- Staff, including personnel with an understanding of identifying suspicious enquiries and an ability to judge the risk of an export;
- Denied entity/persons lists or a screening list to judge requests for quotations or orders;

- A thorough understanding of the sensitivity and classification (for controls) of the companies' goods and services, including what goods are affected by sanctions. Surprisingly, we learned that some companies in Tier One have not done this type of classification of whether their own goods are subject to export controls;
- Regular training of company officials in the procedures and functions outlined in the internal compliance manual.

As part of outreach, governments should offer companies, institutes, and academic organizations training in setting up and maintaining ICPs. For those countries with fewer resources, the 1540 Committee could sponsor trainings for their companies.

There is an on-going need to maintain a model ICP manual that is easily downloadable, well publicized, and available to all. Private bodies and governments have created such manuals; for example, the Coalition for Excellence in Export Compliance (CEEC), a voluntary group of export professionals, produced and made available an excellent set of draft recommended ICP standards.[13] Ideally, the generic template would be comprehensive in scope but each company could select what it needs from a master list and generate a word file that would serve as its ICP manual. The format of the report would allow the company to tailor the manual for its own goods, local laws, and practices.

CAPACITY BUILDING

The United States,' the European Union's, and others' efforts to fund, build, and implement export control capacities in other countries has been critical to the worldwide creation and improvement of strategic export controls. As such, these efforts deserve sustained budgetary and government wide support.

As U.S. and European capacity-building efforts have matured in higher risk countries, officials in both the provider and recipient countries have realized that the recipient needs to define additional gaps in its export control system. They can then request their partners in the United States and the European Union to provide specific assistance to fill those gaps.

Although the United States and the European Union are critical in funding and targeting capacity building, there is a need for other entities to become more involved. The WCO's outreach to its member states should be expanded to better rectify gaps in its members' customs services. The WCO should receive sufficient resources so that it can independently target gaps in WCO member states and provide capacity training. By having an independent means to target and train, it can better complement U.S. and EU outreach efforts.

In the United States, the following governmental programs are involved in foreign export control capacity building and deserve funding and diplomatic support:

- The Department of State's Export Control and Related Border Security (EXBS) program[14]
- The Department of Defense International Counter-Proliferation (ICP) Program
- The Department of Energy's International Nonproliferation Export Control Program (INECP)

Other assistance providers include the European Union Commission's Peer-to-Peer ("P2P") Program, and several export control-related agencies and governmentally-affiliated commercial associations within the governments of Japan and South Korea.

ELECTRONIC SYSTEMS

Countries should establish electronic licensing systems. For example, the project learned that of the 28 members of the European Union only nine states have electronic licensing systems. The European Union is considering recommending the creation of a common software licensing system that all nations in the European Union could use, after adapting the software for their specific national needs and requirements. Such a common system would facilitate the sharing of data among all EU members, which is vital to prevent proliferators from "port shopping" or "licensing shopping" within the European Union, since goods for the most part flow freely between EU member states.

Keeping in mind that electronic systems cannot replace the establishment of effective inter-agency procedures and communications, including government-industry communications, countries should also modernize or establish information technology systems that harmonize their licensing, denial, export, and import data relating to controlled and sensitive goods. When all relevant data and information are readily available to export control agencies or officials, they are able to more effectively carry out their mission.

Modern electronic systems can ease the task of sharing data among various government agencies involved in implementing and enforcing export control laws. All countries should establish or increase electronic information sharing between licensing authorities, customs, and police or other law enforcement entities.

In addition, Tier One and Two countries should consider utilizing digitized governmental databases of exports and imports as part of counter-proliferation efforts, in particular to better know their industries and detect illicit trading networks. In terms of exports, U.S. suppliers of goods valued over $2,500 or licensed goods must file a digitized Shippers Export Declaration (SED), now called Electronic Export Information, with the Department of Homeland Security that goes into a searchable database called the Automated Export System (AES). This database comprises hundreds of millions of records. Declarations provide critical information about goods, recipients, and shippers.

When sound records are kept, suspect shipments can be detected, thus creating a better way to thwart these exports or establishing a potential red flag for associated actors and countries for future shipments. These records can also be used to cross check so-called "general" licenses to ensure that the terms spelled out under these licenses such as allowed destinations, or the numbers of shipments, are being honored by national suppliers.

To support efforts to better monitor for illicit exports and imports as well as illicit networks, countries should increase or introduce the use of electronic big data import/export monitoring systems, similar to the U.S. Border Enforcement Analytics Program (BEAP) system, which uses import and export information to find anomalies relating to potential illicit procurements and generates investigatory opportunities.[15]

For countries with digitized import and export databases, they should consider sharing data among trading partners, so that a more international and reliable picture of the flow of strategic or sensitive goods can be established. The sharing of data among trading partners, while posing challenges, should be encouraged.

Digital platforms use HS or similar codes. However, in digital export declaration platforms, it must be recognized that a simple use of HS codes, which are defined broadly, can weaken the ability to search for suspect end users and goods. This problem is one reason for the recommendation in the section on HS codes to assign critical goods listed on multinational control lists their own specific code. The United States could modify its Export Commodity Classification Numbers in a similar manner.

In addition to updating ECCN codes and working to improve HS codes, the United States should also improve its export declaration system, or Electronic Export Information. One priority is for the United States to modify its export declaration system to ensure that declarations include the actual end-users of the exported goods, and not freight forwarders or trading companies, which, under the current rules, often forward goods onward without notifying the United States.

FREE TRADE ZONES

Free Trade Zones pose difficult counter-proliferation challenges because entities in those zones can serve as false end destinations of strategic goods and provide a means for secret transshipment to the true destination. For international security reasons, as discussed in Chapter 14, FTZs should be integrated fully into national export control systems and any exemptions from export controls should be gradually ended. All countries should start to ensure that officials can monitor the goods entering and exiting FTZs and seize suspicious cargo. They should work to create systems that can provide assurances that goods are not being transshipped to sanctioned countries, such as Iran, North Korea, and Syria, among others.

Many countries do not appear overly aware of the goods passing through their FTZs. As a result, they should increase physical inspections of shipments and put in place trained personnel at major entry and exit points. They should implement risk-based approaches for inspections such as those used in Europe or the United States. These states also need to actively work with and inform shipping industries located in their FTZs about the need for increased scrutiny. Shippers should be subject to following the strengthened enforcement approaches of those FTZs. Countries planning on establishing new FTZs should first establish export control systems inside planned FTZs.

ROLE OF IAEA SAFEGUARDS AND THE ADDITIONAL PROTOCOL

The IAEA is the pre-eminent international organization in the nuclear area and has long-standing programs of assistance. It could play a positive role in better implementing nuclear export controls.

Traditionally, the IAEA has not been seen as a source of support for nuclear export control systems, but it would be of significant benefit to its member states if the IAEA adapted its programs or developed new ones to reflect more fully the requirements of Resolution 1540, including in the export control area. There, its nuclear expertise, both legal and technical, can assist states in developing and implementing effective export control systems.

Examples would be:

- Adapt its legal advice and model legislation to include the requirements of Resolution 1540 with respect to nuclear export controls and with respect to non-state actors;

- Assist member states with respect to the development of the nuclear component of 1540 voluntary National Implementation Action Plans, perhaps through adaptation of the program to develop Integrated Nuclear Security Support Plans;

- Develop jointly with the 1540 Committee assistance projects to support states' implementation of Resolution 1540 in the nuclear area;

- As requested, assist states to develop well-focused and technically sound assistance requests;

- Provide advice to member states, to the extent possible, about the underlying rationale for nuclear export control guidelines and the items controlled by them;

- Consult with the 1540 Committee about sharing information that would help to improve the depiction of the status of states' implementation of Resolution 1540.[16]

Although it is not common to link export control implementation to IAEA safeguards or the Additional Protocol, they contain provisions that are related to more effective implementation of strategic trade controls. As such, all NPT parties should bring into force both a Comprehensive Safeguards Agreement and an Additional Protocol. All countries should participate in the Additional Protocol Voluntary Reporting Scheme for the import and export of items on the protocol control lists. Countries should also report to the IAEA Incident and Trafficking Database on incidents involving trafficking in nuclear or other radioactive material on their territories.

TRANSPARENCY OF NATIONAL EXPORT CONTROL LAWS

All countries should have available clear information regarding export control laws and regulations. This includes maintaining or creating websites, ideally in local languages for domestic companies, and in English or other relevant languages for foreign business partners. The PPI team observed a striking, general lack of information made available to the public by many countries. Websites were shut down for days at a time. The Pakistani government website, for example, was shut down for several days during one PPI data collection period. Similar inabilities to access websites occurred when seeking information from the governments of Palestine, Philippines, and Saint Kitts and Nevis. In most cases, websites were inaccessible due to construction or maintenance; however, governments should maintain at least a static version of websites for information access during times of web updates.

TIER ONE RECOMMENDATIONS

In general, most Tier One countries rely on NSG, other groups' standards, and in some cases more sophisticated ones for their strategic export control systems. As a result, for the majority of countries surveyed in Tier One, export control laws and regulations appear to be sufficient; however, all systems can be made more efficient, as recent export control reforms by the United States and European Union have highlighted. Moreover, lagging countries in Tier One need to make serious improvements based on their performance fractions and the recommendations above.

Although the PPI project did not attempt to thoroughly analyze the sufficiency of NSG or other guidelines or U.S. or EU standards, as the project evolved, several recommendations for Tier One countries emerged that we believe deserve highlighting. They include:

- Countries should ensure the highest level of export control effectiveness, including, for example, the optimization of control lists and licensing practices, customs and shipping controls, enforcement activities, and IT systems.

- Legislation should include all of the Resolution 1540 language relating to export controls.

- Export control legislation should include lists of materials, equipment, and technology covered by multilateral treaties and arrangements or included on national control lists, which could be used for the design, development, production, or use of nuclear (including radiological), chemical, biological weapons, and explosives, and their means of delivery. Examples are the Parts 1 and 2 lists created by the NSG in the nuclear area. In addition, conventional weapons should be covered. In practice, the EU list covers all of these. A comprehensive list should be adopted into national legislation in such a way that updates to the list are automatically and immediately included in laws. Legislation should also include a catch-all clause.

- Government officials should be well trained and engaged in the mission of preventing strategic commodity trafficking. For example, customs agents should be trained in identifying and stopping strategic commodity trafficking.

- Governments should have in place robust outreach programs to industry and academia as well as to state-owned manufacturers and technology holders, so as to inform company officials about export control laws and best internal compliance practices or programs to ensure sound company compliance with export control laws.

- Internal Compliance Programs should be required for all companies and state-owned enterprises such as national laboratories and state-run defense manufacturers engaged in the export of controlled direct use or dual-use goods and encouraged for all exporters of sensitive dual-use goods.

- Governments should make available a point of contact and provide information to companies to assist their efforts in determining the *bona fides* of potential customers of controlled or sensitive goods. They should provide companies with information about the latest illicit procurement schemes geared toward the goods they sell.

- Companies should be encouraged to provide information voluntarily to their government on suspicious approaches by potential or actual customers for price quotations or other types of enquiries. Any proposed sale that invokes suspicion should be shared with the government. Toward this goal, governments should establish official, easy to use points of contact where companies can provide this information confidentially to their national authorities.

- Governments should offer voluntary disclosure platforms for companies to come forward to share information about inadvertent, potentially illegal exports, as well as information about intentional illegal exports. Penalty mitigation should be considered for companies that subsequently take steps to improve their internal compliance systems and for non-egregious or non-repeat lapses.

- Countries should have in place robust prosecutorial and investigatory efforts to ensure that export control laws are enforced and violators are held accountable or deterred from committing export control related crimes.

- Illicit procurement committed by members of Tier One should be stigmatized and discouraged, publicly reported at the United Nations, and pressure put on countries to fully prosecute perpetrators. If persistent, the United States, European Union, and other countries should systematically sanction entities engaged in this conduct.

- Suppliers should take into consideration domestic and regional stability and corruption levels of end-user countries before exporting sensitive goods.

- Tier One countries should apply extra scrutiny, including a denial to the supply of nuclear facilities or nuclear (NSG Part 1) goods to countries that are lagging in their fulfillment of sub-criteria and fall low in the PPI rankings.

- Countries should work closely with the FATF and its regional bodies on proliferation financing, and work to improve compliance with proliferation financing-relevant FATF recommendations. This includes helping financial institutions with implementing and optimizing financial tracking systems, increasing oversight over sanctions compliance by financial institutions, and monitoring and engaging the efforts of financial institutions to freeze suspicious transactions associated with sanctioned individuals or entities.

- In cooperation with suppliers, Tier One countries should improve their end-use and end-user verification efforts. If not already doing so, countries should require verified end-use statements for goods prior to leaving their territories. If there are any doubts about the shipment, the country should conduct investigations on a case-by-case basis.

- Few countries currently conduct periodic post-shipment end-use checks on sensitive exports to ensure that the goods are used for the stated use and by the stated end user. Only a few suppliers have the resources to conduct such checks. Nonetheless, Tier One countries should on a case-by-case basis devote or expand resources for this practice for several key strategic goods, particularly those goods known to be critical to sanctioned and banned programs in pariah countries. Any supplier country should consider requiring end-use checks as a condition of export, potentially even relying on the greater resources of other countries, such as Britain, Germany, or the United States, which can carry out the end-use check in the recipient nation. An alternative is to require the reported "end-use" countries to do follow-up end-use checks, if requested by the supplying country. Although the last condition would be meaningless in the case of committed violators such as Iran and North Korea, for many states with reliable reputations this alternative could be credible and efficient.

- Any country supplying Iran with NSG Part 2 goods that has received approval from the JCPOA Procurement Working Group should utilize the authority provided by the JCPOA to conduct post-shipment end-use verification in Iran. If it cannot commit to doing so, the PWG should not approve the export.

EXPORT CONTROL SYSTEMS IN TIERS TWO AND THREE

While an overriding goal should be the implementation of internationally-acceptable export control systems in all countries, not all countries are comparable, as exemplified by the PPI's tiering system. A general recommendation is that countries in Tiers Two and Three should improve and, in some cases, create, meaningful and effective strategic trade control systems but with a consideration for their size, economic activity, and resources.

The process of creating effective trade control systems takes considerable time, effort, and resources. In the short term, a priority is ensuring that countries in Tiers Two and Three have minimum attributes to their strategic export control systems.

Tier Two countries, which offer trade benefits to major global economies, should have an incentive to create a minimal level of effective strategic trade controls. Many of the countries in Tier Three have *not* been used as transshipment countries by proliferant states, nor have they illegally procured goods or moved funds illegally. They thus appear to pose a generally lower risk of being involved in illicit trading schemes, but this situation could change as countries develop or illicit procurement agents look to exploit additional states with weak controls (see for example Chapter 16). As a result, Tier Three countries should also be motivated to implement greater controls.

As discussed above, there are many groups and countries that can offer assistance on the development of strategic trade control legislation and its implementation; however, many of these efforts involve providing assistance primarily in establishing comprehensive trade control laws.

Although we fully recommend states contacting these entities for assistance in establishing comprehensive export control systems, the following is an attempt to draw out the key minimal attributes of an export control system in transshipment or non-supplier countries. Of course, it would be best if each country embarked on a path to adopt the type of controls commonly found in Tier One, including legislation that is encapsulated by the green categories in the PPI ranking. However, absent such controls, Tiers Two and Three countries should receive assistance and be offered model strategic export control systems that would have an essential set of elements, such as the starter kit discussed in the section containing recommendations for the 1540 Committee. A key principle in devising these elements is that no country should be a safe haven for strategic commodity trafficking and each country should be able to criminalize a set of actions contained in strategic export control legislation, including prosecuting violators or extraditing them. As an interim step on the path to comprehensive export control laws and systems, the following provides a few critical, specific priorities in the near term that would contribute to reducing the threat posed by countries with non-existent, minimal, or ineffective strategic export controls.

A MINIMAL TIER TWO SYSTEM SHOULD HAVE:[17]

- Export control legislation that includes lists of materials, equipment, and technology covered by multilateral treaties and arrangements or included on national control lists, which could be used for the design, development, production, or use of nuclear (including radiological), chemical, biological weapons, and explosives, and their means of delivery. Examples are the Parts 1 and 2 lists created by the NSG in the nuclear area. In practice, the EU list covers all of these. Legislation should include a catch-all clause to cover, at a minimum, UN-sanctioned countries.

- Legislation that includes Resolution 1540 language as set out in paragraph 3.(c) and (d) of the resolution pertaining to prohibitions on brokering, and on controlling goods in "export, transit, transshipment and re-export."[18]

- The capability to conduct outreach to industry and academia about export control laws and control lists, and to assist them in determining whether to make sales of non-controlled goods that could fall under catch-all clauses.

- Governments should develop good knowledge of their country's supply and transshipment potential, including any listed goods and those non-listed goods that could be covered using catch-all controls. Governments can do so by using, among other resources, the Joint Research Center's *Trade Atlas*, which tracks the flow of potentially controlled goods using the analysis of UN-reported transfers by HS number.[19] In this effort to conduct outreach to industry, the country could rely on the capabilities discussed in the technical reachback section to better identify manufacturers of sensitive goods. For those more developed countries in Tier Two that wanted to develop electronic big data import/export monitoring systems, they could ask to receive lists of U.S. imports to their country from the U.S. Border Enforcement Analytics Program.

- The ability to encourage the creation and maintenance of Internal Compliance Programs, at least in simplified form, for any suppliers or trans-shippers of controlled goods, including trading companies and freight forwarders.

- The ability to issue licenses. Licensing offices can be small but should exist and have points of contact, legal information, and digitized forms available online. In Tier Two countries with few resources, the office may consist of a part-time person. It may also be part of Customs.

- A denied parties list in place, which could be adapted from major supplier countries, and can be administered by licensing staff in conjunction with investigatory, customs, and law enforcement agencies. The government should have knowledge of sanctioned countries.

- The ability to contact or liaise with foreign countries about suspicious end-users of concern that have abilities to check *bona fides* of entities and individuals, as part of the process of granting or denying licenses.

- The ability to enforce export control laws, including having the ability to prosecute violators or extradite them.

- A system in place, including a point of contact, to receive information from another country, and the legal authority to expeditiously stop and seize goods.

- An established method to ensure that relevant branches of government, including licensing, customs, and police officials, can cooperate and share information.

- A capability (drawing on foreign expertise, if necessary) for evaluating seized goods.

- At a minimum, UN ASYCUDA or similar, domestic customs system software in place.

- Cooperation as needed with the WCO on the evaluation, development, and improvement of customs systems.

- Trade control systems in place – preferably digital – that allow officials to monitor goods entering and exiting their countries, including FTZs.

- Full implementation of sanctions as required by the UN Security Council, such as those on Iran, North Korea, and Syria.

- Sufficient import controls since Tier Two countries may pose a transit or diversion concern rather than strictly a supplier concern in strategic commodity trafficking.

- Programs or initiatives to receive and incorporate assistance from international and national organizations on improving export control systems.

- Participation in organizations such as FATF, and if the country has sufficient trade levels, joining of initiatives such as the Proliferation

Security Initiative, and having in place bilateral agreements such as a Customs Mutual Assistance Agreement with the United States.

- Work with FATF and its regional bodies to implement the FATF recommendations, especially the six recommendations judged as most relevant to preventing proliferation financing (see Chapter 5).
- Updating of penal codes to include crimes relevant to the trafficking in nuclear, nuclear-related, and other strategic commodities.
- Close work with the 1540 Committee to assist its understanding of country export control systems, including asking for assistance in improving those systems.

A MINIMAL TIER THREE SYSTEM SHOULD HAVE:

- Export control legislation that includes lists of materials, equipment, and technology covered by multilateral treaties and arrangements or included on national control lists, which could be used for the design, development, production, or use of nuclear (including radiological), chemical, and biological weapons, and explosives, and their means of delivery. Examples are the Parts 1 and 2 lists created by the NSG in the nuclear area. In practice, the EU list covers all of these.
- An industry outreach effort to sectors or companies that could be affected by export control laws. The government should develop a basic knowledge of the country's supply and transshipment potential and which goods are affected by sanctions. This effort could be aided by the measures discussed in the technical reachback section.
- The assignment of a few officials (or in some cases a single individual) to conduct industry outreach, issue licenses, and serve as a point of contact for other countries and international organizations. The staff should widely disseminate contact information and work to create a simple website with trade control law information, licensing information, and points of contact for assistance.
- A denied parties list in case a license is requested along with knowledge of sanctioned countries.
- A minimal capability to stop strategic goods in transit, including a point of contact to receive information from other countries. The country should have legal authority to act upon this information, including to expeditiously seize goods, and have a capability (including

drawing on foreign expertise, if necessary) for evaluating seized goods.

- Updating of penal codes to include crimes relevant to the trafficking in nuclear and other strategic commodities.
- The ability to enforce export control laws, including having the ability to prosecute violators or allow for their extradition if they are being sought for prosecution by other countries.
- Sufficient import controls since these countries may pose a transit or diversion concern rather than strictly a supplier concern in strategic commodity trafficking.
- Work with the 1540 Committee to assist its understanding of the country's export control systems, including asking for assistance in improving those systems.
- For countries scoring low on the Corruption Perceptions Index and not reaching a score of 50 percent on the PPI, strategic export control systems should be more robust. In general, these countries should also seek to reduce national corruption.

The United States should continue to provide foreign assistance using its national programs and prioritize how Tier Two and Three states could implement these elements in phases with the eventual aim of creating comprehensive strategic export controls.

NOTES

1. United Nations Security Council, *Security Council resolution 1540 (2004)*, S/RES/1540 (2004), April 28, 2004, http://www.un.org/ga/search/view_doc.asp?symbol=S/RES/1540%20(2004)

2. Albright, *Peddling Peril* (New York: Free Press, 2010).

3. World Customs Organization, "Strategic Trade Control Enforcement," http://www.wcoomd.org/en/topics/enforcement-and-compliance/instruments-and-tools/~/media/7A05799E8D3A46C8B8355175EEBA4322.ashx

4. U.S. National Nuclear Security Administration, International Nonproliferation Export Control Program, "World Customs Organization Strategic Trade Control Enforc[e]ment (STCE)," https://csis-prod.s3.amazonaws.com/s3fs-public/legacy_files/files/attachments/150625_PerryPresentation.pdf

5. A list of HS codes characterizing strategic commodities can be found in: Table 2 in Cristina Versino and Peter Heine, "Harmonized System codes associated with their strategic commodities," *Strategic Trade Atlas: Country Based Views,* Joint Research Center, European Atomic Energy Community, 2016.

6. One example is the EU TARIC Correlation Table. For more information see: Renaud Chatelus and Pete Heine, "Rating Correlations Between Customs Codes and Export Control Lists: Assessing the Needs and Challenges," *Strategic Trade Review,* Volume 2, Issue 3, 2016, http://www.str.ulg.ac.be/wp-content/uploads/2016/10/Rating-Correlations-Between-Customs-Codes-and-Export-Control-Lists-Assessing-the-Needs-and-Challenges.pdf

7. World Customs Organization, 'Sharing, connecting and bridging,' CEN Suite Brochure, Brussels, Belgium, 2015, http://www.wcoomd.org/-/media/wco/public/global/pdf/topics/enforcement-and-compliance/tools-and-instruments/cen/cen-brochure.pdf?db=web

8. If a licensing agency is yet to be established in a country, depending on individual circumstances, it may make sense to create the licensing agency as part of Customs. This way, both authorities have access to shared databases and can share reachback capabilities.

9. See for example, Sibylle Bauer, "WMD-Related Dual-Use Trade Control Offences in the European Union: Penalties and Prosecutions," *EU Non-Proliferation Consortium: Non-Proliferation Papers,* No. 30, July 2013, https://sipri.org/sites/default/files/EUNPC_no-30.pdf

10. In light of Iran's demonstration of its political commitment to reforming its financial system and the relevant steps it took, the FATF decided in June 2017 to continue the suspension of counter-measures. The action plan expires on January 31, 2018 and the FATF urges Iran to proceed swiftly in the reform path to ensure full and accurate implementation of the Action Plan, addressing all remaining AML/CFT

deficiencies, in particular those related to terrorist financing. At its February meeting, the FATF will assess progress made by Iran and take all appropriate action.

11. U.S. Department of Justice, National Security Division, "Guidance Regarding Voluntary Self-Disclosures, Cooperation, and Remediation in Export Control and Sanctions Investigations Involving Business Organizations," October 2, 2016, https://www.justice.gov/nsd/file/902491/download

12. See also for example, *Nunn-Wolfowitz Task Force Report: Industry 'Best Practices' Regarding Export Compliance Programs,* July 25, 2000, http://www.usexportcompliance.com/Papers/nunnwolfowitz.pdf; U.S. Department of Commerce, Bureau of Industry and Security, *Export Compliance Guidelines: The Elements of an Effective Export Compliance Program,* https://www.bis.doc.gov/index.php/documents/pdfs/1641-ecp/file; Bureau of Industry and Security, *BIS "Best Practices" for Industry to Guard Against Unlawful Diversion through Transshipment Trade,* August 31, 2011, https://www.bis.doc.gov/index.php/forms-documents/pdfs/625-best-practices/file; CEEC, "Best Practices for Export Controls, Draft Standards," November 28, 2011, http://www.ceecbestpractices.org/best-practices-standards-workgroup.html

13. CEEC, "Best Practices for Export Controls, Draft Standards," November 28, 2011, http://www.ceecbestpractices.org/best-practices-standards-workgroup.html

14. EXBS provides financial support and direction to INECP, as well as to a range of other U.S. federal agencies, including the Departments and Commerce and Treasury, and the Department of Homeland Security's Homeland Security Investigations, and Customs and Border Protection. In addition, EXBS sponsors a number of non-profit and for profit non-governmental organizations with the ability to provide logistical and substantive support to its export control outreach-related activities.

15. As described by the United States Department of Homeland Security, "The Border Enforcement Analytics Program (BEAP) will provide advanced computing and analytical solutions that enable Immigration and Customs Enforcement (ICE) Homeland Security Investigation (HSI) to effectively combine and analyze multiple, large disparate data sets to increase enforcement effectiveness. The initial Big Data operating capability is currently supporting counter-proliferation casework." United States Department of Homeland Security, "Border Enforcement Analytics Program Apex Infographic," Science and Technology, accessed November 2017, https://www.dhs.gov/science-and-technology/beap-apex-infographic

16. These recommendations are adapted with permission from a paper by Michael D. Rosenthal, *The Role of United Nations Security Council Resolution 1540 (2004) in Supporting Effective Nuclear Security Measures World-Wide,* Presented at the International Conference on Nuclear Security, Vienna, Austria, December 5-9, 2016.

17. Some countries in Tier Two are extremely poor in resources, such as Afghanistan or Bangladesh. They may not be able to meet Tier Two standards. These countries may need further evaluation to see if they should be considered more like Tier Three countries in terms of implemented export control systems but with a recognition that assistance should be provided so that they can eventually reach Tier Two standards.

18. United Nations Security Council, Security Council resolution 1540 (2004), S/RES/1540 (2004), April 28, 2004, http://www.un.org/ga/search/view_doc. asp?symbol=S/RES/1540%20(2004)

19. Cristina Versino and Peter Heine, *Strategic Trade Atlas: Country Based Views,* Joint Research Center, European Atomic Energy Community, 2016, http://publications.jrc. ec.europa.eu/repository/handle/JRC100392

SECTION IV
ADDITIONAL GROUPINGS AND APPLICATIONS

CHAPTER 13
COUNTRIES WITH THEIR FIRST NUCLEAR POWER REACTORS PROPOSED, PLANNED, OR UNDER CONSTRUCTION

One group the PPI team decided to evaluate is comprised of countries that have recently and publicly proposed, planned, or started the construction of their first nuclear power plants. The countries in this group include, alphabetically: Bangladesh, Belarus, Chile, Egypt, Indonesia, Jordan, Kazakhstan, Malaysia, Poland, Saudi Arabia, Thailand, Turkey, the United Arab Emirates, and Viet Nam.[1]

Receiving a nuclear power reactor from an international supplier requires considerable preparation and the establishment of infrastructure. The state must create a regulatory regime to ensure that the reactor is operated safely, nuclear waste is handled properly, and in general, that the environment is protected. The procedures for the physical protection of the nuclear material and equipment have to be enshrined in national laws in order to prevent nuclear terrorism. The state needs to apply IAEA safeguards to the nuclear material and activities to assure the international community of exclusively peaceful purposes.

Often overlooked, but lying at the heart of the PPI, is the need for robust export controls that can assure that newly gained nuclear know-how, designs, technology, and materials are protected from entering a potentially unregulated market in which sensitive goods and intellectual property easily cross borders. Export control regimes are even more important in countries such as Saudi Arabia that desire to first import nuclear power reactors as a prelude to becoming an international nuclear supplier. Those countries that intend to supply nuclear reactors should fulfill a higher standard in creating robust export controls than those countries that do not intend to export them. However, there are basic standards that all these countries should meet.

FINDINGS AND ANALYSIS

The rankings are shown in Figure 13.1. From highest to lowest, the overall ranks are: Poland, Malaysia, Turkey, Kazakhstan, United Arab Emirates, Chile, Bangladesh, Jordan, Saudi Arabia, Thailand, Belarus, Indonesia, Viet Nam, and Egypt.

Overall, most of the countries planning to acquire nuclear power reactors did poorly in the PPI. Twelve out of these 14 countries receive less than 50 percent of all PPI points (see Figure 13.1). Two received less than 25 percent. Six of the countries lack adequate export control legislation, meaning their existing legislation was categorized as Yellow, Orange, or Red. They also showed deficiencies in the super criteria covering Ability to Monitor and Detect Strategic Trade and Ability to Prevent Proliferation Financing (see Figure 13.2). For example, collectively, the countries scored poorly on internal stability/absence of violence or terrorism which is one of the Ability to Monitor and Detect Strategic Trade sub-criteria. When corruption was evaluated as one of the Adequacy of Enforcement sub-criteria, it was noted that five of the countries that have their first nuclear power reactors publicly proposed, planned, or under construction rank below 100 in the Corruption Perceptions Index. On a positive note, and also measured in the Adequacy of Enforcement super criterion, all countries recently received some kind of training or international assistance to bolster their counter-proliferation efforts.

The following countries in this group that have not yet signed or ratified the Convention on the Physical Protection of Nuclear Material include: Egypt, Malaysia, Poland, and Thailand.

The following countries in this group that have not yet signed or ratified the Additional Protocol include: Belarus, Malaysia, and Thailand have signed but not ratified the Additional Protocol. Egypt has yet to sign the AP.

The following states in this group that have signed but not ratified the Convention for the Suppression of Acts of Nuclear Terrorism include: Egypt, Malaysia, and Thailand.

Egypt scores exceptionally low in the International Commitment super criterion.

RECOMMENDATIONS

The states in this group should all ratify and adapt into national legislation the key conventions on physical protection such as the CPPNM and the Additional Protocol prior to receiving major components for their first nuclear power reactors.

These states should also have in place export control legislation that is comparable to countries in Tier One prior to receiving major components.

Nuclear suppliers should consider not providing nuclear power reactors to states that received fewer than 25 percent of the available points in the total PPI score until such time as they significantly improve their export control and regulatory systems. These countries include: Belarus, Indonesia, Viet Nam, and Egypt (see Figure 13.1).

Total PPI scores of countries with their first nuclear power reactors proposed, planned, or under construction

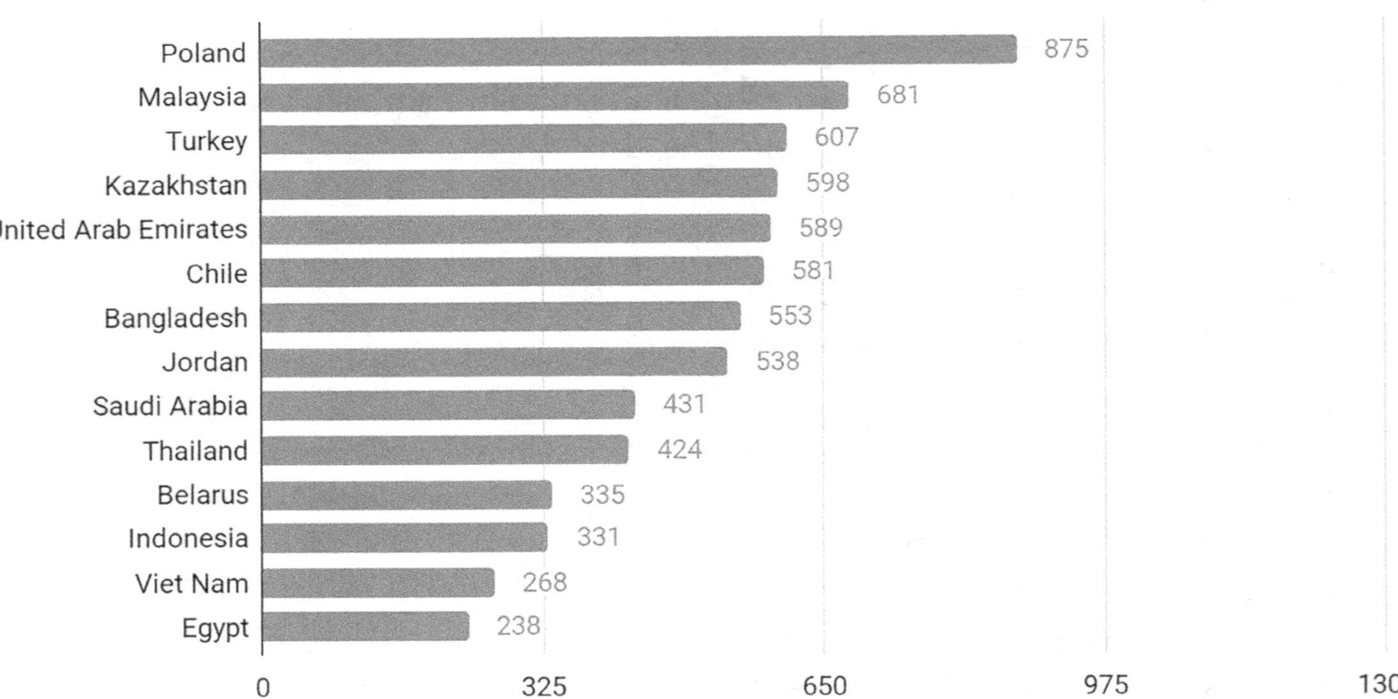

Figure 13.1. The overall PPI ranking for the 14 selected countries. All of these countries have proposed, planned, or started the construction of their first nuclear power plants.

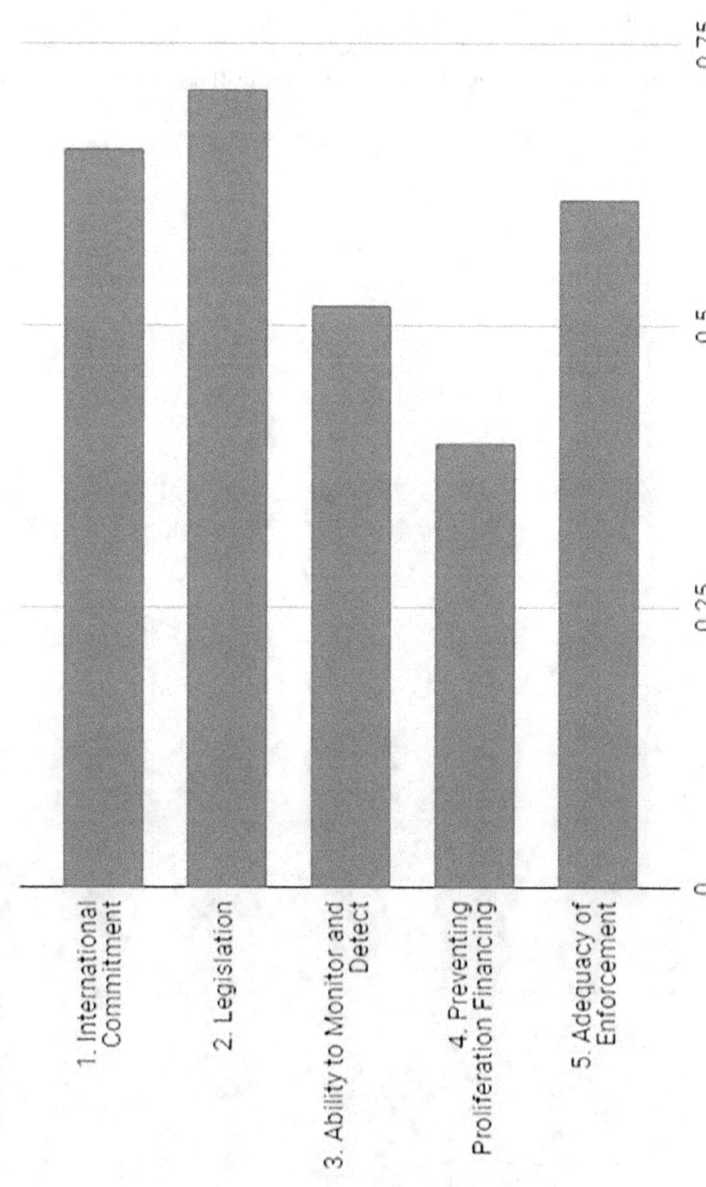

Figure 13.2. The overall performance fractions for the 14 countries. It clearly shows room for improvement in all five super criteria, but especially within the latter three super criteria.

NOTE

1. The Institute has written comprehensive country profiles on the future nuclear ambitions and associated proliferation risks of Egypt, Saudi Arabia, Turkey, and the United Arab Emirates. See: *Saudi Arabia's Nuclear Ambitions and Proliferation Risks*, by Sarah Burkhard, Erica Wenig, David Albright, and Andrea Stricker, March 30, 2017, Available at: http://isis-online.org/isis-reports/detail/saudi-arabias-nuclear-ambitions-and-proliferation-risks/; *Nuclear Infrastructure and Proliferation Risks of the United Arab Emirates, Turkey, and Egypt*, by Sarah Burkhard, Erica Wenig, David Albright, and Andrea Stricker, August 25, 2017, Available at: http://isis-online.org/isis-reports/detail/nuclear-infrastructure-and-proliferation-risks-of-the-united-arab-emirates/

CHAPTER 14
MAJOR FREE TRADE ZONES AMONG TIER TWO COUNTRIES

Free Trade Zones (FTZs), one type of Special Trade Zone, are designed to incentivize trade and offer exceptions and exemptions from trade regulations within a country. Depending on their specific economic purpose, FTZs can have a variety of names, such as Export Processing Zones, Enterprise Zones, Freeports, or Special Economic Zones.[1]

FTZs are typically within a geographic area, often a port, where commodities enter the country, are stored, handled, and often transferred or re-exported. They are generally not subject to customs duties. Some FTZs include manufacturing sites that receive components and assemble them into finished products before sending them onward.

For example, the UAE alone has 37 Free Trade Zones.[2] Most (27 of 37) are located in Dubai, which has historically been involved in many cases of illicit nuclear and other strategic commodity procurement. Only about 50 countries worldwide do not have FTZs.

In general, many FTZs operate outside rigorous national trade control regimes and as a result have been frequently used by proliferant states as transshipment locations, allowing goods to be shipped onward without the knowledge of the supplier. In practice, they allow proliferant states to more easily conceal the transit of goods from a supplier to a proliferant state. A country may have robust and highly effective strategic trade control legislation and regulations outside its special trade zones, but these laws may not apply in the FTZs or they may be applied only partially in the FTZs; moreover, the enforcement of these laws may be ineffective within those zones. In some cases, Tier Two countries, such as the UAE and Malaysia, established FTZs before having national export controls.

Tier Two includes countries that pose greater transshipment concerns than countries in Tier Three but are not in Tier One because they are not nuclear suppliers. For this chapter, the PPI team selected for analysis a subset of Tier Two countries that have major FTZs, based on several criteria, including their trade volume and growth and their likelihood to grow in the future.[3] They include: Bangladesh, Djibouti, Hong Kong, Indonesia, Jamaica, Malaysia, Mauritius, Nigeria, Panama, the Philippines, Singapore, and the UAE. In most cases, these countries established FTZs to generate income and expand their economies. This selection of countries is meant to be representative of Tier Two countries but also to focus on the more important, prolific trading countries in this tier.

There are also many important FTZs in Tier One which are not considered here because Tier One countries, as NSG members and major suppliers, typically have considerably more developed trade control systems. However, the recommendations below may apply to those countries' FTZs as well.

FINDINGS AND ANALYSIS

The rankings in this subgroup of Tier Two are shown in Figure 14.1. From highest to lowest, the overall ranks are: Singapore, Malaysia, Mauritius, Jamaica, United Arab Emirates, Bangladesh, Panama, Philippines, Hong Kong, Djibouti, Indonesia, and Nigeria.

Comparing these countries in the overall rank of all 200 countries, territories, or entities in the PPI, their overall average rank is 87, which is above average for Tier Two countries, but in general, it is not strong. In terms of earning points across all super criteria, these countries in general did not fare well. Singapore, with the highest overall ranking in this group, received 67 percent of all possible points. The great majority, or nine out of 12 countries, received less than half of the total possible points. Even more concerning, four countries received less than one third of the total possible points.

These twelve countries as a group did poorly in their Ability to Monitor and Detect Strategic Trade and their Ability to Prevent Proliferation Financing (see Figure 14.2). In these super criteria, the countries combined received a total normalized performance fraction of 0.5 or less, which is a measure used by the PPI to assess the extent to which requirements of the sub-criteria are met. The results suggest that these countries are not aware of the nature of the goods passing through their FTZs and likely are unaware of any illicit financial activity supporting their movement. In terms of total possible points across each of these two super criteria, Singapore, which has the highest overall ranking in this subgroup and is within the top 20 of all 200 countries, received only 63 percent of the possible points for the super criterion measuring Ability to Monitor and Detect Strategic Trade and only 40 percent of the possible points for Ability to Prevent Proliferation Financing. In none of the five super criteria performance fraction evaluations did these countries fulfill 75 percent of the sub-criteria requirements.

Particularly concerning is that the best performance by these countries was within the Legislation super criterion, where the PPI team assigned points for countries having national legislation in place, even if it applies only to cargo entering and exiting the country in "normal" trade and does not apply rigorously or at all inside the FTZs. Indeed, the legislation and licensing in place for countries that were evaluated in Tier Two are specifically for exports and imports between countries, not through FTZs. Often, it was not possible to determine whether national laws apply in FTZs. Moreover, there is a lack of information about national enforcement entities regulating and monitoring goods that pass through or are re-exported through FTZs. If only legislation known to be valid in FTZs were considered, all of these countries would likely have done worse.

There is evidence that the sufficiency of the export control systems in some of these states is improving. Singapore for example has increasingly implemented more stringent regulations. As pointed out by the United Nations Security Council Panel of Experts on North Korea in 2017, when reporting on recent activity of the sanctioned North Korean company, Glocom/Pan Systems Pyongyang, "Procurement shifted to companies on the Chinese mainland and in Hong Kong, China, owing to lower prices, stringent Singaporean regulations and more direct logistics."[4]

RECOMMENDATIONS

For international security reasons, all major FTZs should be integrated fully into national export control systems and any exemptions from export controls should be gradually ended. Although countries in Tier Two cannot be expected to create export control systems as rigorous as Tier One countries, they do need to have control systems in place that allow officials to monitor the goods entering and exiting the FTZs and to seize suspicious cargo. They should also have systems in place that can provide assurance that goods are not being transshipped to sanctioned countries, such as Iran, North Korea, and Syria, among others.

The largest or most important FTZs should be covered by legislation that includes all major control lists (and a catch-all clause) and countries should train officials to recognize such goods in transit or develop a reliable, timely reachback mechanism (as discussed in Chapter 12). Within these countries' FTZs, it is also important to establish or maintain export licensing regulations, such as requiring additional documentation on listed goods. Examples could be photos and more detailed descriptions of cargo or verified end-use statements.

The countries in this group in particular need to increase their ability to detect and monitor the import and export of sensitive commodities. Because these countries do not appear overly aware of the goods passing through their FTZs, they should increase physical inspections of shipments and put in place trained personnel at major entry and exit points. They should implement risk-based approaches for inspections such as those used in Europe or the United States. Toward that goal, these countries should increase or introduce the use of electronic big data import/export monitoring systems, similar to the Border Enforcement Analytics Program system, which was recently deployed in the United States.[5] These states also need to actively work with and inform the shipping industries involved in their FTZs about the need for increased scrutiny. Shippers should be subject to following the strengthened enforcement approaches of those FTZs.

These countries, along with many others, need to improve mechanisms to prevent proliferation financing and increase cooperation with the FATF. Specifically, eight of the twelve countries in this grouping have not undergone a FATF mutual evaluation based on 2012 standards and have therefore not been evaluated on their ability to implement financial sanctions.[6] Only Bangladesh, Jamaica, Malaysia, and Singapore have been evaluated in this regard and all of them show deficiencies.[7] Djibouti has as of late summer 2017 not been evaluated by FATF. Hong Kong, Indonesia, Malaysia, and Singapore have each been pointed out by the most recent UN Panel of Experts report on North Korea for being involved in UNSCR violations involving North Korea (see Chapter 16).[8]

Major Free Trade Zones in Tier Two Countries - Overall PPI scores

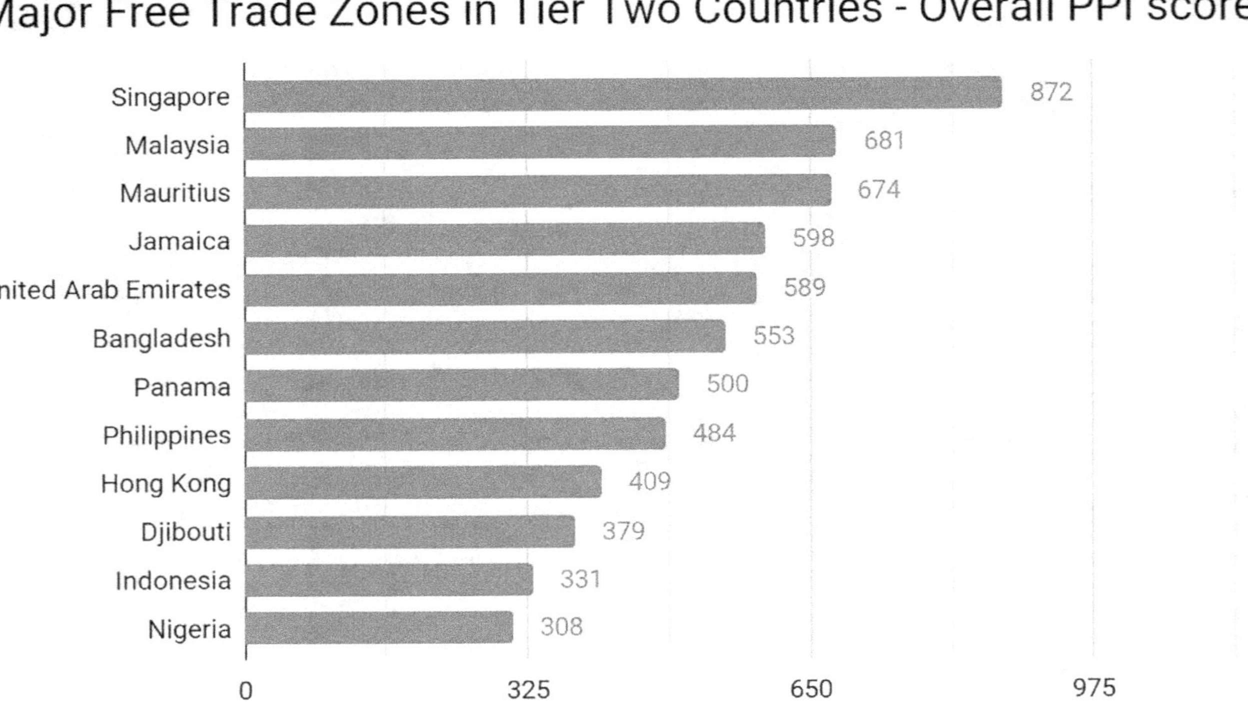

Figure 14.1. Overall PPI ranking for the 12 selected countries in Tier Two with major Free Trade Zones. The majority of countries received fewer than half the possible points.

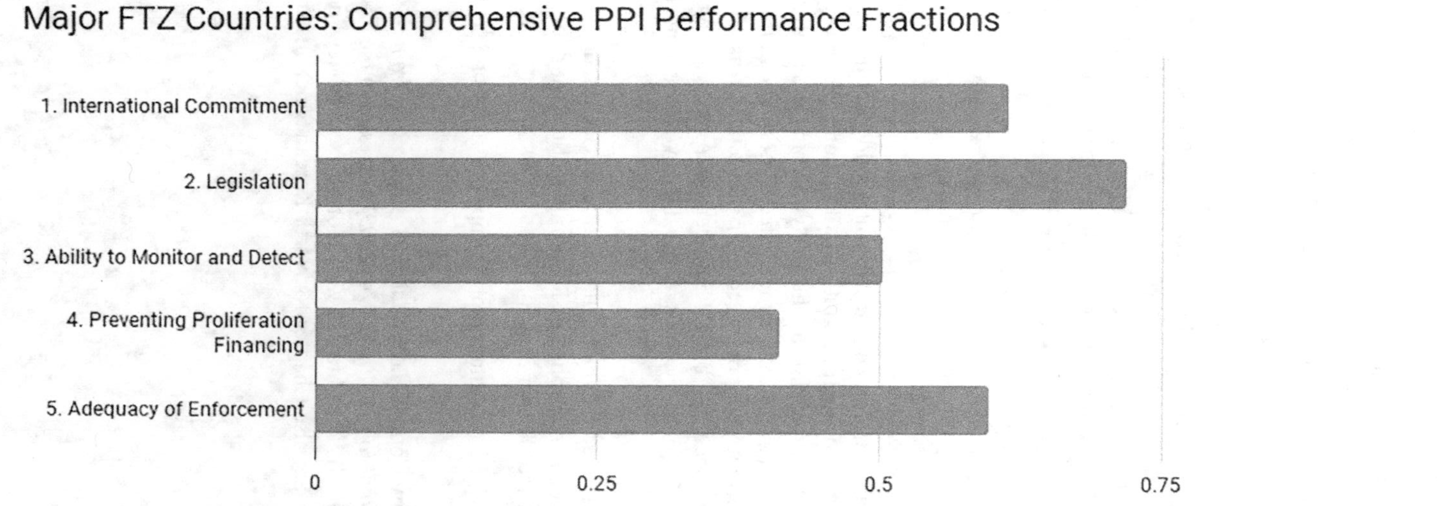

Figure 14.2. Overall performance fractions for the 12 countries in Tier Two. It clearly shows room for improvement in all five super criteria, but especially within Super Criteria Ability to Monitor and Detect Strategic Trade and Preventing Proliferation Financing.

NOTES

1. For more definitions and distinctions see: FATF, "Money Laundering vulnerabilities of Free Trade Zones," 2010, http://www.fatf-gafi.org/media/fatf/documents/reports/ML%20vulnerabilities%20of%20Free%20Trade%20Zones.pdf

2. Dubai-Freezone, "FTZ of the United Arab Emirates," https://en.dubai-freezone.ae/articles-about-bussines-in-uae/full-list-of-free-trade-zones-in-the-uae.html

3. FATF, "Money Laundering vulnerabilities of Free Trade Zones," 2010, http://www.fatf-gafi.org/media/fatf/documents/reports/ML%20vulnerabilities%20of%20Free%20Trade%20Zones.pdf; Economy Watch, "International Free Trade Zone," June 2010, http://www.economywatch.com/international-trade/free-trade-zone.html

4. United Nations Security Council, *Letter dated 17 February 2017 from the Panel of Experts established pursuant to Resolution 1874 (2009) addressed to the President of the Security Council*, S/2017/150, http://www.un.org/ga/search/view_doc.asp?symbol=S/2017/150

5. As described by the United States Department of Homeland Security, "The Border Enforcement Analytics Program (BEAP) will provide advanced computing and analytical solutions that enable Immigration and Customs Enforcement (ICE) Homeland Security Investigation (HSI) to effectively combine and analyze multiple, large disparate data sets to increase enforcement effectiveness. The initial Big Data operating capability is currently supporting counter-proliferation casework." U.S. Department of Homeland Security, "Border Enforcement Analytics Program Apex Infographic," Science and Technology, https://www.dhs.gov/science-and-technology/beap-apex-infographic

6. The 2012 FATF guidelines added the evaluation of financial sanctions implementation in form of a newly phrased Recommendation 7 and the added Immediate Outcome 11. See Chapter 5.

7. None of them had received a denotation of "Compliant" in R7 or a "Highly Effective" in IO11.

8. United Nations Security Council, *Letter dated 28 August 2017 from the Panel of Experts established pursuant to resolution 1874 (2009) addressed to the President of the Security Council*, S/2017/742, http://www.un.org/ga/search/view_doc.asp?symbol=S/2017/150; See also Chapter 16: North Korean Sanctions and the PPI Rankings.

CHAPTER 15
U.S. STRATEGIC TRADE AUTHORIZATION (STA)

In 2010, the administration of U.S. President Barack Obama launched an Export Control Reform (ECR) Initiative to streamline U.S. exports of controlled or sensitive goods. As part of the ECR Initiative, the administration moved hundreds if not thousands of dual-use goods from one of the United States' key export control lists, the U.S. Munitions List (USML), to the Commerce Control List (CCL), under a newly created 600-series category of goods. The 600 series of goods includes many dual-use military items of proliferation concern. The administration did so because the CCL allows for country group licensing exceptions; it then created on the CCL a licensing exception called the Strategic Trade Authorization, or STA. Countries eligible for STA status are now allowed to import 600-series goods license-free under certain conditions. The goods' ultimate end user must be an approved government entity, even though the initial importing entity can be a company. Pre-authorization for these companies includes the requirement that they have received a prior U.S. government license.[1] Eligibility for the STA exception is extended only to a pre-approved list of 36 countries — a total of eight additional countries and territories have more limited eligibility — for a total of 44.

The list of 36 countries includes most North Atlantic Treaty Organization (NATO) members and several other allies that enforce or are party to the four major export control and non-proliferation conventions – the Wassenaar Arrangement, the MTCR, Australia Group, and the NSG.[2]

> *Argentina, Australia, Austria, Belgium, Bulgaria, Canada, Croatia, Czech Republic, Denmark, Estonia, Finland, France, Germany, Greece, Hungary, Iceland, Ireland, Italy, Japan, Latvia, Lithuania, Luxembourg, Netherlands, New Zealand, Norway, Poland, Portugal, Romania, Slovakia, Slovenia, South Korea, Spain, Sweden, Switzerland, Turkey, and United Kingdom. (Of these, Argentina, Australia, Austria, Finland, Japan, New Zealand, South Korea, and Sweden are not NATO members but qualify under their adherence to non-proliferation regimes).*

The additional eight countries or territories eligible for transfers of goods controlled only for national security reasons but not for nuclear, chemical, biological, or missile proliferation reasons include:

> *Albania, Hong Kong, India, Israel, Malta, Singapore, South Africa, and Taiwan.[3] (Of these, Albania is a NATO member).*

This accounts for 44 eligible destinations in total.

The STA exception was designed to ease burdensome licensing restrictions on U.S. exporters and known importing counterparts that frequently purchase large pieces of U.S. military equipment and need to maintain them by easily and quickly replacing parts. They no longer face the administrative hurdle of waiting for the U.S. State Department, which administers the USML, to process a license for each item. However, the exception has prompted proliferation concerns from some U.S. export control experts and practitioners.[4] Concerns include that vetted companies could exploit the STA over time and onward proliferation may occur outside the awareness or scrutiny of the United States. The lack of licensing requirements reduces the number of opportunities for the United States to review importing entity *bona fides*. It is also possible that an approved government recipient could send goods to unauthorized end users. At least one country eligible for STA, Turkey, could also use sensitive goods in its domestic repression campaign or use them against Kurds in neighboring Iraq. Moreover, three categories of goods that the Obama administration did not finish transferring from the USML to the CCL, or Categories 1-3 covering firearms, artillery, and ammunition, are of special concern because as originally envisioned they would become eligible for the STA, allowing governments and authorized companies to import large quantities of these deadly weapons. These weapons, experts fear, could contribute to local and regional conflicts, and, due to their nature, would be prone to being bought and sold and spreading to nefarious users on the global black arms market. They could even be used against U.S. troops abroad. The Trump administration, as of the early winter of 2018, was considering finishing the transfer of these categories of firearms, artillery, and ammunition.

For these reasons, the PPI decided to investigate how the export control systems of countries and territories eligible for the STA rank compare to one another.

FINDINGS AND ANALYSIS

Of note, the STA countries include the top 35 scorers in the PPI overall rank (Annex I). However, only 20 of these countries achieved a score of more than two-thirds of all the possible points (see Figure 15.1). The majority of STA countries are Tier One countries (only Albania, Hong Kong, and Singapore are Tier Two countries), where the PPI team applied the same standard of achieving two-thirds of all possible points. Here, 867 points indicates a sufficient export control system. Ideally, a high standard should be set for STA countries since they should have sound export control systems in order to receive a licensing exception. But the PPI team found that a handful of STA countries did not rank in the top 25 percent (or the top 50 countries) in the overall PPI ranking. With a rank of 50, South Africa barely made the top 25 percent. It did not receive half of all possible points.[5] Four countries or territories received below 50 percent of the points: Albania, Turkey, India, and Hong Kong (see Figure 15.1). This finding underscores that the United States is correct in its approach of not offering certain countries eligibility for the full set of STA-eligible items.

Of all the super criteria, STA countries as a group achieved the highest points in Legislation. On average, they received 95 percent of all possible points under that super criterion. Under the remaining super criteria, listed from high to low, the point averages for countries are: International Commitment (81 percent), Adequacy of Enforcement (78 percent), Ability to Monitor and Detect Strategic Trade (61 percent), and Ability to Prevent Proliferation Financing (27 percent). There is a marked discrepancy between countries enacting legislation and their subsequent actions with regard to Ability to Monitor and Detect Strategic Trade and Adequacy of Enforcement. As shown in Figure 15.2, not all countries give rise to concern about the adequacy of their enforcement against strategic commodity trafficking; this concern applies mainly to countries that received fewer than 50 percent of the total points in this super criterion, namely Turkey and Hong Kong, that cause the greatest concern under this super criterion.

RECOMMENDATIONS

In general, countries with STA eligibility should score highly in the PPI. Those that receive less than 50 percent of the total points, namely 650 points, deserve scrutiny whether their export control system is adequate. The United States should consider reviewing STA eligibility for Turkey and Hong Kong until they improve their export control systems. U.S. dual-use military goods have a higher chance of being diverted via these two countries, or in the case of Turkey, of being used in domestic repression or problematic border security efforts.

The United States should investigate the ultimate end uses of goods it has already transferred under STA, even to highly scoring countries. It should periodically audit and track the whereabouts and uses of these goods to ensure they are not being diverted or the STA exploited.

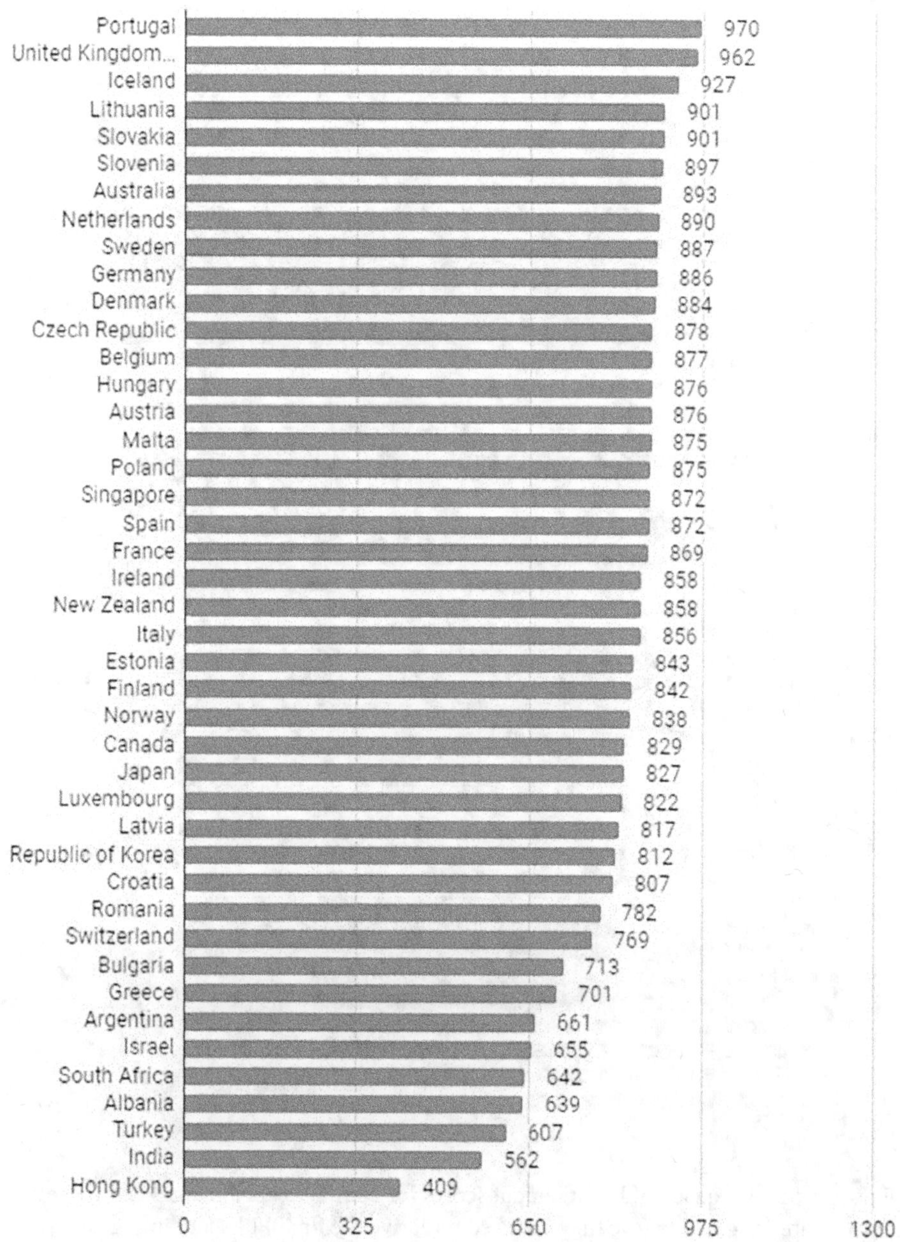

Figure 15.1. The STA-eligible countries' final PPI scores and resulting rank. A score of two thirds of the total points is 867 points; a score of half of the points is 650 points.

Strategic Trade Authorization Countries: Enforcement Rank

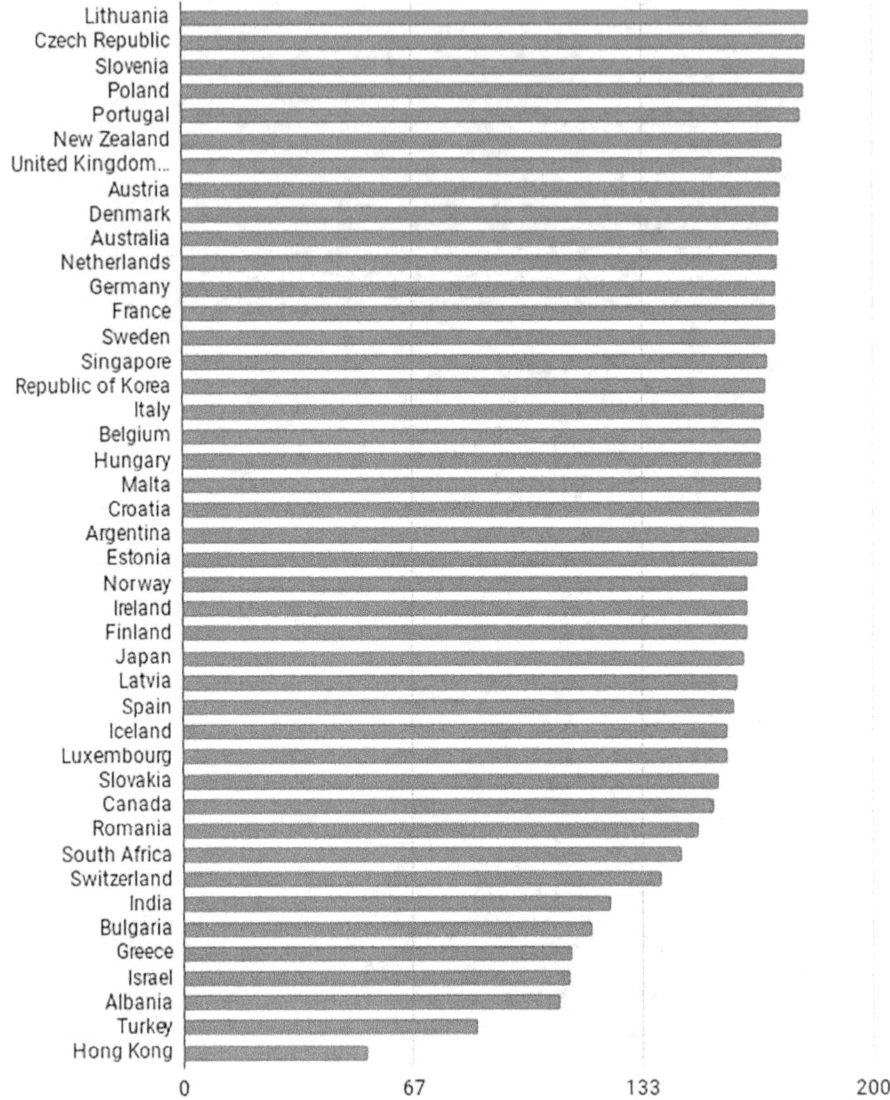

Figure 15.2. Adequacy of Enforcement scores for countries eligible for STA. These raw scores are weighted before they are used to derive the final PPI score in Figure 15.1.

NOTES

1. Venable LLP, "International Trade Alert: License Exception Strategic Trade Authorization: Understanding How it May Work for You," September 2013, https://www.venable.com/license-exception-strategic-trade-authorization-understanding-how-it-may-work-for-you-09-30-2013/

2. Kevin Wolf, Assistant Secretary of Commerce for Export Administration, Bureau of Industry and Security, Department of Commerce, *Training Slides: Implementation of Export Control Reform,* Last revised November 14, 2014. Available at www.bis.gov

3. William Arvin, Senior Export Policy Analyst, Regulatory Policy Division, Bureau of Industry and Security, Department of Commerce, *Briefing Slides: License Exception STA*, July 11, 2012, Available at https://www.bis.doc.gov/index.php/forms-documents/compliance-training/export-administration-regulations-training/596-license-exception-sta/file

4. See Stricker with Albright, *U.S. Export Control Reform: Impacts and Implications for Controlling the Spread of Proliferation-Sensitive Goods and Technologies–A Policy Document for the New President and Congress* (Washington, D.C.: Institute for Science and International Security, May 2017).

5. Due to its special status and subsequent difficulties in deriving its scores, Taiwan is excluded from the following statistics.

CHAPTER 16
NORTH KOREAN SANCTIONS AND THE PPI RANKINGS

In its efforts to further its nuclear, missile, and conventional military programs, North Korea seeks to undermine international sanctions and the export control laws of other countries. It has long attempted to find sympathetic governments or countries with weak or nonexistent export controls that will supply these programs or be more conducive to military and commercial cooperation. North Korea also targets states that are otherwise strong enforcers of export controls and uses deceptive methods, such as front companies or actors to bypass these countries' export control laws. To better understand North Korea's strategies and methods to defeat sanctions, the Institute collected and analyzed North Korea's procurement activities as reported in United Nations Panel of Experts reports from March 2014 to September 2017.[1] A total of 49 countries were found to be complicit in various forms of violations of UNSC sanctions resolutions on North Korea. Using the PPI, we considered these 49 countries in terms of 1) their overall ranking in the index; 2) the rigorousness of their export control legislation; and 3) their Ability to Prevent Proliferation Financing.

MILITARY-RELATED SANCTIONS, ALLEGED OR PROVEN

Thirteen governments were found to be involved in military related cases of North Korean sanctions violations, including: Angola, Cuba, Democratic Republic of the Congo, Eritrea, Iran, Mozambique, Myanmar, Namibia, Sri Lanka, Syria, Uganda, and the United Republic of Tanzania. Egypt is included because it reportedly received a shipment of arms from North Korea.[2] In some cases, these mostly undemocratic regimes received military training from North Korea; in others, they received or exported military related equipment to or from North Korea. This includes North Korea's alleged export of surface-to-air missiles or related equipment to at least two African countries.[3]

The overall PPI scores of these 13 countries are low. The mean for these countries is 254 points out of 1,300 total points. In the PPI, a sufficient strategic export control system in Tiers Two and Three typically would require a score of at least 650 points. The highest scoring country received only 40 percent of all possible points (504 out of a possible 1,300). The PPI scores are shown in Figure 16.1.

Eleven of these 13 countries have inadequate export control legislation according to the PPI's definitions (see below). Six of these countries have barely any export control legislation. This is shown in the pie chart in Figure 16.2.

Total PPI scores of countries involved in military related cases of NK's sanctions violations

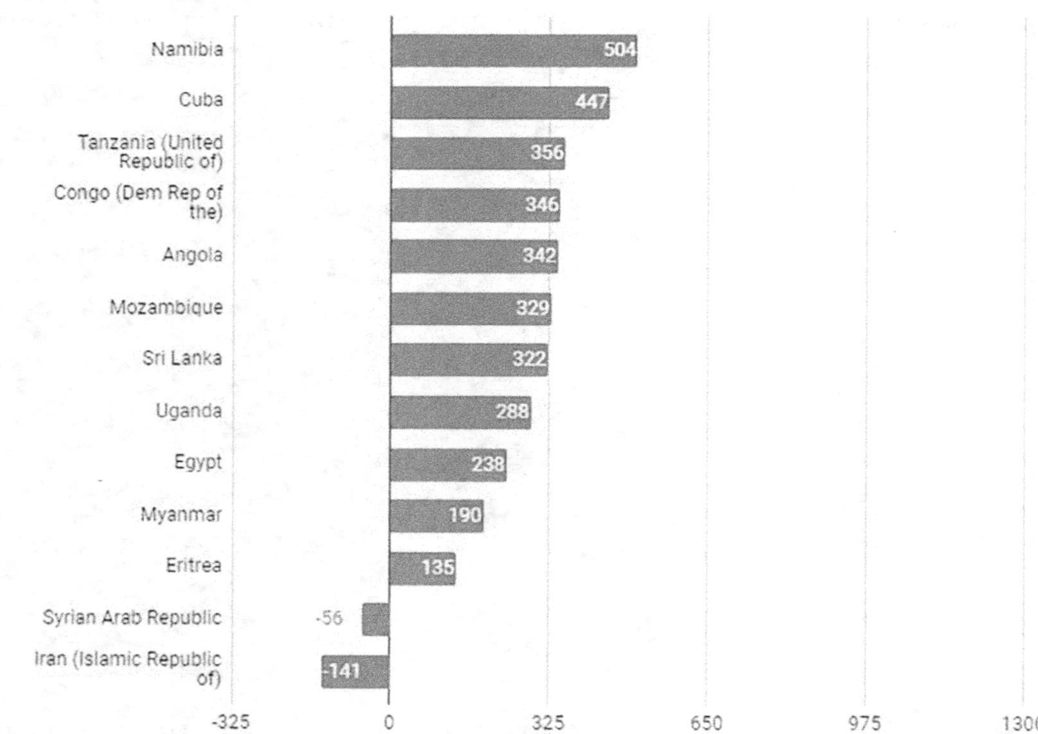

Figure 16.1. All 13 countries received less than 50 percent of the possible 1,300 points. Six received less than 25 percent. The mean is 254 points out of 1,300 points.

Comprehensiveness of export control legislation of countries involved in military related violations of NK UNSC resolutions

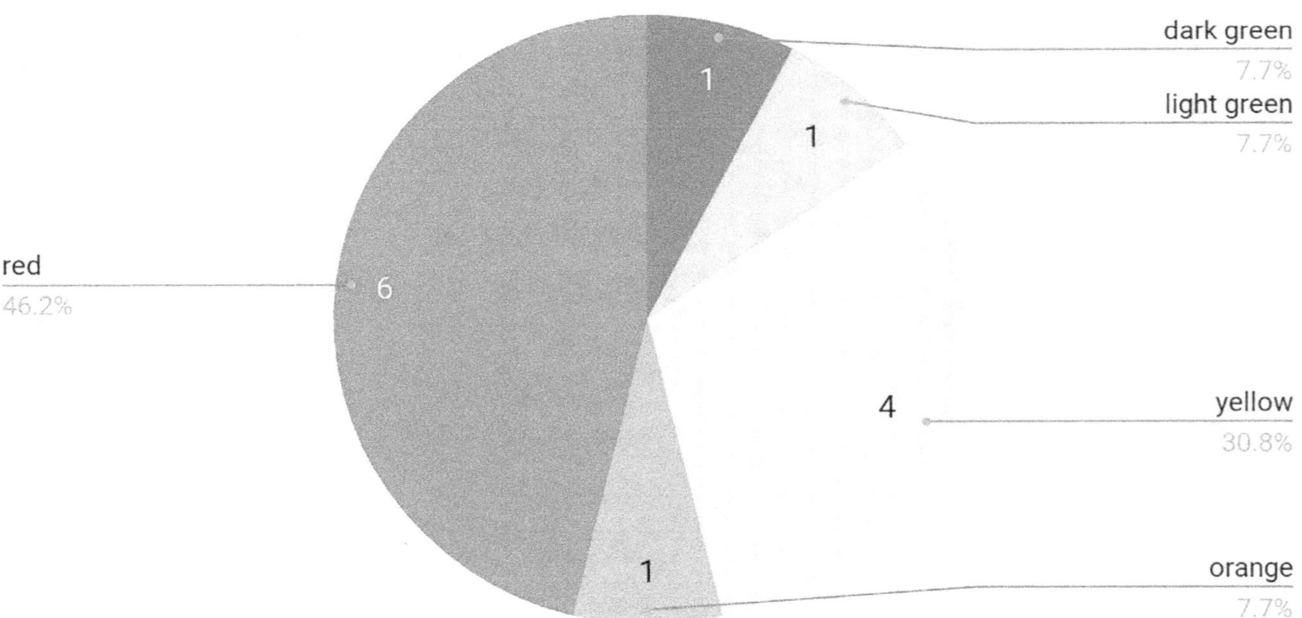

Figure 16.2. Six out of the 13 countries in this category have barely any or no export control legislation (Red color designation). The legislation color key described qualitatively and in brief is: **Dark Green**- legislation is comprehensive; **Light Green**- legislation is somewhat comprehensive; **Yellow**- legislation is deficient; **Orange**- legislation has serious deficiencies; and **Red**- legislation is non-existent or severely deficient. See Chapter 3 for legislative categories.

HIGH CORRUPTION AMONG THESE 13 COUNTRIES

Also noteworthy is that all 13 countries do poorly on the Corruption Perceptions Index, which ranks 176 countries on a scale from 1 to 176, where a ranking of 176 is most corrupt.[4] The above 13 countries have an average rank of 127 in the CPI. None of them ranks above 50. All except two countries rank in the bottom half of the index, and eight out of the 13 countries rank in the bottom third.

OTHER ALLEGED SANCTIONS VIOLATIONS

Based on the project's survey of recent UN Panel of Experts reports, a range of countries were reported as involved in other violations of North Korean UNSC sanctions, as outlined below. These alleged and proven violations were organized into three broad areas, namely non-military-related cases, imports of sanctioned goods and minerals from North Korea, and activities associated with the re-flagging of vessels and providing other assistance for shipments. In total, 44 countries, including all but five of the 13 countries with military-related violations above, were identified as involved in violations in these three other areas. Some countries had multiple violations, although the total number for each country was not tabulated.

Nineteen countries were involved in non-military related cases of sanctions violations that involved facilitating front companies, financial transactions, and other business activities. These countries include Angola, Brazil, Bulgaria, China, Egypt, Ethiopia, Germany, India, Iran, Malaysia, Namibia, Poland, Romania, Russia, Singapore, Sri Lanka, Sudan, Syria, and the United Arab Emirates.

Eighteen countries were involved in imports of sanctioned goods and minerals from North Korea, including: Barbados, China, Costa Rica, Egypt, El Salvador, France, Germany, India, Indonesia, Iran, Ireland, Malaysia, Mexico, Pakistan, Philippines, Sri Lanka, Syria, and Viet Nam.

To transport these illicitly traded technologies, goods, and minerals to and from North Korea, North Korea often relies on receiving shipping assistance from other countries. Twenty countries associated with re-flagging of vessels and providing other assistance for shipments include: Brazil, Cambodia, China, Egypt, Fiji, Greece, Japan, Kiribati, Malaysia,

Marshall Islands, Mongolia, Palau, Panama, Peru, Russia, Sierra Leone, Singapore, Tanzania, Thailand, and Togo.

Of those countries, Cambodia, Marshall Islands, Mongolia, and Panama, are identified as Flags of Convenience (FOC) by the International Transport Workers' Federation (ITF). ITF defines a Flag of Convenience as, "one that flies the flag of a country other than the country of ownership," leading to little oversight and much leeway to break laws and regulations.[5] Flags of Convenience have just recently been declared a national security risk by the Australian government, because "there are features of FOC registration, regulation and practice that organized crime syndicates or terrorist groups may seek to exploit."[6]

The UN reports surveyed by the project list other sanctions violations that are not included in this analysis because the participation of the countries appears entirely inadvertent. The following 13 countries and territories were targeted by North Korea to procure equipment with potential military applications: Canada, China, Czech Republic, Denmark, Egypt, Hong Kong, Japan, Malaysia, Russia, Singapore, Switzerland, Taiwan, and the United States.

TAKING STOCK

In total, 49 countries were identified as involved in sanctions violations in one of the four areas discussed above. Some countries had multiple violations, although the total number for each country was not tabulated.

These 49 countries have a mean score in the PPI of 458 out of 1,300 points, again a relatively low average and lower than the overall PPI average of 486 points. Thirty nine out of the 49 countries scored fewer than 50 percent of the overall points assigned in the PPI, a mark of less than sufficient export controls, and ten scored less than 25 percent (see Figure 16.3). Figure 16.4 shows the PPI score distribution, where there is a maximum peak in the 300-499 point intervals. This peak reflects that many of the countries involved in sanctions violations in general lack sufficient strategic export controls. Moreover, it should be noted that there are many other countries that have received similar or lower PPI scores, making them potentially vulnerable to North Korean exploitation.

Sixteen of the 49 countries are in Tier One; 17 are in Tier Two; and 16 are in Tier Three (see Table 16.1). The average scores of this subset of countries in Tiers One and Three are considerably lower than the Tier averages. For Tier One, the averages of the subset and the entire Tier are 604 and 710 points, respectively. For Tier Three, the averages of the subset and the entire Tier are 336 and 420 points, respectively. For Tier Two, the averages are comparable, 434 vs. 420 points. Similar trends are apparent in the average rankings of these countries in each tier.

Half of the 49 countries that were involved in violating UNSC resolutions on North Korea have poor export control legislation, and many of the countries that do have sufficient legislation have a high degree of corruption relative to their peers, as measured by the CPI. Figure 16.5 shows that out of 49 countries, 26 have inadequate export control legislation, categorized as Red, Orange, or Yellow colors.

In total, 20 countries out of the 49 involved in violations of UNSC resolutions on North Korea have Dark Green color-coded export control legislation, which means their legislation is judged as comprehensive. However, many of the 20 countries listed show a higher degree of corruption on the CPI compared to other Dark Green countries. Their average CPI rank is 63 out of 176, with a median of 63. For all Dark Green countries in the PPI the average CPI rank is 54 and the median is 47.

On the issue of proliferation financing, 18 of the 49 countries on the list rank below 150 or in the bottom fourth of countries. The average rank of the countries in the super criterion on the Ability to Prevent Proliferation Financing is 117 out of a total rank of 200, where the larger numbers are worse. As can be seen in Figure 16.6, no country received more than 50 percent of the available points. This means that many of these 49 countries do poorly on preventing proliferation financing.

Total PPI scores of countries involved in violations of UNSC resolutions on North Korea

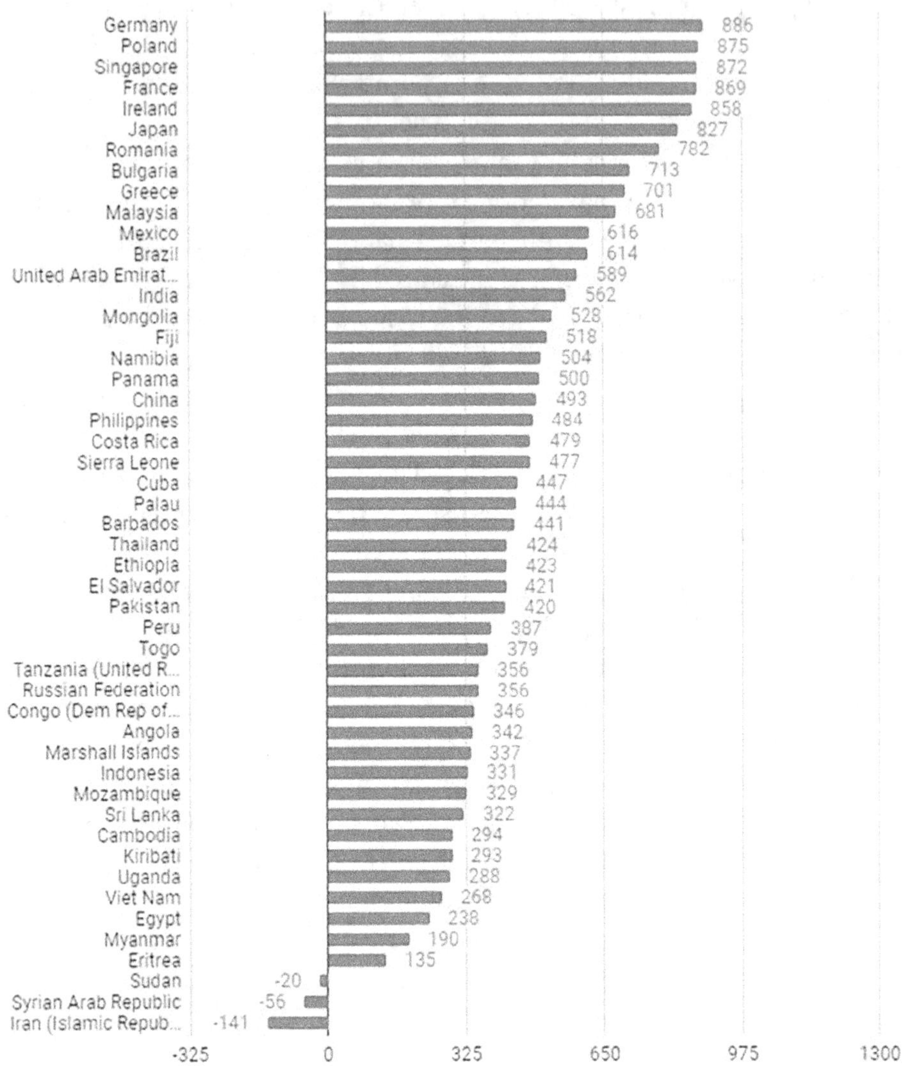

Figure 16.3. Overall PPI performance of countries involved in violating UNSC resolutions sanctions on North Korea. Out of the available 1,300 points, the great majority of countries did not reach the halfway marker of 650 points. (This figure excludes 13 countries that were targeted by North Korea using illicit procurement schemes to procure equipment with potential military applications).

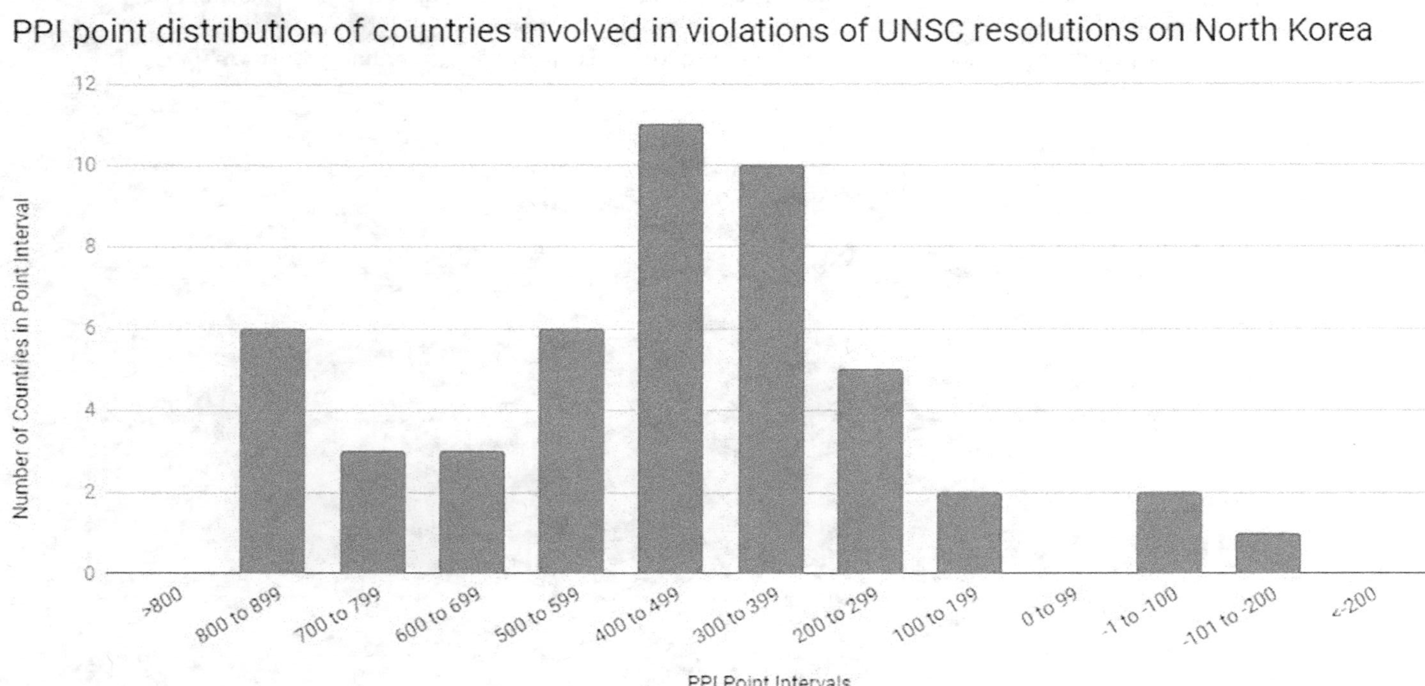

Figure 16.4. Distribution of PPI scores for the 49 countries that were involved in violating UNSC sanctions on North Korea.

Comprehensiveness of export control legislation of countries involved in violations of UNSC resolutions on North Korea

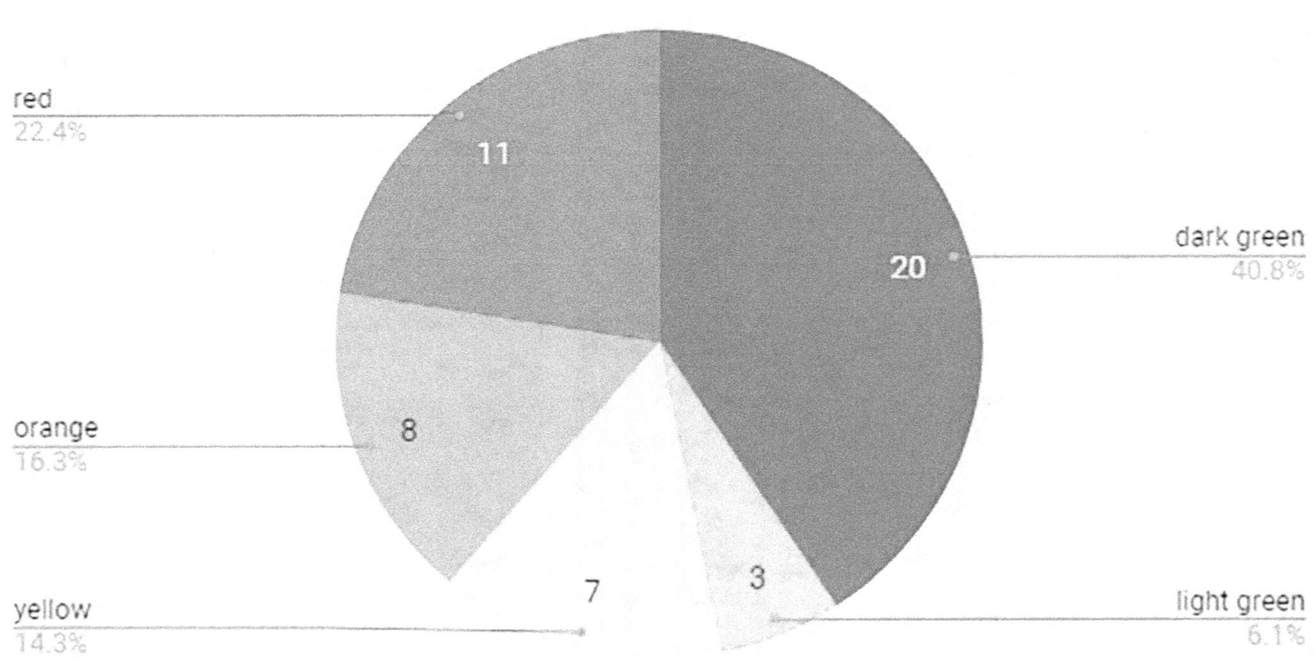

Figure 16.5. Comprehensiveness of export control legislation of all 49 countries identified as involved in violations of UNSC sanctions resolutions on North Korea. Anything but Green is considered inadequate legislation in the PPI. (This figure excludes 13 countries that were targeted by North Korea using illicit procurement schemes to procure equipment with potential military applications).

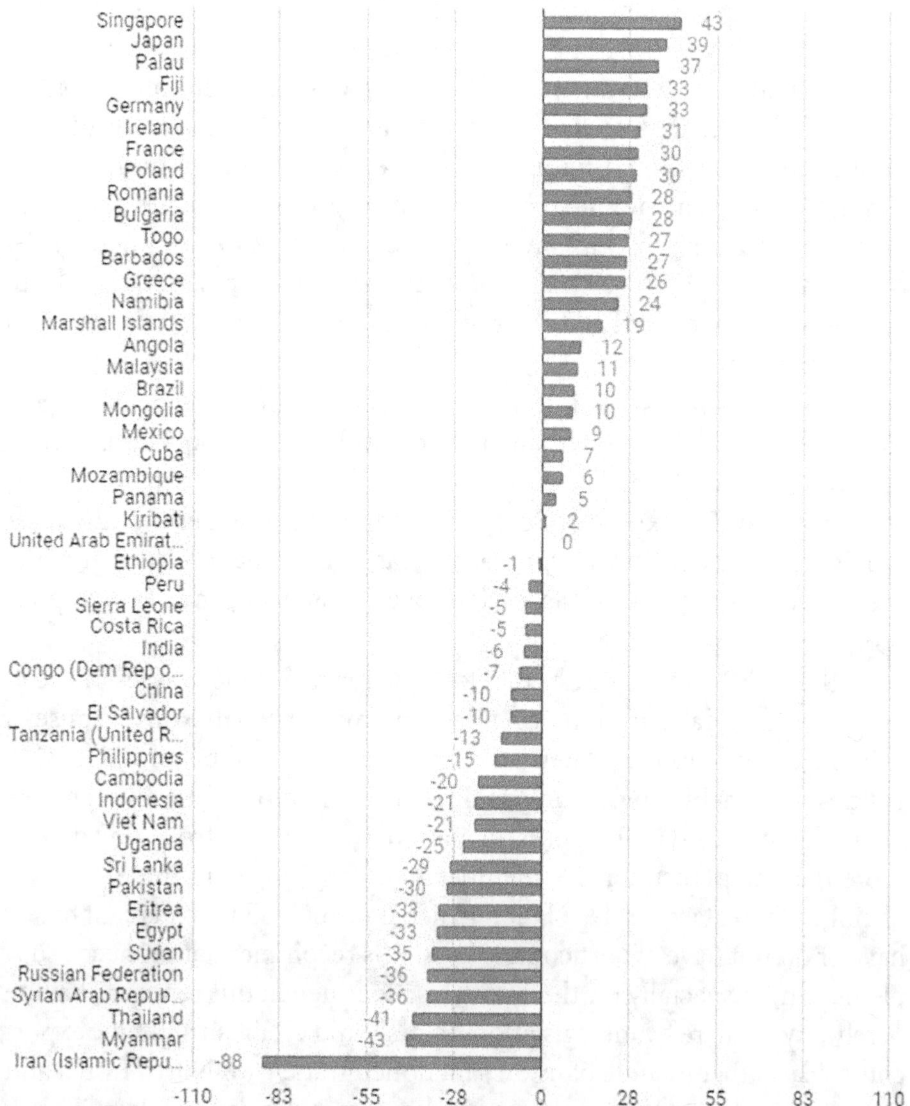

Figure 16.6. Countries that violated UNSC sanctions on North Korea in terms of their Ability to Prevent Proliferation Financing. In this assessment for the PPI, countries could receive a maximum raw score of 110 points.

RECOMMENDATIONS

All countries should fully implement UNSC sanctions on North Korea and limit military, scientific, or commercial cooperation with the country. The UN Security Council and major countries should accelerate the designation of individuals and entities that violate UNSC resolutions on North Korea. Countries that have engaged with North Korea in arms trade and military training should be urged to expel North Korean military personnel and suspend any further cooperation. Other countries should be discouraged from starting any such cooperation. As recommended by the United States, and given the wide-scale sanctions violations by North Korea, countries should end their non-humanitarian-essential trade with North Korea.

The effectiveness of international pressure in achieving this goal can be seen in the case of Uganda, where military and police forces had received training from the North Korean army for years. Nonetheless, recently Uganda "expelled North Korean military experts and representatives of North Korean companies…as African nations face growing pressure to comply with UN sanctions over Pyongyang's nuclear weapons program."[7]

The UN Panel of Experts on North Korea has made a series of excellent recommendations in their reports on limiting North Korea's abuse of shipping, transshipping, and financial transactions, and better identifying entities for sanctioning.[8] One panel recommendation urges all members to implement catch-all clauses in national export controls. Given that more than 50 percent of UN member states are judged in the PPI as not having sufficient export legislation in general, and about 25 percent barely have or do not have export control laws, this recommendation needs supplementing. Especially for the countries identified in this report as having barely any or no relevant legislation, they should establish strategic export control laws that include bans on sanctioned trade with North Korea and other sanctioned states, as the panel also recommends (see also Chapter 12: Recommendations for Tiers Two and Three countries).

Based on our analysis, we offer several other targeted recommendations relevant to export control implementation:

- Countries that have violated the UNSC resolutions with respect to financing should turn to the Financial Action Task Force, its regional bodies and guidelines, and specifically ask for assistance in implementing FATF recommendation 7 as laid out in its updated 2012 framework. This recommendation states: "Countries should implement targeted financial sanctions to comply with United Nations Security Council resolutions relating to the prevention, suppression and disruption of proliferation of weapons of mass destruction and its financing. These resolutions require countries to freeze without delay the funds or other assets of, and to ensure that no funds and other assets are made available, directly or indirectly, to or for the benefit of, any person or entity designated by, or under the authority of, the United Nations Security Council under Chapter VII of the Charter of the United Nations."[9]

- Countries that imported large quantities of minerals or ore or other controlled goods should increase physical inspections of incoming shipments, especially from ships under Flags of Convenience or other flags that have been used by North Korea before.

- Countries that have provided shipment assistance to North Korea should re-evaluate and, if violations exist, ban North Korea's access to their flags and registries.

Overall, the results indicate that in pursuing its banned or illegal activities North Korea often cooperates with or otherwise exploits countries with weak or nonexistent export and proliferation financing controls and those that suffer on average from more corruption than other countries. Although a range of remedies are needed to fix the poor performance of many of the countries identified in this report as involved in sanctions violations, the creation of punitive measures is an effective means to accelerate more compliant behavior in the short term not only in these countries but among all countries that may do business with North Korea.

TIER ONE COUNTRIES	TIER TWO COUNTRIES	TIER THREE COUNTRIES
Germany	Singapore	Fiji
Poland	Malaysia	Sierra Leone
France	United Arab Emirates	Cuba
Ireland	Mongolia	Palau
Japan	Namibia	Barbados
Romania	Panama	El Salvador
Bulgaria	Philippines	Togo
Greece	Costa Rica	Congo (Dem Rep of the)
Mexico	Thailand	Angola
Brazil	Ethiopia	Marshall Islands
India	Peru	Mozambique
China	Tanzania (United	Cambodia
Pakistan	Republic of)	Kiribati
Russian Federation	Indonesia	Myanmar
Egypt	Sri Lanka	Eritrea
Iran (Islamic Republic of)	Uganda	Sudan
	Viet Nam	
	Syrian Arab Republic	

Table 16.1. The 49 countries arranged in terms of their tiers, and within each tier, their rank, from better to worse.

NOTES

1. UN Panel of Experts reports 2014–2017. All reports can be found on the website of the United Nations Security Council Subsidiary Organs: 1718 Sanctions Committee (DPRK), Panel of Experts reports, https://www.un.org/sc/suborg/en/sanctions/1718/panel_experts/reports

2. Joby Warrick, "A North Korean ship was seized off Egypt with a huge cache of weapons destined for a surprising buyer," *The Washington Post,* October 1, 2017, https://www.washingtonpost.com/world/national-security/a-north-korean-ship-was-seized-off-egypt-with-a-huge-cache-of-weapons-destined-for-a-surprising-buyer/2017/10/01/d9a4e06e-a46d-11e7-b14f-f41773cd5a14_story.html?tid=a_inl&utm_term=.b879ddf1b124

3. They were Mozambique and Tanzania. See http://www.un.org/ga/search/view_doc.asp?symbol=S/2017/742

4. Transparency International, *Corruption Perceptions Index 2016,* https://www.transparency.org/news/feature/corruption_perceptions_index_2016#table

5. International Transport Workers' Federation, "Flags of Convenience," Transport Sectors, http://www.itfglobal.org/en/transport-sectors/seafarers/in-focus/flags-of-convenience-campaign/ (Accessed October 2017).

6. International Transport Workers' Federation, "Australian Senate Inquiry Finds Flag of Convenience Shipping Poses Serious Risks To National Security," ITF Press Releases, July 19, 2017, http://www.itfglobal.org/en/news-events/press-releases/2017/july/australian-senate-inquiry-finds-flag-of-convenience-shipping-poses-serious-risks-to-national-security/

7. Rodney Muhumuza, "Uganda expels North Korea military experts over UN sanctions," Associated Press. October 20, 2017, https://apnews.com/9dbf7a31e93e414f8db339021be6d30f

8. UN Panel of Experts reports 2014–2017. All reports can be found on the website of the United Nations Security Council Subsidiary Organs: 1718 Sanctions Committee (DPRK), Panel of Experts reports, https://www.un.org/sc/suborg/en/sanctions/1718/panel_experts/reports

9. 2012 FATF Recommendation 7: Targeted financial sanctions related to proliferation. See: http://www.fatf-gafi.org/media/fatf/documents/recommendations/pdfs/FATF_Recommendations.pdf

CHAPTER 17
INCARCERATION PENALTIES FOR EXPORT CONTROL VIOLATIONS

Criminal or civil penalties for export control violations can serve as an effective deterrent to potential proliferators. The effectiveness of that deterrent is related to the length of incarceration risked by an individual for violating export controls, where a longer potential prison term would typically provide a greater deterrent against individuals breaking the law. The PPI team determined on a country-by-country basis whether people convicted of export control violations can be incarcerated and the potential length of incarceration.

This assessment first had to identify which countries have a strategic trade control (STC) system in place, since without such a system of laws, relevant violations or potential prison terms cannot be identified in that country's penal code. In total, prison sentences from STC violations were identified for approximately one fourth of all countries considered in the PPI, based on internet searches of individual countries' penal codes. Additional countries with STCs have criminal penalties that include incarceration, but they were not all identified here.

FINDINGS AND ANALYSIS

The potential length of incarceration varies across this subset of countries. Some countries, such as the United States, can impose sentences of decades, although in practice, most receive below ten years imprisonment, and below five years is most common. Certain countries with strong export controls, such as those categorized as Green in the PPI assessment on Legislation, nonetheless show a trend of relatively short prison sentences of often less than five years, or even less than one year, for export control violations. This variation in sentencing was striking in Europe, where sentencing varies more widely than expected for a trade zone sharing common export control laws. Although legislation in the European Union is mostly unified, sentencing guidelines or practices seem not to be uniform. Defining penalties for violations of the European strategic trade control on dual-use items (Council Regulation (EC) No 428/2009 of 5 May 2009) is done autonomously by each country. Violating this law, for example, by exporting without a license when one is required, can lead to prison sentences of only three years or less in several countries,[1] including in Cyprus,[2] Denmark,[3] Greece,[4] Luxembourg,[5] Portugal[6] and Sweden.[7] On the other hand, in Austria,[8] Germany[9], Slovakia,[10] Slovenia,[11] and the United Kingdom,[12] relatively long prison sentences of five to 10 years are applied, with longer sentences for severe cases. Hungary has a short prison sentence for minor or unintentional cases, but imposes a long imprisonment for severe cases. For many countries, if an export violation also entails proven assistance to a nuclear weapon or other WMD program, sentences can be longer.[13]

The results show that tougher sentencing is compatible with having a high level of exports. Major export economies such as Britain and Germany have the longest potential periods of incarceration within the European Union.

The reasons for the variation in sentencing across the European Union were not determined, but a question is whether the countries with shorter potential sentencing do not sufficiently deter those who would violate export controls. In general, EU countries with shorter potential prison sentences tend to rank lower in the PPI than EU countries with longer potential prison sentences. All the countries mentioned here are in Tier One, which includes in total 57 countries. Table 17.1 and Figure 17.1 show that countries with longer prison sentences tend to rank better within this Tier. Their average rank is 9, while the average rank for countries with shorter prison sentences is 21. The trend can also be seen in these countries' Adequacy of Enforcement (Figure 17.2). The average rank for countries with longer prison sentences is 13, while the average for countries with shorter prison sentences is 27.

LONGER PRISON SENTENCES	TIER ONE RANK	SHORTER PRISON SENTENCES	TIER ONE RANK
United States	1	Cyprus	35
Austria	16	Denmark	12
Germany	11	Greece	37
Slovakia	6	Luxembourg	29
Slovenia	7	Portugal	2
Hungary	15	Sweden	10

Table 17.1. Tier rankings for countries with longer prison sentences for strategic trade control violations compared to ranks of countries with shorter sentences.

Countries' ranking in Tier One in relation to the length of prison sentencing for STC violation

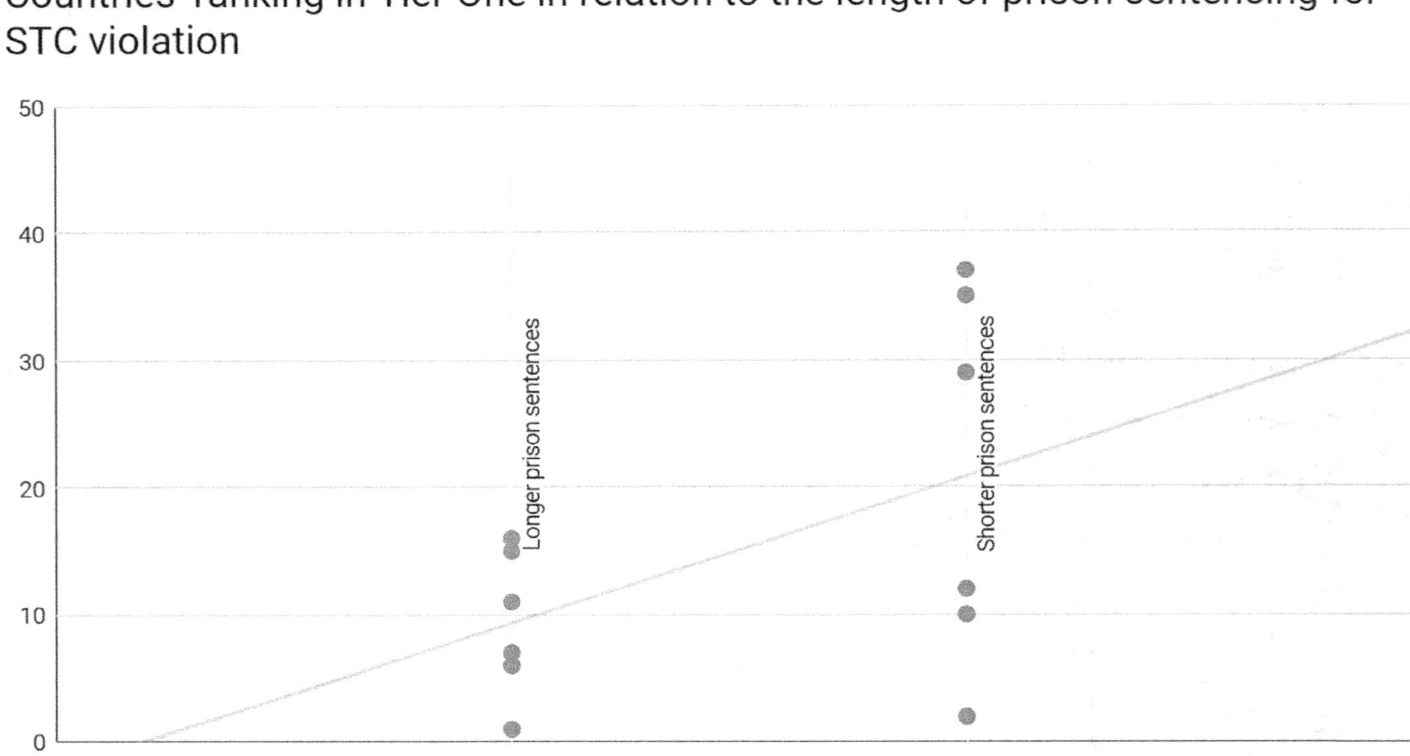

Figure 17.1. All the countries mentioned are in Tier One, which includes in total 57 countries. Countries with longer prison sentencing for strategic trade control violations tend to rank better within this tier. Their average rank is 9, while the average rank for countries with shorter prison sentences is 21.

Countries' ranking in Tier One in Enforcement in relation to the length of prison sentencing for STC violation

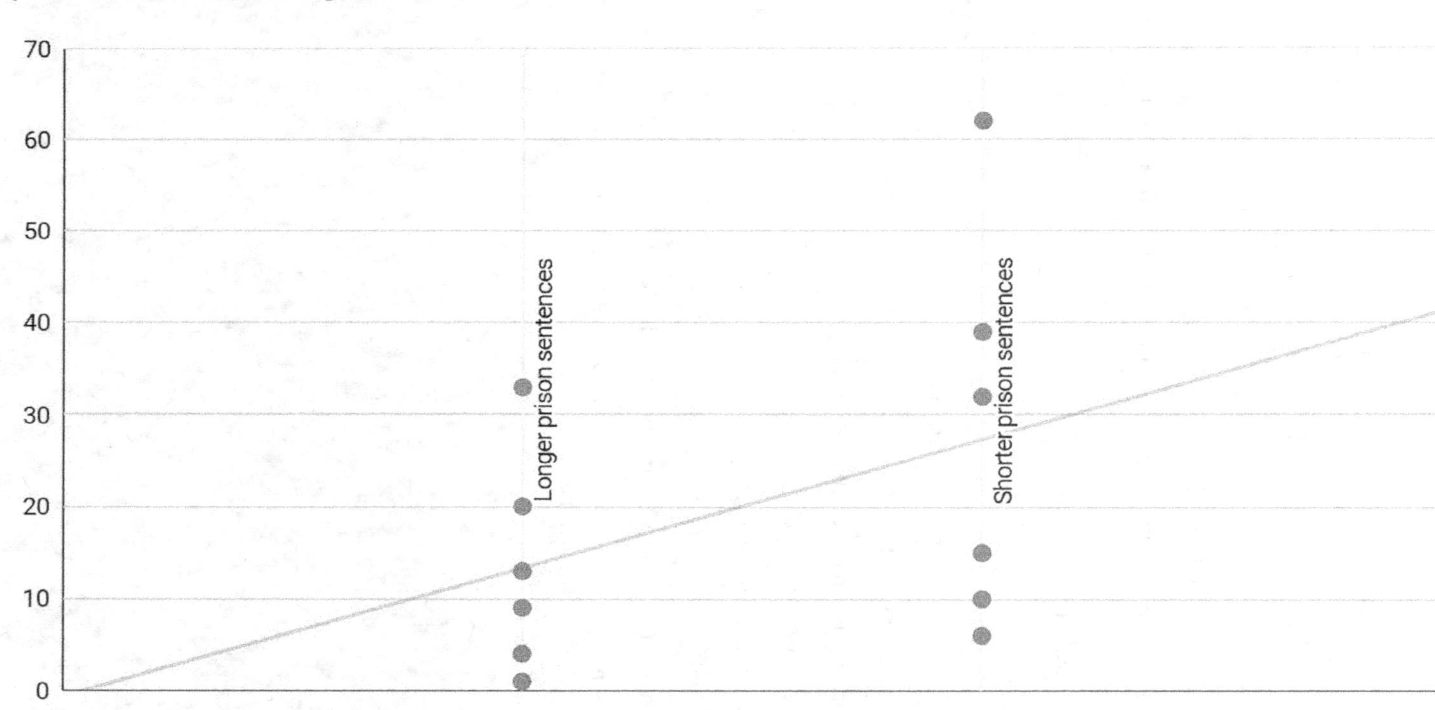

Figure 17.2. A similar trend as in Figure 17.1 can also be seen in these countries' Adequacy of Enforcement. The average rank for countries with longer prison sentences is 13, while the average for countries with shorter prison sentences is 27.

NOTES

1. The length of incarceration for EU countries considered here is from Quentin Michel, "The European Union Export Control Regime: Comment of the Legislation: article-by-article," Liege University, Belgium, March 2011, https://csis-prod.s3.amazonaws.com/s3fs-public/legacy_files/files/attachments/130828_3EUExportControlRegimeCommentary.pdf

2. Imprisonment of up to 3 years.

3. Fines or up to 2 years imprisonment. Imprisonment of up to 6 years in aggravated circumstances.

4. Imprisonment of up to 2 years.

5. Imprisonment of up to 1 year.

6. Imprisonment of up to 2 years (Legislation currently being revised with views to harmonization with community legislation).

7. Fines, imprisonment of 2 years and in severe cases of up to 6 years.

8. Fines and imprisonment of up to 10 years.

9. Prison sentence of up to 15 years.

10. Imprisonment of up to 8 years.

11. Prison sentences of up to 5-10 years.

12. Imprisonment of up to 10 years and/or unlimited fine.

13. Prison sentences are between 2-8 years and in qualified cases up to 5-10 years (15 years for WMD-related criminal acts).

CHAPTER 18
EXPORT CONTROL LEGISLATION IN THE NON-ALIGNED MOVEMENT (NAM) VERSUS NON-NAM COUNTRIES

The Non-Aligned Movement is a group of about 120 countries. It was set up in 1961 by countries that sought not to align with one of the superpowers involved in the Cold War, the United States and the Union of Soviet Socialist Republics (USSR), and instead sought to pursue independently or collectively their own policies.[1] Some of the NAM countries have historically resisted the implementation of stronger export controls, both nationally and internationally. Reasons for this range from a desire to maintain independence from regulations imposed by Security Council members or great powers, to preferences for freer trade, to aspirations to use stronger non-proliferation obligations as leverage against nuclear-weapon states to compel them to reduce nuclear stockpiles or disarm before NAM countries undertake additional obligations. Several members have sought to acquire sensitive goods illegally for nuclear weapons efforts or unsafeguarded nuclear programs and likely have opposed export controls as a result of those activities. The PPI decided to assess the NAM countries as a group on the sufficiency of their export control legislation in comparison with non-NAM countries.

The countries that are part of NAM include the following:

Afghanistan, Algeria, Angola, Antigua and Barbuda, Azerbaijan, Bahamas, Bahrain, Bangladesh, Barbados, Belarus, Belize, Benin, Bhutan, Bolivia, Botswana, Brunei Darussalam, Burkina Faso, Burundi, Cambodia, Cameroon, Cape Verde, Central African Republic, Chad, Chile, Colombia, Comoros, Congo (Dem Rep of the), Congo (Rep of the), Côte d'Ivoire, Cuba, DPRK, Djibouti, Dominica, Dominican Republic, Ecuador, Egypt, Equatorial Guinea, Eritrea, Ethiopia, Fiji, Gabon, Gambia, Ghana, Grenada, Guatemala, Guinea, Guinea-Bissau, Guyana, Haiti, Honduras, India, Indonesia, Iran, Iraq, Jamaica, Jordan, Kenya, Kuwait, Laos, Lebanon, Lesotho, Liberia, Libya, Madagascar, Malawi, Malaysia, Maldives, Mali, Mauritania, Mauritius, Mongolia, Morocco, Mozambique, Myanmar, Namibia, Nepal, Nicaragua, Niger, Nigeria, Oman, Pakistan, Palestine, Panama, Papua New Guinea, Peru, Philippines, Qatar, Rwanda, Saint Kitts and Nevis, Saint Lucia, Saint Vincent and the Grenadines, São Tomé and Príncipe, Saudi Arabia, Senegal, Seychelles, Sierra Leone, Singapore, Somalia, South Africa, Sri Lanka, Sudan, Suriname, Swaziland, Syrian Arab Republic, Tanzania, Thailand, Timor Leste, Togo, Trinidad and Tobago, Tunisia, Turkmenistan, Uganda, United Arab Emirates, Uzbekistan, Vanuatu, Venezuela, Viet Nam, Yemen, Zambia, and Zimbabwe.

FINDINGS AND ANALYSIS

Of the countries that belong to the NAM, the PPI color-coding of legislation shows that only 17 percent have adequate export control legislation compared to 80 percent of the 80 countries or territories that do not belong to the NAM (see Figures 18.1 and 18.2).

With regard to the scores in Legislation super criterion, approximately 16.67 percent of NAM countries achieved two-thirds or higher of the possible points in that category; 31.67 percent received more than half but less than two-thirds of the possible points, and the remaining 51.67 percent of countries received less than half of possible points. Comparatively, 75 percent of the 80 non-NAM countries evaluated by the PPI achieved two-thirds of the possible points or higher for the Legislation super criterion; 7.5 percent received less than two-thirds but more than half of the possible points, and 13 percent received less than half of the possible points.

In some respects, these findings are not terribly surprising given many of its members' arguments against strengthening export controls.

The relative lack of strong export control legislation among NAM countries can in part be attributed to this view; however, due to the serious and potential danger of nuclear dual-use and other strategic goods to be misused or proliferated, NAM countries should expand the legal basis of their export controls from which they can then increase their capacity to monitor and enforce controls on strategic trade. Non-NAM countries that have close relations with NAM countries should encourage stronger export control legislation and the broadening of their overall legal basis for monitoring and detecting strategic trade.

Significantly, one of greatest violators of nations' export control laws, namely Iran, is a leader in NAM in opposing export controls. In this sense, the "thief" is making the rules, and Iran's ranking and scoring shows just how abysmal its export control system is. Iran should not have influence over the decisions of international law-abiding NAM countries, and the NAM needs to rectify this situation.

Non-Aligned Movement Countries and Extent of Export Control Legislation

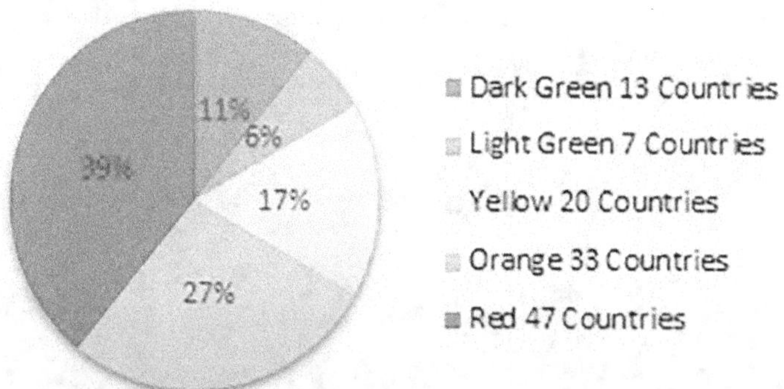

Figure 18.1. The pie chart shows that the majority of NAM countries lack sufficient export control legislation.

Non-NAM Countries and Extent of Export Control Legislation

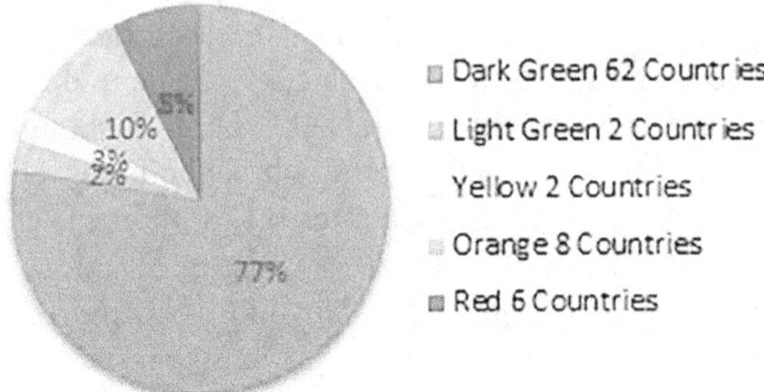

Figure 18.2. The pie chart shows that the great majority of non-NAM countries have sufficient export control legislation.

NOTE

1. Nuclear Threat Initiative, "Non-Aligned Movement (NAM)," last updated April 14, 2017. http://www.nti.org/learn/treaties-and-regimes/non-aligned-movement-nam/

CHAPTER 19
NATIONAL EXPORT CONTROL LEGISLATION VERSUS CORRUPTION

Corruption can heavily disrupt export control implementation and enforcement in a country. Companies engaged in exports may think they can simply ignore legal export requirements, believing that there is little likelihood of being investigated or prosecuted. This chapter seeks to better understand the relationship between national export control legislation and corruption, and in particular, the relationship between corruption and those countries that have minimal or no export controls. As before, corruption is measured using the 2016 Corruption Perceptions Index, or CPI, by Transparency International.[1] Countries that rank low in the CPI tend to be "plagued by untrustworthy and badly functioning public institutions like the police and judiciary. Even where anti-corruption laws are on the books, in practice they're often skirted or ignored. People frequently face situations of bribery and extortion, rely on basic services that have been undermined by the misappropriation of funds, and confront official indifference when seeking redress from authorities that are on the take."[2] In such an environment, export controls are unlikely to be effectively encoded into laws or implemented.

In order to determine the credibility of export control regimes and to target countries more likely to pose transshipment, smuggling, proliferation financing, and black-market risks, the PPI team determined which countries ranked in the bottom half of the CPI and compared them to the quality of their legislation, where the legislation has been categorized into five levels of apparent comprehensiveness of their control lists, as discussed in Chapter 3 and briefly summarized below. Doing so allows for a determination that corrupt countries have little to no legal basis from which to enforce export controls and those which lack export controls are also corrupt.

- **Green (legislation is comprehensive):** This category counted 75 countries.
- **Light Green (legislation is somewhat comprehensive):** This category counted 9 countries.
- **Yellow (legislation is deficient):** This category counted 22 countries.
- **Orange (legislation has serious deficiencies):** This category counted 41 countries.
- **Red (legislation is non-existent or severely deficient):** This category counted 53 countries.

FINDINGS AND ANALYSIS

There is a general relationship between a country's corruption perception and the extent of its export control legislation with regard to nuclear and other strategic commodities. Countries with more expansive legislation tend to be less prone to corruption, or alternatively, there is a positive correlation of poor export controls with higher levels of corruption (see Figures 19.1 and 19.2).

This leads to questions about the number of countries that are in the bottom half of the CPI and have less than adequate legislation, in this case taken as countries with Orange or Red levels of legislation. The following characterizes these countries.

Thirty-four countries rank in the bottom half of the CPI and have Red category legislation, from less to more corrupt:[3]

Columbia, Liberia, Maldives, Egypt, Guyana, Mali, Togo, Djibouti, Honduras, Iran, Nepal, Papua New Guinea, Guinea, Mozambique, Cameroon, Kenya, Madagascar, Comoros, Zimbabwe, Congo (Democratic Republic of), Burundi, Central African Republic, Chad, Congo

(Republic of the), Haiti, Angola, Eritrea, Guinea-Bissau, Afghanistan, Sudan, DPRK, South Sudan, Yemen, and Somalia.

Nineteen countries rank in the bottom half of the CPI and have Orange category legislation, from less to more corrupt:

Benin, El Salvador, Gabon, Niger, Timor-Leste, Trinidad and Tobago, Cote d'Ivoire, Ethiopia, Bolivia, Venezuela, Dominican Republic, Ecuador, Malawi, Lao People's Democratic Republic, Paraguay, Mauritania, Gambia, Turkmenistan, and the Syrian Arab Republic.

Twenty-two countries rank in the bottom half of the CPI and have Green legislation, from less to more corrupt:

Macedonia, Argentina, Kosovo, Philippines, Thailand, Armenia, Viet Nam, Pakistan, Moldova, Mexico, Azerbaijan, Kazakhstan, Ukraine, Russia, Kyrgyzstan, Lebanon, Myanmar, Tajikistan, Uzbekistan, Cambodia, Iraq, and Libya.

There are in total 75 countries (ignoring any yellow legislation countries), which are in the Red, Orange, or Green legislative categories and in the bottom half of the CPI. They represent roughly 38 percent of 200 countries examined by the PPI.

Nineteen of these 75 countries simultaneously are complicit in UNSC sanctions violations on North Korea: Cambodia, Mexico, Myanmar, Egypt, Congo (Democratic Rep of the), Mozambique, Eritrea, Syrian Arab Republic, Sudan, Togo, Angola, Iran, Russia, Pakistan, Thailand, Togo, Philippines, Ethiopia, and El Salvador. See Chapter 16 for a discussion of countries involved in doing business with North Korea.

With the exception of Malawi, Cameroon, Timor-Leste, Gabon, and Trinidad and Tobago, all of the countries with Red or Orange legislation rank below 100 in the full PPI ranking. Malawi was the only country able to achieve more than 50 percent of the possible total points, and the majority received less than a third of the possible total points (see Figure 19.3). With the exception of Macedonia, Argentina, and Moldova, all of the countries with Green legislation ranked below 50 in the PPI with seven ranking between 50 and 100 and the remaining 12 ranking below 100. None of these Green countries were able to achieve 50 percent of the possible points and half received only one third of the potential number of points (see Figure 19.4).

In general, countries that did poorly in the CPI also did not perform well in the PPI (see Figure 19.5 and 19.6). Thirty-seven of the countries of these 75 countries had negative points in the Ability to Prevent Proliferation Financing super criterion. Only nine of the 75 countries were unable to achieve more than half of potential sub-criteria points for the Adequacy of Enforcement super criterion; only two were able to achieve more than half of the sub-criteria points for the Ability to Monitor and Detect Strategic Trade super criterion. Collectively, these results demonstrate a clear inability to prevent financial proliferation, enforce legislation, or aptly monitor and detect illicit inflows and outflows. Any positive or existing effort to do otherwise is mired by states' relatively high susceptibility to corruption and lack of legal basis from which to combat illicit trade and enforce export controls.

RECOMMENDATIONS

A priority is for the international community to assist efforts in states with Orange and Red category legislation to not only battle corruption, but to draft, implement, and enforce export control legislation, or at least the minimal controls discussed in Chapter 12 for Tiers Two and Three countries. While such efforts are ongoing, countries should avoid doing business in controlled or sensitive goods, including conventional military goods, with high corruption countries that have few or no legal export control laws. Suppliers of sensitive or controlled goods should also be extremely wary of any purported end users of such goods in these countries, as the goods could be used illicitly in these countries, including by criminal or terrorist entities, or transshipped through them to sanctioned states, terrorists, or otherwise sanctioned entities.

As discussed in Chapter 16, any country violating UN Security Council sanctions on North Korea deserves special attention. The international community should actively pressure those countries that fall into the corrupt and poor or non-existent export control legislation categories to stop doing business with North Korea and cut back diplomatic relations. This group represents an even more dubious set of states.

Corruption and Export Control Legislation

Figure 19.1. The 176 countries ranked by the Corruption Perceptions Index of 2016 by the quality of their export control legislation. The legislation color key described qualitatively and in brief is (from right to left on the table): **Dark Green**— legislation is comprehensive; **Light Green**—legislation is somewhat comprehensive; **Yellow**—legislation is deficient; **Orange**—legislation has serious deficiencies; and **Red**—legislation is non-existent or severely deficient.

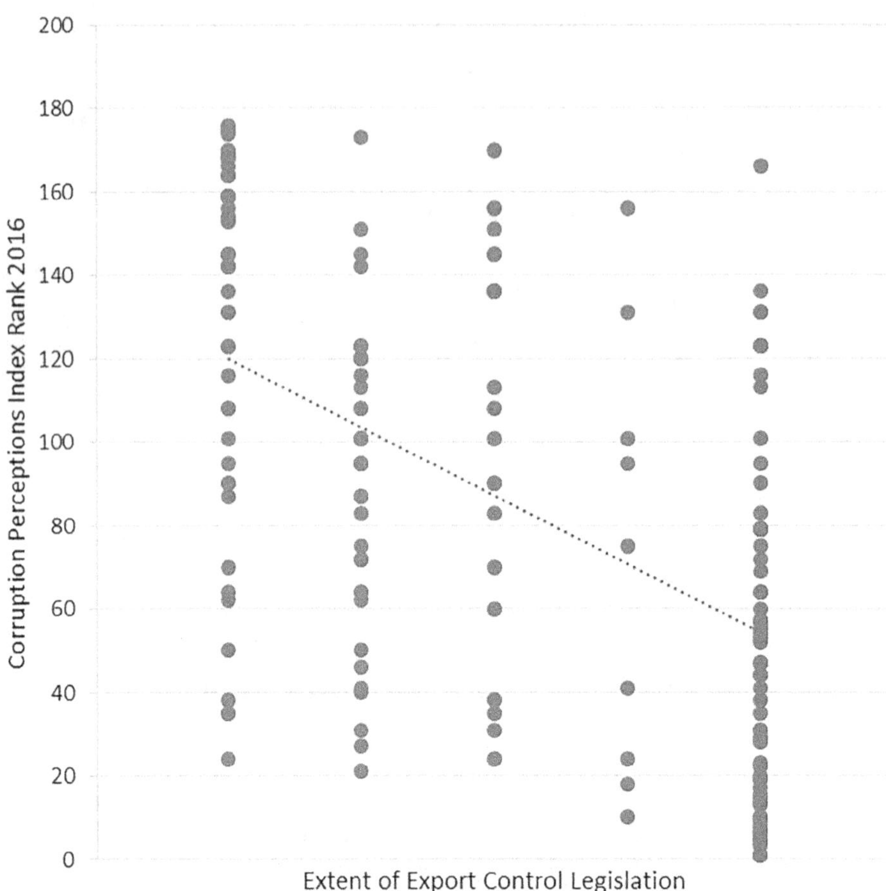

Figure 19.2. The trend line demonstrates the correlation that countries with more extensive legislation tend to be less corrupt. Country color codes are removed and standardized in order to show correlation.

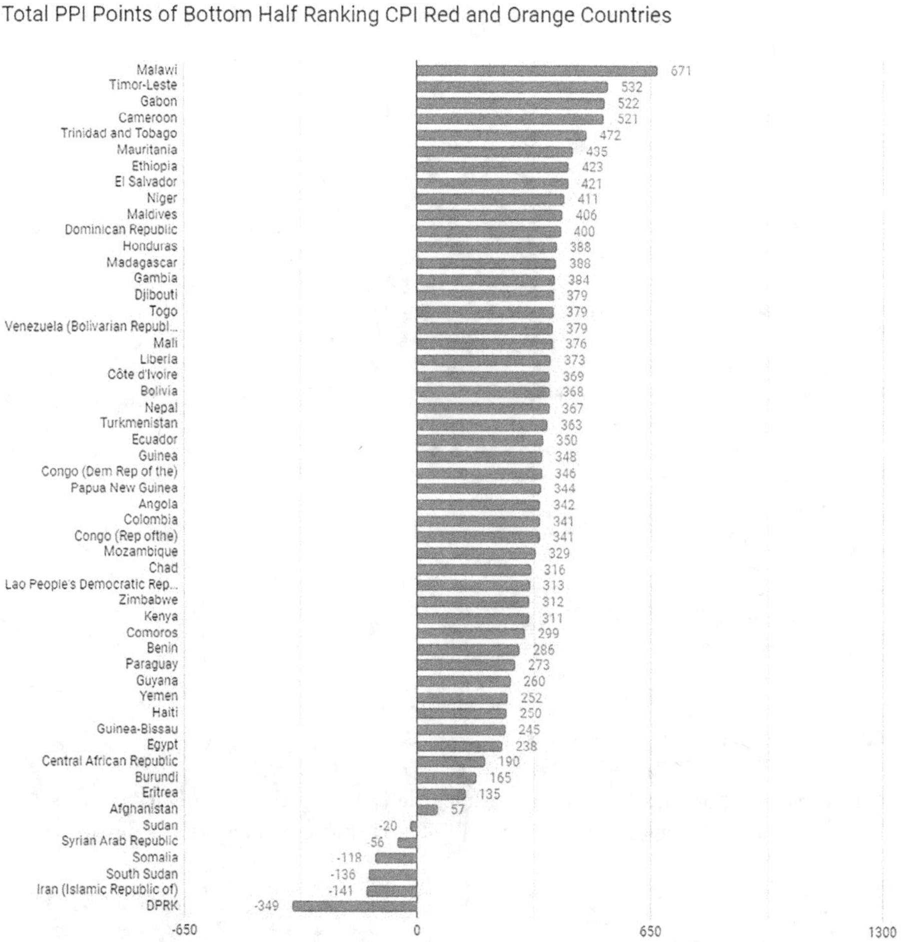

Figure 19.3. Countries categorized with legislation color coding of Red and Orange and ranking in the bottom half of Corruption Perceptions Index for 2016.

Total PPI Points of Bottom Half Ranking CPI Light and Dark Green Countries

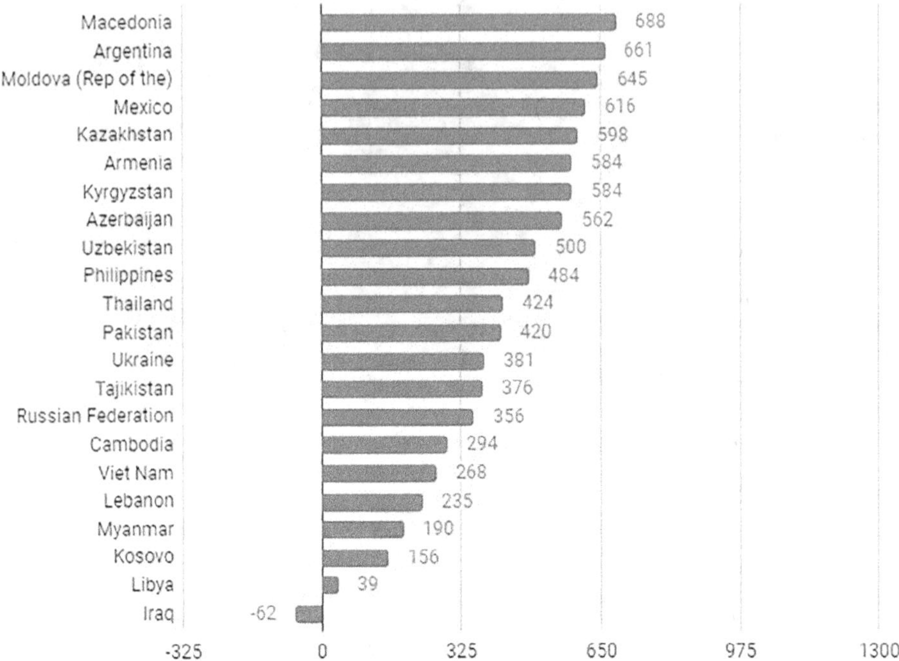

Figure 19.4. Countries categorized with legislation color coding of Dark Green and Light Green and ranking in the bottom half of Corruption Perceptions Index for 2016.

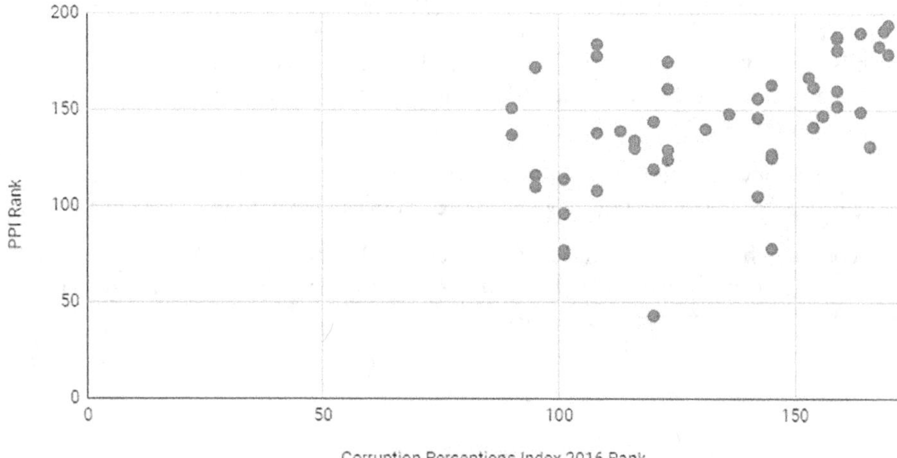

Figure 19.5. Countries categorized with legislation colored as Red or Orange that ranked in the bottom half of the Corruption Perceptions Index. The 53 countries that have high corruption and do poorly in the PPI appear in the upper right-hand corner.

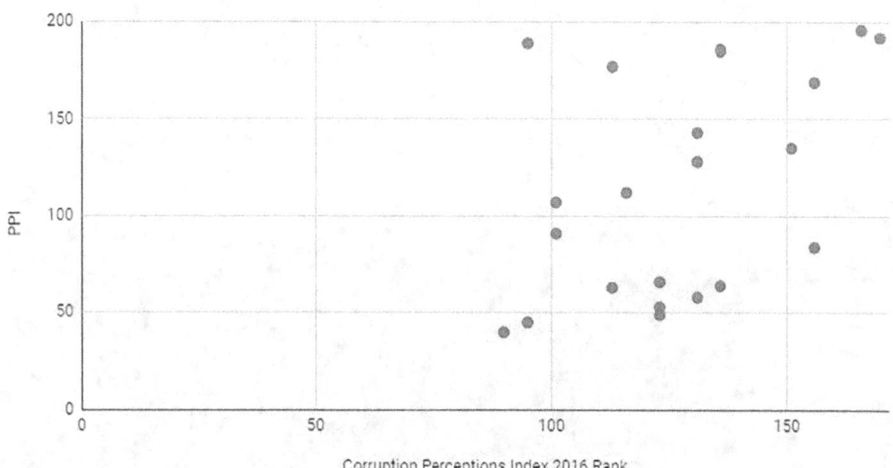

Figure 19.6. Countries categorized with legislation colored as Dark Green or Light Green that rank in the bottom half of the Corruption Perceptions Index. The 22 countries that have high corruption and do relatively poorly in the PPI are on the right-hand side of the graph.

NOTES

1. Those countries not included in the CPI, and thus excluded from this chapter, but were evaluated in PPI are the following: Andorra, Antigua and Barbuda, Belize, Cook Islands, Equatorial Guinea, Fiji, Holy See, Kiribati, Liechtenstein, Marshall Islands, Micronesia, Monaco, Nauru, Niue, Palau, Palestine, Saint Kitts and Nevis, Samoa, San Marino, Swaziland, Tonga, and Tuvalu.

2. Transparency International, *Corruption Perceptions Index 2016,* https://www.transparency.org/news/feature/corruption_perceptions_index_2016#table

3. If countries had the same rank they are then listed alphabetically. See: Transparency International, *Corruption Perceptions Index 2016,* https://www.transparency.org/news/feature/corruption_perceptions_index_2016#table

ANNEX I
FULL RANKING AND SUPER CRITERIA SCORES

TABLE A.1. TOTAL PPI RANK AND TOTAL POINTS

PPI RANK	COUNTRY	TOTAL POINTS (1300 points possible; negative scores also possible)
1	United States of America	1027
2	Portugal	970
3	UK (Great Britain & Northern Ireland)	962
4	Iceland	927
5	Lithuania	901
6	Slovakia	901
7	Slovenia	897
8	Australia	893
9	Netherlands	890
10	Sweden	887
11	Germany	886
12	Denmark	884
13	Czech Republic	878
14	Belgium	877
15	Hungary	876
16	Austria	876
17	Malta	875
18	Poland	875
19	Singapore	872
20	Spain	872
21	France	869
22	Ireland	858
23	New Zealand	858
24	Italy	856
25	Estonia	843
26	Finland	842
27	Norway	838
28	Canada	829
29	Japan	827
30	Luxembourg	822
31	Latvia	817
32	Republic of Korea	812
33	Croatia	807
34	Romania	782
35	Switzerland	769
36	Cyprus	749
37	San Marino	736
38	Bulgaria	713
39	Greece	701
40	Macedonia	688
41	Malaysia	681
42	Mauritius	674
43	Malawi	671
44	Andorra	663
45	Argentina	661
46	Israel	655
47	Liechtenstein	647
48	Zambia	645
49	Moldova (Rep of the)	645
50	South Africa	642

PPI RANK	COUNTRY	TOTAL POINTS (1300 points possible; negative scores also possible)
51	Albania	639
52	Solomon Islands	620
53	Mexico	616
54	Montenegro	615
55	Brazil	614
56	Turkey	607
57	Jamaica	598
58	Kazakhstan	598
59	Monaco	593
60	Burkina Faso	593
61	United Arab Emirates	589
62	Antigua and Barbuda	584
63	Armenia	584
64	Kyrgyzstan	584
65	Chile	581
66	Azerbaijan	562
67	India	562
68	Guatemala	560
69	Bangladesh	553
70	Serbia	541
71	Jordan	538
72	Georgia	536
73	Lesotho	536
74	Botswana	536
75	Timor-Leste	532
76	Mongolia	528
77	Gabon	522
78	Cameroon	521
79	Uruguay	519

PPI RANK	COUNTRY	TOTAL POINTS (1300 points possible; negative scores also possible)
80	Samoa	519
81	Fiji	518
82	Tonga	512
83	Namibia	504
84	Uzbekistan	500
85	Panama	500
86	Grenada	495
87	Bahrain	494
88	China	493
89	Saint Lucia	488
90	Nauru	487
91	Philippines	484
92	Costa Rica	479
93	Bahamas	478
94	Sierra Leone	477
95	Qatar	475
96	Trinidad and Tobago	472
97	Ghana	469
98	Cape Verde	464
99	Bhutan	453
100	Cuba	447
101	Palau	444
102	Swaziland	442
103	Barbados	441
104	Brunei Darussalam	441
105	Mauritania	435
106	Saudi Arabia	431
107	Thailand	424
108	Ethiopia	423

PPI RANK	COUNTRY	TOTAL POINTS (1300 points possible; negative scores also possible)
109	Bosnia and Herzegovina	422
110	El Salvador	421
111	Seychelles	420
112	Pakistan	420
113	Suriname	418
114	Niger	411
115	Hong Kong	409
116	Maldives	406
117	Tunisia	404
118	Dominica	402
119	Dominican Republic	400
120	Algeria	397
121	Taiwan	395
122	Nicaragua	391
123	Vanuatu	391
124	Honduras	388
125	Madagascar	388
126	Peru	387
127	Gambia	384
128	Ukraine	381
129	Djibouti	379
130	Togo	379
131	Venezuela (Bolivarian Republic of)	379
132	Sao Tome and Principe	377
133	Saint Vincent and the Grenadines	377
134	Mali	376

PPI RANK	COUNTRY	TOTAL POINTS (1300 points possible; negative scores also possible)
135	Tajikistan	376
136	Saint Kitts and Nevis	374
137	Liberia	373
138	Côte d'Ivoire	369
139	Bolivia	368
140	Nepal	367
141	Turkmenistan	363
142	Tanzania (United Republic of)	356
143	Russian Federation	356
144	Ecuador	350
145	Senegal	350
146	Guinea	348
147	Congo (Dem Rep of the)	346
148	Papua New Guinea	344
149	Angola	342
150	Oman	342
151	Colombia	341
152	Congo (Rep of the)	341
153	Marshall Islands	337
154	Belarus	335
155	Indonesia	331
156	Mozambique	329
157	Tuvalu	328
158	Sri Lanka	322

PPI RANK	COUNTRY	TOTAL POINTS (1300 points possible; negative scores also possible)
159	Rwanda	320
160	Chad	316
161	Lao People's Democratic Republic	313
162	Zimbabwe	312
163	Kenya	311
164	Nigeria	308
165	Niue	305
166	Morocco	301
167	Comoros	299
168	Micronesia (Federated States of)	297
169	Cambodia	294
170	Kiribati	293
171	Uganda	288
172	Benin	286
173	Kuwait	281
174	Cook Islands	278
175	Paraguay	273
176	Holy See	269
177	Viet Nam	268
178	Guyana	260
179	Yemen	252
180	Equatorial Guinea	251

PPI RANK	COUNTRY	TOTAL POINTS (1300 points possible; negative scores also possible)
181	Haiti	250
182	Belize	246
183	Guinea-Bissau	245
184	Egypt	238
185	Lebanon	235
186	Myanmar	190
187	Central African Republic	190
188	Burundi	165
189	Kosovo	156
190	Eritrea	135
191	Afghanistan	57
192	Libya	39
193	Palestine (State of)	30
194	Sudan	-20
195	Syrian Arab Republic	-56
196	Iraq	-62
197	Somalia	-118
198	South Sudan	-136
199	Iran (Islamic Republic of)	-141
200	DPRK	-349

TABLE A.2. TIER ONE RANKS AND SCALED, WEIGHTED SUPER CRITERIA SCORES (SEE CHAPTER 7)

TIER ONE RANK	COUNTRY	PPI RANK	TOTAL POINTS (1300 max)	INT'L COMMITMENT (100 max)	LEGISLA-TION (200 max)	ABILITY TO MONITOR & DETECT STRATEGIC TRADE (200 max)	ABILITY TO PREVENT PROLIFERATION FINANCING (400 max)	ADEQUACY OF ENFORCEMENT (400 max)
1	United States of America	1	1027	86	199	145	217	380
2	Portugal	2	970	90	198	142	181	359
3	UK (Great Britain & Northern Ireland)	3	962	86	199	149	180	347
4	Iceland	4	927	73	183	140	214	316
5	Lithuania	5	901	76	197	140	125	363
6	Slovakia	6	901	76	198	131	186	311
7	Slovenia	7	897	78	197	109	152	361
8	Australia	8	893	96	199	136	115	346
9	Netherlands	9	890	88	200	137	121	345
10	Sweden	10	887	90	200	137	117	344
11	Germany	11	886	90	199	131	121	344
12	Denmark	12	884	90	199	133	115	346
13	Czech Republic	13	878	82	198	128	108	362
14	Belgium	14	877	90	199	134	119	335
15	Hungary	15	876	84	197	131	129	335
16	Austria	16	876	90	199	127	113	347
17	Malta	17	875	76	198	118	148	335

TIER ONE RANK	COUNTRY	PPI RANK	TOTAL POINTS (1300 max)	INT'L COMMITMENT (100 max)	LEGISLATION (200 max)	ABILITY TO MONITOR & DETECT STRATEGIC TRADE (200 max)	ABILITY TO PREVENT PROLIFERATION FINANCING (400 max)	ADEQUACY OF ENFORCEMENT (400 max)
18	Poland	18	875	84	198	123	110	360
19	Spain	20	872	90	198	126	139	320
20	France	21	869	88	199	129	110	344
21	Ireland	22	858	86	199	135	111	327
22	New Zealand	23	858	100	185	135	90	348
23	Italy	24	856	90	197	125	108	337
24	Estonia	25	843	70	199	128	112	333
25	Finland	26	842	90	200	122	103	327
26	Norway	27	838	90	184	136	100	327
27	Canada	28	829	86	184	136	115	308
28	Japan	29	827	86	146	129	142	326
29	Luxembourg	30	822	86	200	134	87	316
30	Latvia	31	817	79	196	114	107	322
31	Republic of Korea	32	812	92	183	117	82	338
32	Croatia	33	807	82	195	116	80	334
33	Romania	34	782	82	196	103	103	299
34	Switzerland	35	769	86	192	133	80	278
35	Cyprus	36	749	67	197	84	109	291
36	Bulgaria	38	713	80	195	101	100	237
37	Greece	39	701	86	196	97	96	225

TIER ONE RANK	COUNTRY	PPI RANK	TOTAL POINTS (1300 max)	INT'L COMMITMENT (100 max)	LEGISLATION (200 max)	ABILITY TO MONITOR & DETECT STRATEGIC TRADE (200 max)	ABILITY TO PREVENT PROLIFERATION FINANCING (400 max)	ADEQUACY OF ENFORCEMENT (400 max)
38	Argentina	45	661	90	194	83	-40	334
39	Israel	46	655	42	137	96	155	224
40	Liechtenstein	47	647	49	169	88	91	250
41	South Africa	50	642	86	198	117	-49	289
42	Mexico	53	616	80	181	114	31	211
43	Brazil	55	614	76	150	103	38	248
44	Turkey	56	607	90	195	116	36	171
45	Kazakhstan	58	598	73	163	71	10	280
46	Monaco	59	593	45	123	54	181	190
47	India	67	562	59	166	110	-21	248
48	Serbia	70	541	65	193	110	-135	306
49	China	88	493	67	197	118	-37	148
50	Pakistan	113	420	37	193	106	-110	194
51	Taiwan	121	395	0	137	80	0	177
52	Ukraine	128	381	82	170	106	-184	207
53	Russian Federation	143	356	78	178	94	-131	137
54	Belarus	154	335	65	177	95	-143	141
55	Egypt	184	238	34	132	75	-119	116
56	Iran (Islamic Republic of)	199	-141	35	94	68	-321	-17
57	DPRK	200	-349	12	0	31	-272	-120

TABLE A.3. TIER TWO RANK AND SUPER CRITERIA SCORES

TIER ONE RANK	COUNTRY	PPI RANK	TOTAL POINTS (1300 max)	INT'L COMMITMENT (100 max)	LEGISLA-TION (200 max)	ABILITY TO MONITOR & DETECT STRATEGIC TRADE (200 max)	ABILITY TO PREVENT PROLIFERATION FINANCING (400 max)	ADEQUACY OF ENFORCEMENT (400 max)
1	Singapore	19	872	71	177	126	158	340
2	Malaysia	41	681	57	183	94	39	308
3	Malawi	43	671	59	116	88	168	239
4	Zambia	48	645	55	116	120	114	239
5	Moldova (Rep of the)	49	645	61	193	113	17	261
6	Albania	51	639	55	193	82	91	219
7	Jamaica	57	598	55	147	122	7	268
8	United Arab Emirates	61	589	57	153	112	2	266
9	Armenia	63	584	53	147	107	132	144
10	Kyrgyzstan	64	584	55	177	74	28	249
11	Chile	65	581	67	102	97	117	197
12	Azerbaijan	66	562	61	170	90	22	219
13	Bangladesh	69	553	51	143	92	76	191
14	Georgia	72	536	57	141	69	27	242
15	Mongolia	76	528	63	113	92	35	224
16	Namibia	83	504	53	108	87	88	168
17	Uzbekistan	84	500	57	110	58	83	192
18	Panama	85	500	69	110	85	17	218
19	Philippines	91	484	63	158	96	-53	220

TABLE A.3. TIER TWO

TIER ONE RANK	COUNTRY	PPI RANK	TOTAL POINTS (1300 max)	INT'L COMMITMENT (100 max)	LEGISLA-TION (200 max)	ABILITY TO MONITOR & DETECT STRATEGIC TRADE (200 max)	ABILITY TO PREVENT PROLIFERATION FINANCING (400 max)	ADEQUACY OF ENFORCEMENT (400 max)
20	Costa Rica	92	479	63	142	69	-20	225
21	Bahamas	93	478	51	85	59	94	190
22	Qatar	95	475	55	110	105	61	143
23	Ghana	97	469	57	155	108	-23	173
24	Brunei Darussalam	104	441	47	104	77	20	192
25	Saudi Arabia	106	431	53	96	84	28	170
26	Thailand	107	424	49	150	118	-149	256
27	Ethiopia	108	423	43	139	40	-2	203
28	Bosnia and Herzegovina	109	422	57	162	86	-41	157
29	Niger	110	411	49	90	85	64	123
30	Hong Kong	115	409	22	122	79	79	107
31	Tunisia	117	404	59	88	72	-18	202
32	Dominican Republic	119	400	69	93	85	-70	223
33	Algeria	120	397	55	121	86	-42	178
34	Nicaragua	122	391	57	143	63	-52	180
35	Vanuatu	123	391	53	83	61	79	116
36	Madagascar	125	388	59	86	85	4	154
37	Peru	126	387	67	108	62	-15	165
38	Venezuela (Bolivarian Republic of)	131	379	45	114	52	69	99

TIER ONE RANK	COUNTRY	PPI RANK	TOTAL POINTS (1300 max)	INT'L COMMITMENT (100 max)	LEGISLA-TION (200 max)	ABILITY TO MONITOR & DETECT STRATEGIC TRADE (200 max)	ABILITY TO PREVENT PROLIFERATION FINANCING (400 max)	ADEQUACY OF ENFORCEMENT (400 max)
39	Tajikistan	135	376	53	133	49	-73	215
40	Tanzania (United Republic of)	142	356	54	100	86	-47	163
41	Ecuador	144	350	61	100	60	-54	183
42	Oman	150	342	47	82	82	13	118
43	Colombia	151	341	61	73	75	17	114
44	Indonesia	155	331	65	92	109	-76	140
45	Sri Lanka	158	322	47	100	71	-106	210
46	Lao People's Democratic Republic	161	313	39	129	93	-66	119
47	Nigeria	164	308	59	105	68	-87	163
48	Morocco	166	301	61	108	73	-121	179
49	Uganda	171	288	51	100	78	-89	148
50	Kuwait	173	281	61	87	84	-47	97
51	Paraguay	175	273	67	92	60	-118	171
52	Viet Nam	177	268	61	128	67	-76	88
53	Lebanon	185	235	49	127	72	-196	183
54	Afghanistan	191	57	53	92	38	-180	54
55	Libya	192	39	61	102	53	-189	11
56	Syrian Arab Republic	195	-56	34	75	63	-133	-95
57	Iraq	196	-62	57	92	66	-331	54

TABLE A.4. TIER THREE RANK AND SUPER CRITERIA SCORES

TIER ONE RANK	COUNTRY	PPI RANK	TOTAL POINTS (1300 max)	INT'L COMMITMENT (100 max)	LEGISLA- TION (200 max)	ABILITY TO MONITOR & DETECT STRATEGIC TRADE (200 max)	ABILITY TO PREVENT PROLIFERATION FINANCING (400 max)	ADEQUACY OF ENFORCEMENT (400 max)
1	San Marino	37	736	49	177	63	166	280
2	Macedonia	40	688	59	172	83	179	195
3	Mauritius	42	674	55	113	80	173	252
4	Andorra	44	663	47	154	81	141	240
5	Solomon Islands	52	620	35	121	64	173	227
6	Montenegro	54	615	63	194	84	-25	299
7	Burkina Faso	60	593	51	113	96	127	206
8	Antigua and Barbuda	62	584	63	85	84	128	224
9	Guatemala	68	560	55	146	111	55	194
10	Jordan	71	538	63	136	111	-12	239
11	Lesotho	73	536	51	90	79	141	175
12	Botswana	74	536	43	132	81	115	165
13	Timor-Leste	75	532	29	113	55	101	234
14	Gabon	77	522	61	139	79	68	174
15	Cameroon	78	521	51	109	72	113	176
16	Uruguay	79	519	61	86	100	94	177
17	Samoa	80	519	41	113	69	119	176
18	Fiji	81	518	61	113	88	121	134

TIER ONE RANK	COUNTRY	PPI RANK	TOTAL POINTS (1300 max)	INT'L COMMITMENT (100 max)	LEGISLA-TION (200 max)	ABILITY TO MONITOR & DETECT STRATEGIC TRADE (200 max)	ABILITY TO PREVENT PROLIFERATION FINANCING (400 max)	ADEQUACY OF ENFORCEMENT (400 max)
19	Tonga	82	512	41	77	79	139	176
20	Grenada	86	495	33	90	62	110	200
21	Bahrain	87	494	63	90	80	123	138
22	Saint Lucia	89	488	51	108	67	46	216
23	Nauru	90	487	33	98	45	131	181
24	Sierra Leone	94	477	43	144	73	-19	236
25	Trinidad and Tobago	96	472	53	95	101	40	183
26	Cape Verde	98	464	33	96	71	53	211
27	Bhutan	99	453	24	106	67	136	120
28	Cuba	100	447	55	104	91	24	173
29	Palau	101	444	45	83	37	133	147
30	Swaziland	102	442	45	108	54	30	204
31	Barbados	103	441	39	90	52	97	163
32	Mauritania	105	435	59	107	67	34	168
33	El Salvador	111	421	63	140	57	-38	200
34	Seychelles	112	420	55	106	46	31	182
35	Suriname	114	418	31	90	80	17	199
36	Maldives	116	406	37	77	73	75	144
37	Dominica	118	402	45	100	54	8	195
38	Honduras	124	388	61	118	59	11	139

TABLE A.4. TIER THREE

TIER ONE RANK	COUNTRY	PPI RANK	TOTAL POINTS (1300 max)	INT'L COMMITMENT (100 max)	LEGISLA-TION (200 max)	ABILITY TO MONITOR & DETECT STRATEGIC TRADE (200 max)	ABILITY TO PREVENT PROLIFERATION FINANCING (400 max)	ADEQUACY OF ENFORCEMENT (400 max)
39	Gambia	127	384	43	83	61	79	119
40	Djibouti	129	379	55	108	63	-19	173
41	Togo	130	379	51	100	68	97	63
42	Sao Tome and Principe	132	377	27	85	64	84	117
43	Saint Vincent and the Grenadines	133	377	41	85	53	50	148
44	Mali	134	376	55	103	54	-8	173
45	Saint Kitts and Nevis	136	374	41	83	47	34	169
46	Liberia	137	373	39	88	89	6	151
47	Côte d'Ivoire	138	369	53	92	66	8	149
48	Bolivia	139	368	45	138	57	-71	200
49	Nepal	140	367	37	88	69	33	140
50	Turkmenistan	141	363	59	75	40	17	173
51	Senegal	145	350	57	94	74	64	62
52	Guinea	146	348	37	85	57	30	139
53	Congo (Dem Rep of the)	147	346	55	131	98	-26	87
54	Papua New Guinea	148	344	47	77	62	39	120
55	Angola	149	342	51	85	67	45	95
56	Congo (Rep ofthe)	152	341	47	100	65	-14	144
57	Marshall Islands	153	337	43	46	40	71	137

TIER ONE RANK	COUNTRY	PPI RANK	TOTAL POINTS (1300 max)	INT'L COMMITMENT (100 max)	LEGISLA-TION (200 max)	ABILITY TO MONITOR & DETECT STRATEGIC TRADE (200 max)	ABILITY TO PREVENT PROLIFERATION FINANCING (400 max)	ADEQUACY OF ENFORCEMENT (400 max)
58	Mozambique	156	329	55	94	57	23	99
59	Tuvalu	157	328	27	67	42	-18	210
60	Rwanda	159	320	47	102	76	-14	109
61	Chad	160	316	41	85	53	10	127
62	Zimbabwe	162	312	43	85	52	-20	151
63	Kenya	163	311	63	87	82	-58	136
64	Niue	165	305	16	58	45	115	70
65	Comoros	167	299	51	69	47	35	96
66	Micronesia (Federated States of)	168	297	8	85	55	-18	167
67	Cambodia	169	294	61	110	89	-73	108
68	Kiribati	170	293	35	62	45	6	146
69	Benin	172	286	37	92	71	12	73
70	Cook Islands	174	278	22	46	58	121	30
71	Holy See	176	269	39	38	61	61	70
72	Guyana	178	260	47	62	51	-60	161
73	Yemen	179	252	53	69	52	71	7
74	Equatorial Guinea	180	251	24	69	40	42	75
75	Haiti	181	250	48	85	47	-36	106
76	Belize	182	246	45	69	43	-37	126

TIER ONE RANK	COUNTRY	PPI RANK	TOTAL POINTS (1300 max)	INT'L COMMITMENT (100 max)	LEGISLATION (200 max)	ABILITY TO MONITOR & DETECT STRATEGIC TRADE (200 max)	ABILITY TO PREVENT PROLIFERATION FINANCING (400 max)	ADEQUACY OF ENFORCEMENT (400 max)
77	Guinea-Bissau	183	245	41	85	44	-41	117
78	Myanmar	186	190	45	102	51	-156	148
79	Central African Republic	187	190	50	85	35	-105	125
80	Burundi	188	165	45	93	69	-137	95
81	Kosovo	189	156	6	87	38	-38	63
82	Eritrea	190	135	27	77	26	-119	124
83	Palestine (State of)	193	30	12	69	35	-42	-44
84	Sudan	194	-20	45	69	56	-126	-64
85	Somalia	197	-118	21	54	26	-200	-20
86	South Sudan	198	-136	6	54	23	-200	-20

SUPER CRITERIA RANKS WITHIN TIERS

The PPI project developed several charts which show how countries rank in their tier for each super criterion. These charts were too large to include here but can be found in color at www.isis-online.org/ppi. While some countries show a consistent low or high rank, other countries show significant differences in rank when it comes to individual super criteria. Countries are sorted from left to right by deviation within the ranks. In this way, countries with clustered ranks are represented on the left side of the graphs, while countries with great deviations in rank are represented towards the right side.

MAPS SUMMARIZING PPI SCORES AND LEGISLATION CATEGORIES

The following two maps illustrate key PPI findings on global maps. The first map represents the country scores for all 200 countries and territories by blue shading, where a darker shade represents a higher score (see table A.1). The second map shows the legislative color category defined in chapter 3, where in brief: **Dark Green**- legislation is comprehensive; **Light Green**- legislation is somewhat comprehensive; **Yellow**- legislation is deficient; **Orange**- legislation has serious deficiencies; and **Red**- legislation is non-existent or severely deficient.

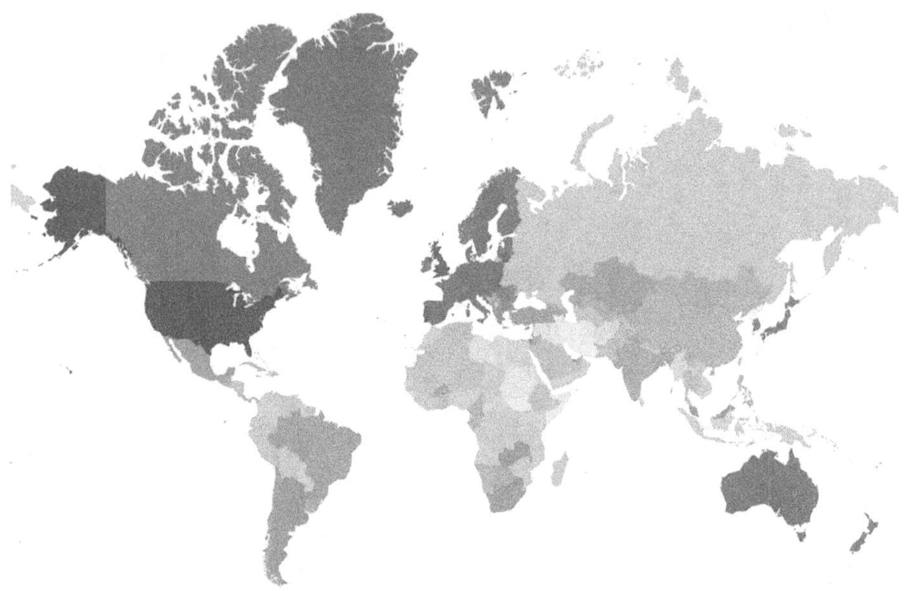

Figure A.1. The strength of export control systems around
the world, according to the PPI scoring.

KEY:

Darkest = highest points (maximum available 1,300; actual maximum reached 1,027)

Lightest = lowest points (negative points possible; lowest actual score -349)

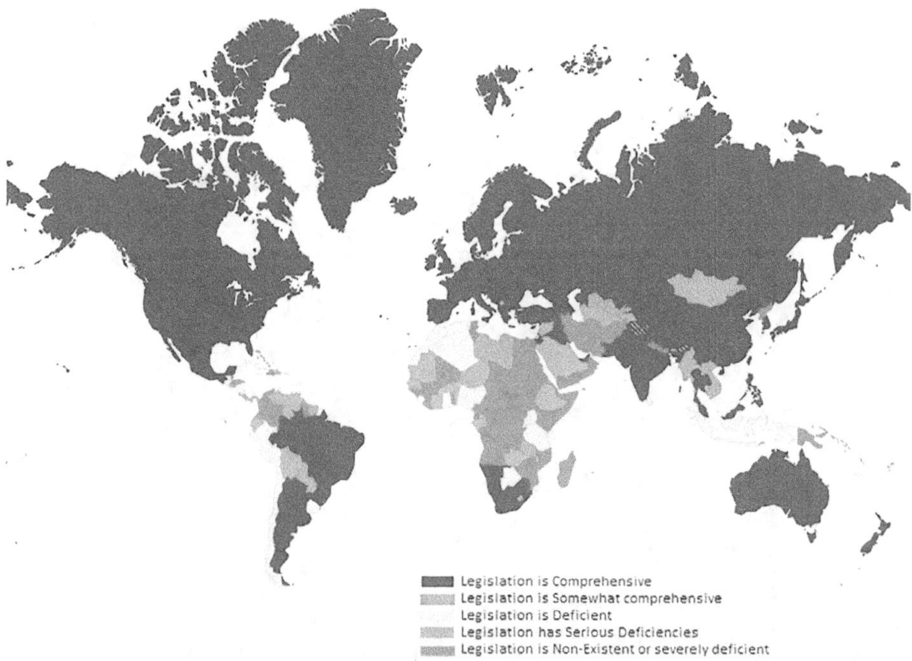

Figure A.2. World map indicating legislation color categories. The legislation color key described qualitatively and in brief is: **Dark Green**- legislation is comprehensive; **Light Green**- legislation is somewhat comprehensive; **Yellow**- legislation is deficient; **Orange**- legislation has serious deficiencies; and **Red**- legislation is non-existent or severely deficient. See Chapter 3 for legislative categories.

www.ingramcontent.com/pod-product-compliance
Lightning Source LLC
Chambersburg PA
CBHW061622250726
48659CB00004B/1054